FROM
FURY
TO
PHANTOM

FROM
FURY
TO
PHANTOM

Flying for the RAF
1936–1970

THE MEMOIRS OF
GROUP CAPTAIN RICHARD 'DICKIE' HAINE,
OBE, DFC

Pen & Sword
AVIATION

First published in Great Britain in 2005 by
Pen & Sword Aviation
an imprint of
Pen & Sword Books Ltd
47 Church Street
Barnsley
South Yorkshire
S70 2AS

ISBN 1 84415 202 2

A CIP catalogue record for this book is
available from the British Library.

Typeset in 10/12pt Palatino by
Phoenix Typesetting, Auldgirth, Dumfriesshire

Printed and bound in England by
CPI UK

Pen & Sword Books Ltd incorporates the imprints of Pen & Sword Aviation,
Pen & Sword Maritime, Pen & Sword Military, Wharncliffe Local History,
Pen & Sword Select, Pen & Sword Military Classics and Leo Cooper.

For a complete list of Pen & Sword titles please contact
PEN & SWORD BOOKS LIMITED
47 Church Street, Barnsley, South Yorkshire, S70 2AS, England
E-mail: enquiries@pen-and-sword.co.uk
Website: www.pen-and-sword.co.uk

Contents

CHAPTER ONE

My Family

1916 to 1934

I was born in the midst of that other dreadful war. In 1917 the news of the horrors of Ypres and the Somme were being received at home with incredulity and despair. The frightening casualties suffered during the taking of Paschendaele Ridge brought home the horrors of the war in the trenches in France, and now, at home, rumours were rife that the German airships had dropped bombs on British soil. Indeed, it was revealed that for months the Zeppelins had freely roamed the night skies of England unchallenged, and on one night alone as many as fourteen had been reported over the home counties. The physical damage and casualties they inflicted were comparatively slight, but there was something uniquely horrible about these great dark menacing craft cruising almost silently above the English countryside. I was spared that feeling of terror, for I was only one year old at the time, but in later years any mention of Zeppelins encouraged me to tell an amusing family story in which I jokingly used to claim that I was a casualty of the First World War.

Old Eckits, the loyal and willing family retainer, although getting on and a bit slow, was only too glad to do anything that was asked of her. One Sunday morning, my parents had gone to church, asking Eckits to put the Sunday roast in the oven at noon, and at the same time keep an eye on the two baby boys. On returning home, as they approached the gate they heard a loud explosion, and to their horror were met by the sight of Eckits, her face blackened, her hair singed and in disarray, rushing out of the back door with a screaming child, equally be-sooted, clutched under each arm. 'The Zeppelins have come, the Zeppelins have come!', her hysterical shouts setting the dogs off barking. While Mother tried to calm the victims and settle the dogs, Father rushed into the house to turn off the gas oven before there was another explosion.

I was the baby of the family, and as well as the other casualty, my young brother, there was an older son and three girls in the family. Father had founded, and now ran, a small builders' merchant firm in Gloucester. It was a hard struggle in the Depression following the war, but through considerable personal efforts he managed to keep the Firm alive, and in later years he was able to hand over to his eldest son a thriving company with excellent prospects. My second brother Mike was the brainy one, and understandably was favoured by my parents to go to university. Even in his schooldays he showed considerable interest and ability in electronics and physics, and he graduated later with a doctorate in electronic engineering. He became Director of the AEI Research Laboratory at Harlow and was Director of their Laboratory at Aldermaston, from where he visited the United States of America during the Second World War in connection with the current experimentation with nuclear physics. Back at Harlow he worked with a colleague in his laboratory and became the co-inventor of the electron microscope, an example of which can now be seen in the London Science Museum. His outstanding abilities were clearly a hard act to follow, but fortunately I, his younger brother, had no aspirations in the field of either business or electronics, and my preordained course was clearly defined in my mind. I was going to fly, and this ambition transcended all else. In those early days I must admit I would not have believed, even in my wildest dreams, that one day I would be one of the Few in the Battle of Britain, would be shot down in Holland and would return to England with a Queen, and at the end of my flying career would have flown more than a hundred different types of aircraft.

The three girls in the family were kind and considerate sisters to me, being the baby of the family. My mother spoilt me madly and my father was a most kind and generous man who never failed to support me in my ambitions. I suffered the inevitable mild bullying and ribbing of my elder brothers and their friends, but survived to relatively happy days of youth. To fly was my obsession, and all my efforts and energy were directed along this well-defined course. I spent many hours at home in my shed making aircraft models, and Christmas and birthdays brought more model aeroplanes, which I would fly with great enthusiasm, on their elastic power, around the tennis court. But there were also school exams to get through, the growing pains of early adulthood and the agony of first love affairs to suffer. There were several girls whom we shared among ourselves and our friends, and it was seldom that a weekend passed without an expedition into Wales or touring the Cotswolds.

We had learned to drive at an early age, and Father was always generous in letting us have the use of his large Buick or one of the firm's cars. The girls were usually enthusiastic spectators on the touchline for our rugby matches, and all our escapades together were always the greatest fun. As these happy relationships developed I began to realize that there was only one girl for me. Suzette became the love in my life, and we were constant companions, sharing a love of sport and outdoor life. Those early days together were some of the happiest that I can remember, full of innocent comradeship and fun. But even Suzette took second place to the achievement of my ambition to fly. My father, ever mindful of my interests, took me out to a field at Higham where Alan Cobham had arrived one weekend with his flying circus. My father soon parted with the princely sum of five shillings, and I was clambering into that amazing old biplane, an Avro 504K G-EBIZ. As we taxied out I became very aware of the way the Gnome Monosoupape rotary engine was blipped on and off to regulate the aircraft's speed: no throttle on this aeroplane. We turned into wind in the far corner of the field, and by this time I was completely captivated and mad with excitement. The Gnome's tick-over changed to a mighty roar, and the whole aircraft shook alarmingly as it accelerated across the field. But the awkward, trundling gait soon became a blissful smoothness as the aircraft was borne on the air into its natural element, and at last I experienced for the first time the magic of flight. The slipstream tearing at my hair in the open cockpit, the unforgettable smell of hot castor oil and the view of the captured countryside below were always to remain in my memory. As we climbed up out of the field we saw below Churcham Court, my father's old home, and the church in whose graveyard he would one day be buried and where I would later be married.

As we turned I saw below us the curve of the Severn and beyond it the whole city of Gloucester, with its lovely old cathedral, and the backdrop of the Birdlip hills behind. Turning further I could see May Hill with its crown of Scotch Pine and the Malverns dimly in the misty distance. I twisted around in the cramped cockpit with some effort to see if I could get a glimpse of our home at the foot of Robinswood Hill, but all too soon we began to lose height and were turning over the river on our landing approach. The rotary was now just ticking over, with the occasional blip as the pilot adjusted his speed. And as we straightened up we slipped between the great elms that then lined the road, touched down gently in the long grass and lumbered awkwardly back to where Dad awaited with a glad smile as he saw that my face was a picture of gleeful happiness. My obvious pleasure was probably a source of some encouragement to the rather apprehensive-looking queue awaiting the next flight!

A few weeks later, my mother, not to be outdone and also mindful of my passion, drove me down in the sidecar of her Douglas motorbike to

Filton, where she had made arrangements for a tour of the Bristol Aircraft Factory. Again I was in a state of excited expectation. I was not disappointed as we were escorted through the workshops to the sound of turning machinery, screeching lathes and pounding hammers. I was fascinated by the work in the wing and tail assembly shop where girls were busy stitching sturdy linen to the assembled framework with uncanny skill and dexterity. The completed wings were stacked against the far wall waiting to go into the paint shop, whence came the all-pervading and exciting smell of aircraft dope. But the ultimate thrill was, of course, when we came to the final assembly hangar. The wings and tail had now been sprayed and stood in their silver glory ready for assembly. As we moved on down through the sheds, the shape of real aeroplanes began to emerge. Finally, my heart gave a leap as the hangar doors were swung open and a completed machine was rolled out. God made beautiful birds, but surely this wondrous product of man's and woman's skills that now stood for the first time, its silver wings shimmering in the sunlight like a newly-born butterfly emerging from its chrysalis, was a worthy prototype. But no gentle, docile butterfly was this; with its blunt, pugnacious Jupiter engine it looked every inch just what it was: a 'Bulldog'. Born in the mid-1920s, it was probably one of the most perfectly proportioned fighters to enter the service, and very much a product of its age. I was amazed to learn later on that the Bulldog had flown against the Russians in Finland with some success in 1939/40.

On the tarmac apron at Filton mechanics fussed around the Bulldog, and a Hucks starter was driven to the front of the aeroplane and preparations were made to start the Jupiter engine. The Hucks was an extraordinary machine, a Model 'T' Ford modified with a gantry affair carrying a long drive-shaft projecting over its front. This shaft fitted into a claw on the propeller boss of the aircraft, and as the Ford was persuaded into life, the shaft was engaged and the propeller was turned. After the odd preliminary puff of blue smoke the Jupiter came to life in a thrilling roar, and the Hucks backed away in a hurry, anxious to get clear of that whirling propeller. Only someone with a name like Cyril Uwins could possibly fly this wonderful machine, and as we watched, the chief test pilot, already in the cockpit, taxied out to get into wind and took off over the houses of Patchway. To a young boy it was a breathtaking experience to witness this splendid fighter aircraft with Royal Air Force tricoloured roundels on its silver wings, shaking off its earthly ties and climbing up into the blue. With impatient expectation we waited for the Bulldog to reappear, and after a few minutes it flew in low from the south, and we were thrilled by a display of superb aerobatics over the airfields until Captain Uwins with admirable judgement slipped in over the downwind hedge and set the aircraft down as lightly as any bird. He taxied the Bulldog briskly back to the apron, and as he climbed from the cockpit my mother, as bold and self-assured as always, hurried across the tarmac and thanked him, as though his thrilling display was all for our exclusive benefit. He was very kind and shook me by the hand and wished me success in my endeavours. So ended a most wonderful day. I never dreamed that in a few years' time I too would be bringing in an aircraft over that same hedge to a gentle landing on Filton's field.

CHAPTER TWO

First Solo

1934 to 1935

Now exams were passed, school was finished and it was time to start making serious efforts to get into the flying game. Father again was of great help, but despite his efforts there was little sign of positive progress. But in the interim he did give me a temporary job in his building company and also arranged for me to work as an apprentice at the Gloster Aircraft Company at Brockworth. Here I had to start work at 7.30 a.m., which meant leaving home at 6.30 on my bike and cycling through the length of Gloucester city to reach Brockworth. However, I did not mind and was thrilled at being close to real aeroplanes; besides, the ten shillings that I was paid each week came in handy. At the slightest excuse I would help to open the huge hangar doors and help the servicing crews to push out the Hawker Hind medium bombers that were being built at that time under contract by Gloster Aircraft Co. for an overseas customer. Once out on the tarmac, although it was not part of my job, I would busy myself around the aircraft, cleaning and polishing, until the chief test pilot came out to fly it.

Hiding round the corner of the hangar, I watched enthralled as Gerry Sayers taxied out, and with a thrilling roar from the Kestrel climbed away from Brockworth over the Cranham Woods, the silver wings of the Hind reflecting in the sunlight. I watched as long as I dared, but much to my disappointment had to creep back to my job in the hangar before the Hind landed. While I revelled in my experience at Brockworth, my father got to know two aviation enthusiasts in Gloucester. One was a pharmacist and the other a garage proprietor, both of whom flew out at Staverton at the Cotswold Aero Club. So he kindly took the trouble for me to meet them out at the club in the hope that that they might be able to take me flying. I used to cycle the seven miles out to Staverton whenever I had a spare moment, always hoping to scrounge a flight with one of them. They were very kind and sympathetic, but flights were difficult to come by and in great demand. However, I did succeed in getting one flight in a Gipsy Moth and on another occasion in a French Desouter monoplane, an early cabin light-aircraft. I enjoyed them both, but far preferred the open cockpit of the Moth and feeling the wind rushing through my hair and making the flying wires sing.

I am the first to admit that I was shy by nature, and it was a great credit to me that I persisted in making myself useful around the club, cleaning and oiling the machines and pushing out the aircraft on a flying day. I was prepared to talk to anyone who I thought could teach me anything about flying and maintenance of aircraft. With ever-growing confidence and familiarity with the club environment I lost some of my shyness, and on one occasion I was introduced to the famous one-armed, one-eyed pilot Stewart Keith-Jopp, who later, when in the ATA, flew a Hurricane to France for the British AASF and delivered Spitfires to squadrons at home. He was quite a hero-figure to me, and he encouraged me to take some flying lessons. This was, of course, what I most wanted to do, and quoting Keith-Jopp I went to my father and asked him if it would be possible. Generous and sympathetic as always, he managed to find the money, no doubt at some cost to his own interests, and agreed that I could have ten hours of dual flying instruction.

So it was that in August 1935 I was on my bike to Staverton and reporting to one of the club instructors for flying lessons in the Gipsy Moth G-ABER. I well remembered the first flight when I nervously but firmly first took over the flying controls and the instructor came through on the Gosport communication tube and told me that he could feel me gripping the control column as though it was an axe handle. 'Just finger and thumb and a gentle touch will give you a much better feel of the aircraft's sensibilities and it will respond accordingly.' I never forgot that advice, and it served me well in all my flying years, when it did not take me very long to gain confidence in handling a wide variety of difference types of aircraft.

A week after my first dual flight and a few more lessons we took off from Staverton and followed the Fosse Way to a grass field just north of Cirencester. After two dual circuits and landings at the field the instructor climbed out of the rear cockpit of the Moth, did up the safety harness and sent me off on my first solo flight. I suppose this was the most thrilling moment of my life, but I must admit I felt it was also a decisive moment of truth as well. I realized that my whole flying career was at stake, and although I was not afraid of crashing I was very appre-hensive that I might make a cock-up of the landing and break this lovely machine that had been placed in my care. The grass of the field was lush and long, and I could feel the drag of it on the wheels as I taxied out and turned into wind.

The far hedge looked awfully close, and I thought it a bit unfair that I had been brought out here by my instructor away from the familiar surroundings of the aero club airstrip for my first solo, as I found that the strange environment made judgment that much more difficult in flying an accurate circuit. However, the sheer thrill of the moment made the adrenalin flow to sharpen my concentration, and with cool confidence I opened the throttle and the little Gipsy engine responded at once. I corrected the slight swing on the rudder bar as the nose moved slightly from the gap in the hedge on which I had chosen to line up, and as my speed began to build I eased the Moth into the air with that firm but gentle backward pressure on the stick that I had learnt and remembered. Airborne and alone at last, I enjoyed a wonderful feeling of thrilling exhilaration as I looked along the wings and felt rather than heard the singing of the flying wires and the slip-stream clawing at my face round the small windscreen, and the moment gave me almost painful joy and wonder that it was in my own hands to get the Moth to do my bidding. In my excitement of the moment I forgot that I was supposed to be doing a circuit, and found I was already half-way to Gloucester. In a slight panic I gently turned the Moth around and anxiously scanned the countryside for the field of my departure. To my relief I soon spotted the farm that had been our turning point on our first circuit, and I set up my approach from there as the instructor had demonstrated. It was easy now to line up on the wheel tracks we had made previously in the long grass, and checking my height, throttling back the Gipsy engine and with a quick look at the spring-balance air speed indicator on the right-hand wing strut I knew I had got it about right, and although I floated a little way I managed a satisfying landing. I taxied back to where my instructor stood looking bored and quite unconcerned, but nothing could spoil my moment of triumph. After six flights and four and half hours dual I had gone solo. On the return flight back to Staverton I was in a magic dream, and the celebration shandy back in the clubhouse bar made me feel really confident and grown up. But the best feeling came over me on leaving the clubhouse, when I happened to hear my instructor say in response to a question from within, 'Oh, he's a natural pilot!' I obtained my pilots's licence on 25 September 1935, but did not fly at Staverton again until 1 June 1936, when my logbook showed I took my first passenger, Suzette Corps. As far as I know, Suzette never flew again.

You could say that it was Hitler and the Nazis that gave me my real break. By the middle of 1935 the British Cabinet, urged into action by the military leaders, responded at last by authorizing an expansion of the armed forces.

Too late to act as a deterrent to Germany, but at least it improved the capability for our own defence when the time came. Deficiencies were particularly evident in the Royal Air Force, and the Air Ministry called for applicants to join as direct-entry sergeant pilots. My application must have been the first to arrive in the Air Ministry, and as my service number showed I was the tenth of all the NCO pilots to be selected.

I was accepted on 26 August 1935, and was instructed to report to the Bristol Flying School, Filton, for elementary flying training. My cup brimmed over!

CHAPTER THREE

Fury First

1935

After the preliminaries of signing the arrival forms at Bristol Flying School we were introduced to the head of the school, the senior staff of ground school and the flying instructors. We were still allowed to wear civilian clothes and could find our own accommodation in civilian houses off the base. For a short time I shared accommodation in a large house with Freddy Rosier, Johnny Walker and other characters who became well known later as fighter aces or distinguished themselves in other flying operations. In those days, however, sitting around listening to Freddie on his fiddle, we never talked about the possibility of being involved in air combat in the not too distant future, and certainly never imagined for a moment that Freddie would be terribly burned when attacked by a German fighter during an air battle that was to prove to be of such vital importance in the future.

There was now little time for us to engage in any activities other than our flying training. This was a time of great excitement for me, and I whole-heartedly threw myself into what had always been my ambition. I had one advantage over the rest of the fellows on the course in that not only had I already obtained a pilot's licence but by a coincidence my instructor was the same as the one I had at Staverton, who had first given me dual instruction. He had been moved to Filton in a hurry to meet the now urgent task of training direct-entry service pilots. As a consequence of this advantage I was soon well ahead in the flying programme, having gone solo on the Tiger Moth on the fifth sortie, after two hours' instruction. It also gave my instructor some spare flying time, when we would go off together to do some low passes over his girlfriend's home near Painswick and return to fly up the Avon and *under* the suspension bridge before side-slipping off a bit of surplus height over the hedge at Filton and finishing up neatly parked among the other Tigers. With a sly grin and forefinger to his lips my instructor strolled off to the locker-room to park his flying kit.

Flying instruction continued through September and October with aerobatics, spinning and solo cross-countries to Andover. On the ground we were taught to use navigational aids (a hand-held brass calculator), how to strip and reassemble a Vickers gun, and, of course, the principles of flight and the intricacies of an aero engine. But the flying was what I revelled in. All too soon our flying training was completed, and on my last solo sortie at Filton, as I brought the Tiger Moth in over the hedge for my final landing, I suddenly recalled that visit with my mother not many years before when we watched together as Cyril Uwins approached over that same hedge in the Bulldog. The *ab initio* course was completed on 15 October, and we all went away rejoicing that we were now pilots, although perhaps not yet fully fledged!

But our high spirits were soon dampened as we entered the grim gates of the Royal Air Force Depot at Uxbridge for the next phase of our training. Perhaps we had not read the small print in our joining-up contracts, for it came as a rude shock that we were not entered as sergeants, as we had thought, but as almost the lowest of the low, leading aircraftmen, at least for the time being.

As we entered RAF Uxbridge there were no three stripes for us or the comfort of the sergeants' mess. For a time I felt very disillusioned. After the euphoria of the Bristol Flying School this seemed a betrayal and a mean trick by the Air Ministry, and we all felt strong resentment. However, it soon became clear that we were not going to be in a position to complain about anything, and there was to be a great deal to complain about. The whole course was accommodated in a bleak barrack room, with iron bedsteads, three 'biscuits' as hard as concrete, a bedside locker in which our kit was to be laid out in precision order and all personal effects packed up and carried away. For a fortnight we were ordered around with little consideration for either our pride or our well-being. The NCOs in charge subjected us to daily drill on the square, rifle drill and marches with full back-packs, and as soon as we were released from that we were herded back to our barracks, where everything had to be cleaned, polished and tidied. This included boots, buttons, uniform, bed space and lockers, not to mention basins and latrines. This really was two weeks of unmitigated bullying in the name of discipline, and the NCOs obviously relished every moment of it. I must admit I reached a stage of deep depression and wondered if I would be able to make the grade. Luckily, we all shared the suffering together and managed to retain a fairly collective sense of humour among the course members, refusing to be cowed, much to the frustration of our tormentors.

As we emerged from those grim gates at the end of those horrid weeks it was with a feeling of great relief. At least we emerged as individuals again and could look forward to more reasonable and sympathetic treatment.

And thus it proved: our reception at our Flying Training School at Wittering was encouraging and helpful. We arrived on the night of 7 November 1935 by train from London, and were met at Stamford station and taken to RAF Wittering by three-ton lorry. This late-night arrival in the dark was to cause me some confusion in the following weeks. I assumed that being taken on from Stamford by lorry meant travelling further north. It took me some time to get out of the habit of looking for the airfield to the north of Stamford, not realizing that on our arrival the lorry had brought us back on our tracks and south to Wittering: a strange quirk of the human navigation machinery. Wittering was alongside the Great North Road, with Stamford a few miles further north. The intensity of our training did not allow much time off the station, but occasionally a few of the more venturesome of our course walked into the town primarily to get a meal of fish and chips and a beer. I thought it was a great pity that we did not have the time or inclination at that time to explore the lovely old town. Built on either slope of the Welland valley, its houses of locally quarried limestone were fine examples of medieval and Georgian buildings which seemed to glow in the sunshine. Happily the town is now protected by a bypass, but not long ago the Great North Road ran through the middle, and athwart it was the 'gallows' arch of the George Hotel, one of the oldest post-houses between London and Scotland. As long ago as Norman times the Knights of St John were providing shelter here for pilgrims finding their way to the Holy Land. At one time the hostelry boasted stabling for eighty-six horses, and some forty coaches a day used to pass through the cobbled street for a rest at the inn. I remember how we had all admired this grand hotel but felt it was much too posh a place to go in for our fish and chips and a beer.

Just across the road to the east was Burghley House standing in its vast estates. The house was built by William Cecil, and its forty rooms now contain one of the finest collections of Elizabethan furniture, paintings and tapestries in the country. But to our small band of would-be fliers the treasures that lay beyond this estate wall beside which we plodded back to the airfield still remained undiscovered.

We were the junior term at the training school and would be flying Hawker Harts and Audaxes. I was pleased to have Sgt Craigie as my instructor, a soft-spoken and kindly man of considerable experience who was quite unflappable in the air. We got on well together, and after eight flights in the Hart I was sent off solo. This was another milestone in my avowed career, to fly alone in a real Royal Air Force aeroplane with those red, white and blue roundels on the silver wings, just as I had so avidly looked upon all those years ago in the Bristol hangar. And what a thrill it was, to handle what felt to me like a great big flying machine with its 500 hp Rolls-Royce Kestrel engine. I just loved every moment in the air, but even then I yearned to be on my own and looked forward to my solo flights. It always gave me a lift when I saw the mechanics carrying out those heavy round lead weights to fit onto the bars under the rear cockpit that were necessary when the back seat was to be unoccupied.

A week later I flew the Audax solo. It was a similar aircraft to the Hart, but heavier and with a more powerful Kestrel. After about twenty-three hours on the Hart and Audax, including cross-country flights to Abingdon and Upper Heyford, we were all subjected to a flight test by the senior flying instructor. I may not have realized it at the time, but this was a vital test of our flying ability that would have a profound effect on our future in the Air Force. Nevertheless I tried very hard to turn in an immaculate flight for the senior instructor. While all the course eagerly awaited the findings of the flight tests that might influence their future, the good news came through that at the start of the senior term we would be gazetted as sergeants. And more good news: on the same day there would be a parade during which we would be presented with our flying brevet. So 14 January 1936 was a proud date, and members of the senior term, at the end of the day, could not get into Stamford quickly enough to show off to the girls and boys the coveted wings proudly displayed on our chests. And for me the good streak continued, as I and a few others on the course learned that we had been selected to go onto fighters. Our elation was in stark contrast to the gloom and grumbles of the remainder of the course, who were probably committed to flying the heavies in Bomber Command or in flying-boat squadrons. This selection was of special importance to me, for it was the culmination of my ambition to fly fighters. I began to feel that my service career was really on course for the future of which I had dreamed. Strangely enough the majority of those selected for the fighter role were already my closer friends on the course.

In particular I got on very well with John Tanfield, a young enthusiast with common interests. But sadly a year later he was killed in his Fury when it crashed at Tangmere. He was only 19. We only suffered one catastrophe during the period of our course training, and this occurred because the maverick of the pupils, Mac, failed to pay sufficient attention to the briefing on the cooling system of the Kestrel and made a stupid mistake in the air, which had disastrous results. The radiator of the Hart could be moved in and out of its housing between the undercarriage to regulate the engine cooling by means of a wheel in the cockpit. When carrying out aerobatics, if negative G was applied the radiator would fall into the fully retracted position. We were specifically warned to watch out for this, and if it occurred, to remember to wind the radiator out again to restore normal cooling. Well, Mac did his aerobatics, including a slow roll, and the inevitable happened unnoticed, so that after a while the engine overheated. Finally the coolant boiled and white smoke poured out of the exhausts. Mac, in panic, assumed the aircraft to be on fire, undid his harness, turned the Hart on its back and fell out and parachuted to the ground. As a salutary lesson we were all taken out to see the wreckage. The heap of twisted metal, torn fabric and shattered glass that was but an hour ago a beautiful flying machine was a heartbreaking sight. At the time I made the rash and rather high-minded resolve always to put the safety of the aircraft first, before thought of self-preservation. As it happened, never in the whole of my flying career did I abandon an aircraft of which I had control. On 20 February Sgt Craigie led me out to the flight line, but instead of going to the familiar Harts and Audaxes he walked over to one of the Fury aircraft, and my heart missed a beat as I feasted my eyes on what must have been the most elegant of all the biplanes ever built. And, wonder of wonders, I was now going to have the chance to fly it.

Craigie had already given me a full briefing on the aircraft's flying characteristics and switches and instruments in the cockpit, and as I climbed in it already felt familiar to me. However, I was mindful of the vicious swing on take-off that the aircraft was reputed to have, although I guessed it had been exaggerated by my fellow students still flying Harts. What a thrilling sound the Kestrel made on start-up, with its stub exhausts spitting flames and smoke, and how responsive I found the engine to even small throttle movements. The long sleek nose impaired forward visibility a little while taxiing, but gently swinging the aircraft from side to side was made easy with the use of the new toe brakes once I had mastered them. At that time Wittering was just a large grass area with a large dip at the north end. With no runway to line up on it was necessary to pick a conspicuous mark on the far boundary to aim for. I turned into wind and chose a gap in the trees as an aiming point, and firmly moved the throttle forward. Acceleration was exhilarating, and anticipating the swing I applied gentle but firm pressure on the right rudder pedal even before the nose had time to wander from the gap ahead. With the slightest backward pressure on the stick, the Fury leapt into the air and rocketed into an impressive climb. Even though I was very inexperienced I found that I was already beginning to appreciate the fundamental characteristics that made up the performance of an aircraft. I sensed that the Fury flew as well as it looked with its light powerful controls, well harmonized to give superb manoeuvrability and a dazzling performance, making it an ideal aerobatic aircraft.

I revelled in every moment of that flight, my first in a Royal Air Force fighter; another milestone passed and ambition achieved. I returned to Wittering by reference to the plume of white smoke from the Ketton Cement Works, a landmark that we found useful in locating the airfield. I joined the circuit with reluctance, but was thrilled by the crackle that came from the exhaust stubs as I throttled back the Kestrel over the hedge, and found the approach and landing straightforward and the brakes a joy to help park the aircraft back on the Fury flight line. Envy showed on every face as I returned to the locker-room, and I couldn't find the words to express my elation.

The Fury was designed by Sidney Camm and was said to be his favourite aircraft; with its good looks and enhanced performance it was a worthy predecessor to the Hurricane. The specification given to Hawkers was for an interceptor fighter that would dispense with the perceived need for standing patrols. It must therefore have a good turn of speed, a high rate of climb and good manoeuvrability. The Fury achieved all these in full measure, and was, in addition, a beautiful aircraft. As it went into squadron service its charisma made it the perfect vehicle for pre-war fighter boys, for it exuded the glamour that came to epitomize the lifestyle of the breed who, all too soon, were to be faced with the brutal realities of air combat. Several future 'Aces' and many of those who paid the ultimate price were nurtured in the Fury's cockpit.

I found the following weeks a thrilling time, enjoying to the full the superb manoeuvrability of the Fury in aerobatics and formation flying. When I was not flying or at lectures, I started to play serious rugby again, soon being picked for the station's team, and I was most fortunate to be selected as stand-off half to Tom Morgan at scrum-half who later was to play for Wales. He was a wonderful inspiration and without doubt helped me on the rugby field, and I began to play a reliable game and enjoyed it immensely.

As I became more familiar with the Fury I enjoyed flying it more and more. Returning from a flight one evening I became aware, perhaps for the first time, of the significance of the two .303 Vickers guns sitting on either side of the decking in front of me. It came as a rude awakening to me that the 'fun' flying must now give way to the real purpose of my training. I was flying a fighting machine and must treat it as such. A few days later this realization was confirmed when the senior term of our course was taken up to the Armament Training Camp at Catfoss for gunnery training. From the start I did not enjoy firing guns, and it soon became clear that I could fly much better than I could shoot. Despite my best efforts, my results in firing at an airborne sleeve towed on a 200 feet wire behind a Fairey Gordon were barely average, and just when I began to obtain better results our flight was ordered back to Wittering to make way for another squadron needing gunnery practice. But I soon realized that a good aim was going to be vital for survival in the years ahead, and so I took every opportunity to practise shooting, and eventually became a passable shot.

CHAPTER FOUR

Nearly Fatal

1936 to 1937

On 10 May, a date that I would have occasion to remember all too well in the future, I received my first posting, and much to my delight it was to No. 25 Squadron. This was a prestigious fighter squadron flying Hawker Furies, and I could not have wished for anywhere better. It was based at Hawkinge, a small grass airfield in a unique position on the cliff tops above Folkestone. It was a beautiful position with wide views across the green belt of South Kent. Attractive to look at but a menacing trap to unwary aviators when the sea fog rolled in to cover the South Downs and visibility at Hawkinge was reduced to nil. It was only a few months after I joined the squadron that two of our officers were caught in this trap and were killed in the subsequent crash into the hillside.

On my arrival at Hawkinge I was well received on the first day when I rather nervously reported to the squadron adjutant and he told me to find the A Flight commander in number one hangar. Slim was all one could wish for in a fighter pilot – tall and slim with a real press-on attitude and leading his flight from the front with dash and confidence. He suffered my inexperience and nervousness with kindly understanding, and I was soon able to take my place in all details of the flying programme. I enjoyed every moment of flying the Fury and was prepared to suffer the taunting and kidding of the other NCO pilots in the flight who had, of course, had to get in several years of service before they got their three stripes, and they understandably resented the direct-entry sergeants such as myself. However, as I gained experience and caught up with their capabilities, I was soon accepted as one of them. I began to fly as No. 3 in Slim's formation aerobatics team, and several times was called on to carry out special flights requiring accurate recordings of in-flight data, etc. These flights, I think, first gave me the idea that I might aspire to be a test pilot, although it was early days to think

17

about that, of course. On the anniversary of King George V's Coronation the squadron was called on to carry out dummy dive-bombing attacks on a target at the Folkestone cricket ground as part of the celebrations, and I again flew as Slim's number three in a close formation. On 22 June I had the first, and the last, engine trouble with the Kestrel that I ever experienced. During a local flight the engine developed an internal water leak, and with white smoke pouring from the exhaust and power being rapidly lost, I managed to land without further trouble on the small emergency landing ground at Littlestone, near the seafront at New Romsey.

On a glorious June day as I was doing a navigation exercise over Canterbury and diving my Fury down to a few hundred feet over a little village of Sturry, I circled round a large house with extensive gardens. A lawn in front of the house was the centre of my attention for there was the lovely sight of several scantily dressed young ladies doing gymnastic exercises on the green sward. My arrival was by no means accidental, as I had previously found out that this was the home of the Women's League of Health and Beauty, and I knew that Suzette would be there. The short display of aerobatics over Sturry that morning was one of my best, and I returned to Hawkinge with a happy heart. This was not the last time that Suzette would receive my salute from the air. From time to time the other NCO pilots from the squadron and I used to go down to the Wellington Hotel in Folkestone for a darts and table-tennis evening. Here I met Maisie, the daughter of Captain and Mrs Lister who ran the hotel, and we became close companions.

Life at Hawkinge was most fulfilling in every way, and I revelled in it. When weather permitted there was flying every day, either on individual training or flight formation exercises. The station also sported a good rugby team and had regular fixtures with the Army at Shorncliffe Barracks and local towns like Dover and Maidstone. I would never claim that I was a brilliant stand-off half, but I always found a place in the first team. Life continued happily until 16 October, when I came very close to tragedy. During a high-level cross-country squadron formation flight in Furies to RAF Tangmere, we had been flying westwards at 20,000 feet for some time when my flight commander, who was leading the formation, was astonished to see my aircraft leave the formation and start to do the most alarming antics, rapidly losing height in a series of stalls and spins. Slim called me desperately on the radio, as did other members of the formation, but there was no answer. Getting dangerously near the ground, I slowly became aware that I had passed out, but I finally regained consciousness and was lucky enough to have sufficient height to regain control of my Fury. After a shaky landing at Tangmere, to a group of anxious faces gathered round I was able to explain that apparently my oxygen supply had somehow become disconnected, and I could remember nothing until waking up at 2,000 feet and being amazed to find myself in the air. Safely on the ground, we found that the Fury, on inspection, was a bit 'stretched', and the doc said I had burst a lot of blood vessels in my eyes, but I did not seem to have suffered further damage. I managed to fly back to Hawkinge under the watchful eyes of the rest of the formation led by Slim, who kindly remained at low altitude. On 11 December the members of 25 Squadron were delighted when the squadron was re-equipped with the Fury Mk2. We had looked on the Fury 1 as the ultimate in grace and elegance, but this Super Fury soon received all the superlatives for looks and performance. With an uprated, fully supercharged Kestrel engine, streamlined spats on the wheels and a new wing plan, it gave the squadron an élite reputation, soon to be affirmed by its being chosen to perform at the Royal Air Force Display at Hendon in June 1937. This turned out to be the last of these famous pageants ever to be held. On 29 January 1937 I was asked to report to my squadron commander, who gave me the sad news that my father had died. It was a very sad blow, particularly as I had planned to write to him that very night to tell him that I would be flying at Hendon. I knew that he would have been proud and pleased to know that it was largely through his help and support that his son had done so well in the Royal Air Force. Now he would never know. Slim sent me off on a week's leave, and after the funeral I returned to my squadron a very saddened sergeant.

But I had little time to dwell on the loss of a father who had helped me so much in my career, as we were busily engaged during the next few weeks in practising for our event in the coming Hendon Display. Our part was to be a squadron of 'goodies' called in to attack and destroy a party of 'pirates' assembled in a fort: a canvas erection in the centre of the airfield. They were to be armed, so the squadron had to devise tactics to confuse their return fire. Sufficient to say that on the day, the screaming of our Kestrels as the Furies dived in to the attack, the aerobatics in tight formation, together with the howling of the pirates and bomb and gun-firing noises broadcast over the PA system, made this a very popular event. This was the last of the famous Hendon Displays, and as the squadron re-formed and did a last flypast I thought how fortunate I was to have taken part. Unfortunately the Furies had to return direct to Hawkinge after the show, and so I did not have the chance of seeing my family party, who were among the 200,000-odd spectators assembled below, together with the King and Queen, princes and princesses, foreign diplomats and a crowd of air marshals. But it was not for them that I had been flying, not even the air marshals. As we swept over Hendon in our farewell flypast I only had a moment to scan the upturned faces of the great crowds below, and hoped that Suzette would know that it was she for whom I was flying and would be proud.

As the news from Europe became more and more ominous, our flying was concentrated on war exercises. It had already become clear that Germany had abrogated the terms of the Versailles Treaty and had announced the formation of the *Luftwaffe*. Details of German aircraft began to appear in the crew room, and aircraft recognition became a daily subject for our attention. The Germany–Italy Axis had been proclaimed and German aircraft had been used to uplift Franco's Army in Africa back to Spain. The Spanish Civil War was being used by Germany, Italy and Russia as a testing-ground for their war weapons. The bombing of the City of Guernica by the German Condor Legion shocked the world and gave a grim warning of what was in store, being clear evidence that Germany was bent on armed conflict in Europe.

In August 1937 the squadron suffered a flying accident when one of our flying officers crashed while flying his flight commander's Fury and attempting a forced landing at Dymchurch. Happily he was only slightly injured. On the same day I took off in a Fury on a climb to maximum ceiling of 34,000 feet, and as I looked down from that great height the whole of south-east England in all its tranquil beauty was spread out below. I was still at that innocent and impressionable age, and could not imagine that this land, so precious to every Englishman, might be threatened by a hostile invasion, and I could not even imagine the vital air battles that would be fought in this very piece of sky in a few years' time. I contemplated the future as I saw it, with the prospect of meeting superior German aircraft, in this beautiful but wholly in-adequate Hawker Fury that I was flying.

In August the squadron flew to Biggin Hill and Kenley on short 'war' detachments, and when these were completed we were released on a long summer leave. I took the opportunity to drive down to Gloucestershire in my splendid little Riley Imp (surely the most desir-able sports car ever made?) to see my mother and brother and sisters. We had a great deal to talk about, and had long discussions about the future prospects and what we might do to safeguard the family inter-ests now that father was gone.

Before returning from leave I went to Hatfield to see the end of the King's Cup Air Race, won that year by Alex Henshaw flying the stylish Mew Gull. On the way home Leslie, my big brother, took me to the Shelsley Walsh Hill Climb, where we entered his Riley Gamecock in the race. We were outclassed and were not placed. Although we were not placed we had a lot of fun, and I always enjoyed doing exciting things with my elder brother. We were, and always continued to be, very close until Leslie emigrated to New South Wales with his wife to live near the beautiful coast at Ocean Shores, to play golf, and all too soon to die after a painful cancer, nursed by his devoted wife. In his last days he could look out of his bedroom window and for the last time see the whole length of the beautiful Byron Bay, the most easterly point of Australia. I missed him badly.

I spent my twenty-first birthday at my sister's home at Longhope with my mother, and next day returned to my squadron to find a new CO and station commander. The latter would prove to be a good friend some weeks in the future.

CHAPTER FIVE

Furies to Demons

October 1937 to June 1938

On 28 October the unbelievable happened and the squadron was told that it must give up its splendid Super Furies and exchange them for the clapped-out Demon two-seater fighters of No. 41 Squadron at Catterick. This order considerably dented our pride, for we really thought 25 Squadron was held in high esteem, particularly after its acclaimed performance at the Hendon Air Pageant. However, Slim, my flight commander, optimistic as always, convinced us that the exchange was no detriment to our squadron but was probably intended to prop up the morale of 41 Squadron, and he soon had us flying tight-formation aerobatics in our acquired Demons. But the loss of our splendid Furies was deeply felt and strongly resented.

As our training continued with the added needs of our air gunners we couldn't help wondering just what plans the Air Ministry had in mind for our future role. It was clearly a retrograde step to re-equip the squadron with an aircraft of inferior performance to our single seaters. The Fury was capable of 223 mph, with a good climb performance, whereas the Demon's top speed was only 202 mph, with much inferior manoeuvrability. It seemed that the Air Staff planners' policy exemplified the compromise of economy enforced by the Treasury (the Demon was a comparatively cheap aircraft to produce) and the needs of a sound defence strategy. But plans for the introduction of a heavy multi-gun turret for the Demon supported the idea that the planners believed that our future fighters needed only to have heavy firepower to shoot down bombers, and ignored the likelihood that they might also have to tangle with high-performance escorting fighters. The fighter pilots only hoped that this thought would get through to the planners in Whitehall and that new suitable fighters would be in the pipeline, but at squadron level we were kept in ignorance of the pending arrival of the monoplane eight-gun fighters. In any event, the squadron had to make the most of its Demons for a further eight months until our Gladiators arrived, but even these were, of course, still one step behind the Hurricanes.

As our squadron training continued we suffered a bad accident. Two Demons of the squadron collided while flying in formation between Dover and Deal. One aircraft spun out of control and the pilot parachuted to safety, but the gunner died later when the aircraft crashed on Sandwich golf course. The sergeant flying the other aircraft, with commendable skill and a lot of luck, managed to land his Demon back at Hawkinge, with badly damaged mainplanes and interplane struts.

During the winter months Wednesday afternoons at Hawkinge were usually devoted to rugby games or away matches with local units like Manston or Lympne and Army teams at Shorncliffe Camp or Colchester. However, on Wednesday 9 December 1937 I was ordered to report to Headquarters No. 11 Group at Uxbridge. After my previous experience at the station I felt nervous of what was in store for me. But I was relieved and excited when I was called in to an interview with the Air Officer Commanding to discuss the prospects of a commission. I knew that I had been recommended by my commanding officer but never thought that it had progressed so far. After the interview, which seemed to have gone reasonably well, I went on from Uxbridge to Gloucestershire, where I was eager to tell the family this good news. A few days later the whole family foregathered for a Christmas party at my sister Noni's delightful home at Longhope, which nestles under the shadow of May Hill.

On my long drive back to the squadron at Hawkinge, I boosted my little Riley to its maximum performance in the hope that the thrill would cheer me up. The next day I applied myself with enthusiasm to the intensive night-flying programme in which the squadron was now engaged. On 25 February I was airborne on my first-ever solo night-flying, and I found it both frightening and demanding. In the daylight I never tired of the thrill of first getting off the ground and feeling that I was fully in control of the aircraft with a clear horizon to refer to. But at night, as I lifted off from take-off, there was a moment of anxiety, particularly on a dark night, as I searched for a reference point on which to confirm the aircraft's attitude. It took a good deal of training before I learned to refer to the instruments at once and wholly rely on them and rid myself of these moments of panic. This first night solo in the Demon was made all the more scary when I was conscious of the long exhaust pipe that ran down the side of the fuselage, glowing a fiery red down the whole of its length. No one had warned me of this phenomenon. Hawkinge was not a very big grass field and it had a high hedge on rising ground on the western approach and the cricket field leading up to Hawkinge village and its burial ground at the other end. In the course of our first night-flying programme one of the Demons overshot on landing and finished up in the village cemetery through an error of judgment, but understandable in view of the short runway available and the inexperience of the pilot.

In those days the night-flying lights consisted of a row of paraffin flares (goose-necks) and a large floodlight (Chance Light) at the touchdown end of the runway. The latter was only switched on as an aircraft was on the final approach and was not always fully reliable. I was made aware of this some months later when it was the part-cause of my first crash, when I ended up in my mangled Blenheim over the end of the runway at Northolt, the squadron's war base.

Tactical exercises were being held regularly, and flights from the squadron were detached for several days at a time to Biggin Hill and Kenley. During one visit to Kenley the resident squadron had just received the first of its Hurricane 1s, which was an early production version and had the large fixed-pitch wooden propeller. This aircraft was quite a handful for an inexperienced pilot perhaps coming from a Fury squadron, and was unforgiving on the approach and landing if its pilot was at all careless in maintaining adequate flying speed. At the very moment of my landing approach to Kenley airfield I had one of their Hurricanes ahead of me. I watched in horror as it turned slowly, much too slowly, towards the airfield, and suddenly dropped a wing, flipped over and struck the ground in a ball of fire. A very sad sight when both pilots and Hurricanes were going to be desperately short in the coming battle that now seemed inevitable.

In May we had the last of our rugby games, a match against Rydden's Brewery of Faversham. This was a most popular fixture, and although there is no record of who won, the hospitality afterwards was most generous. But the game remains in my memory because I foolishly drove home in my muddy football boots, and parking my beloved Riley in front of the sergeants' mess my foot slipped off the brake pedal and we rammed the car in front. I could have cried! Luckily not too much damage was done, and in due course the Folkestone garage managed a very good repair job.

Later in the month our popular flight commander, for the first time, let us down. He was leading nine Demons of the squadron to Northern Ireland, staging at Catterick and West Freugh. We took off in formation with Slim leading as usual, but after an hour's flying the weather deteriorated and the cloud forced us down to a few hundred feet above the ground, and we grimly hung on to Slim's wingtips in deteriorating visibility. After a while he started to circle round, and it was clear that he was lost, and therefore so were we. Fuel was getting low and so he did the only sensible thing and told us all to break formation and find a suitable field in which to force-land. It is surprising how many large green fields there are below on a normal cross-country flight, but when the weather is closing in, fuel is running short and one is lost, no suitable field seems to appear. Whichever way I turned I seemed to run into sloping ground covered in cloud. In desperation and determined not to wait until I was out of fuel, I opted to attempt to land in the first field with any possibility at all. I reduced height and speed, and looking ahead I saw a minute field with a wood on one side and a low hedge to approach over, and luckily the field seemed to slope towards me. I set up a low approach, and just about on the stall I slammed the throttle shut, cut the ignition and turned off the fuel and let the Demon drop into the field. The ground was soft, the grass was long and I managed to come to a stop some few yards from the far end of the field.

Relieved to be safely down I felt very silly as I climbed down from the cockpit to be standing there, miles from anywhere, in the depth of the country, with an aeroplane. But it did not take long for the village bobby to appear on his bike, puffing up the hill of an adjoining lane. He obviously didn't deal with this situation every day, but he soon caught on and pedalled off to the nearest telephone with the number of RAF Catterick and the map reference of the field where I had landed the Demon. Within an hour an officer and a refuelling tanker had arrived. A small amount of fuel was pumped into the Demon's tank, as Catterick turned out to be quite close, and discussions took place as to whether I was capable of taking the aircraft off again from such a small field or whether a more experienced pilot should come over from Catterick. Considering my inexperience it certainly was a challenge, and I would look pretty stupid if, having got it safely down, I was to crash it on take-off. The difficulty was not so much the short field but the considerable slope on it. There was little wind and the cloud had lifted, so the decision having been made I decided to take off down the slope, which would give me added acceleration and a low hedge to clear. I soon had the two 'erks', one either side of the engine cowling, frantically turning the engine starting handles. The Kestrel roared into life and they extricated themselves from the force of the slipstream and the rigging wires and at my signal, pulled away the chocks that they had brought with them. I taxied up the hill to the top of the field, and with a slight wind behind sent the Demon bowling down the hill, the far hedge getting closer all too rapidly. I could feel the difference that the bit of tailwind was making to the build-up of flying speed, but with a silent prayer and gentle backward pressure on the stick we lifted over the hedge with feet to spare, and I was soon in the Catterick circuit and landed happily. It turned out that most of the squadron's other aircraft had found Catterick and had landed safely.

The squadron aircraft were soon reassembled at Catterick, and took off for Ireland next day for bombing and gunnery training at the Practice Camp at Aldergrove. A few days later it was Empire Air Day, and the squadron, together with No. 23 Squadron, carried out a Wing Formation Flypast over Belfast and adjacent towns led by Sqn Ldr Eccles. We managed to put up a total of eighteen aircraft, and this considerable armada duly impressed the Irish populace, according to the Belfast press. After a day of low-bombing attacks with smoke bombs and days of more gunnery exercises, the squadron aircrew were stood down for a day and were taken on a tour of Ulster.

Few of us had ever visited the country before, and inevitably our opinion of the Irish people was tainted by the stories we had heard of IRA atrocities and the bigotry and violent hatred that still seemed to be prevalent between the two sides. We found it hard to believe that the kind and generous folk whom we now met were the same race of people who continued to harbour within their society a few wicked terrorists intent upon their own policy of gaining their political ends by fear and intimidation and the threat and use of violence. Such thoughts went through my head as we were driven down to see the Giant's Causeway, the most unusual rock formation that I had ever seen: thousands of hexagonal columns of basalt, apparently formed by the flow of a volcanic river many aeons ago, seeming to march out into the sea. Perhaps the mythical giant's road to Scotland? The scenery that we saw that day, the rugged unforgiving wildness of this coast exposed to the cruel Atlantic, compared dramatically with the benign softness of the green and pleasant hinterland, providing, perhaps, a clue to the unpredictable and volatile nature that seemed to exist in the make-up of the people of Ulster.

On 20 June we flew back from Ireland in a formation of six Demons from Aldergrove (Ireland), toWest Freugh (Scotland), to Sealand (Wales) and back to Hawkinge (England) – six hours' flying on a most glorious summer's day, and a nice change from the flight out to Ireland during the previous week when we had got lost. A few days later the squadron suffered a tragic accident when our popular Canadian officer crashed his Demon into the side of the hill just below Hawkinge trying to scrape in for a landing when thick cloud clung to the hills. He and his gunner were killed instantly. I was a bearer at the funeral a few days later. It was a particularly sad occasion because none of the Canadian officer's relatives were able to get over to be there, and it was only his colleagues from the squadron who mourned his passing. Many years later I paid a nostalgic visit to Hawkinge to try and recapture the spirit of those days, but little remained to help me recall the happy comradeship of my first squadron. As we drove down the hill towards

Folkestone I imagined that I could still see the scar in the chalk of the hillside where the Demon crashed and killed this Canadian. I thought what a slender thread it was that held our fate, and that this young life so suddenly snuffed out here on this Kentish hillside might easily have been spared to fight and find immortality perhaps in the battle that was to save a country that was not his own. As we drove on down the hill and I woke from this reverie and looked across the valley I could see Capel le Ferne, where the splendid Battle of Britain Memorial now stands with its graphic figure of a fighter pilot gazing sadly from the cliff-top out to sea, remembering, perhaps, the many friends whose watery grave it was. The figure evoked such graphic memories that it brought to my mind the words of a poem written, I think, by a former Secretary for Air:

> On Weald of Kent I watched once more
> And thought I heard the thundering roar
> Of fighter planes, but none were near
> And all around the sky was clear.
> Born on the wind a whisper came
> Though men grow old THEY stay the same.
> And then I knew, unseen to eye
> The immortal FEW went sweeping by.

CHAPTER SIX

Demons to Gladiators

June 1938

The melancholy mood that followed the fatal accident at Hawkinge did not persist in the squadron for very long as we received the news that our Gladiator fighters would be arriving shortly. So it was in only a few days that I came down to the flight one morning to hear, not the familiar crackle of Rolls-Royce Kestrels being warmed up by the ground crews, but the strange sound of rattling valve rockers and the swish of the huge slow-turning wooden propeller of the Gladiators and their Mercury engines. And what a welcome sound it was, and what an exciting sight to see these superb, aggressive-looking fighters lined up on the tarmac outside our hangar and to know that I was once again going to be able to fly a real fighter. This was the last of the epoch of silver-winged biplane fighters going back to such unforgettable names as the Snipe, the Camel and the SE.5. Compared with the monoplane fighters already in service in the *Luftwaffe* it was obsolete, but nevertheless it deserves an honoured place in the annals of RAF history for it performed very creditably when put to the test in the early stages of the war when our resources were stretched to the limits. In northern France Gladiator squadrons flew in support of the British Expeditionary Force in the winter of 1940, and later as part of the Advanced Air Strike Force. Very few of those aircraft ever came home, but they contributed to the breathing space that was desperately needed at that time. The Gladiators operated very successfully in North Africa, Norway, Greece and Malta. Where they came up against the Fiat CR.42 of the *Regia Aeronautica* they shot down a great number, and acquitted themselves well in many theatres, including Aden, Syria and Iraq. In the latter case a military coup led by one Rashid Ali, an Arab with strong German sympathies, was seen to be a serious threat to our interests in the Middle East. Our main base at Royal Air Force Habbaniyah, forty miles west of Baghdad, was the key to our defence and was seen to be such by the Germans, who persuaded Rashid Ali to lay siege to the base. A strong Arab artillery force was deployed on the plateau overlooking the airfield, and for several days it pounded the base with heavy gunfire. A spirited defence was mounted in reply by training aircraft from No. 4 Flying Training School, whose base it was. Their aircraft of Airspeed Oxfords and Harvards were fitted with makeshift bomb racks and guns, and their pilots took on their unaccustomed role with bravado. They were hard pressed and suffered quite a few casualties, but help was at hand when a flight of Gladiators, all that could spared, was sent up from Egypt and helped to turn the tide. Rashid Ali was sent packing and calm returned to Habbaniyah, this courageous Royal Air Force strategic base on the Euphrates. Several years later I was reminded of this piece of Arab treachery when I took command of a fighter-bomber wing of Venom fighters at Habbaniyah. They too would take their place in Middle Eastern military history when they were called upon to attack Egyptian installations at the head of the Suez Canal in the Anthony Eden débâcle.

The Gladiator was the most prolific of all the biplanes, and some 450 were manufactured and saw service in many parts of the world. The aircraft was a delight to fly, with a good rate of climb and great manoeuvrability. Originally it had a very flat approach and landing angle because of its excellent streamlining, but the fitting of generous-sized flaps on each of the four mainplanes gave a marked improvement, making the approach much steeper and providing a better view over the nose for the approach and landing. The use of these flaps, however, could be a dangerous trap for the unwary because there was a considerable downward change of trim when they were lowered, and this had to be appreciated and the aircraft trimmed accordingly. However, it was only a matter of getting used to it, and it presented no problem as experience was gained on the aeroplane.

The Munich Crisis brought an end to those halcyon days of air shows, formation aerobatics and any fun flying, and everything was sharply focused on states of readiness, combat tactics and interception practices against formations of Battles, Hampdens and Blenheims. The lovely silver wings that epitomized my original romantic ideas of flying military aircraft were gone now, repainted with drab warlike camouflage. But these extra months of 'phoney war' provided an opportunity for the Royal Air Force to get its act together and put in place our ground radar stations that were to play a vital part later on. With the Gladiator the squadron felt that we now had a chance of putting up a reasonable fight, even against the Me 109s, if we could be directed by the developing ground radar stations and put into a favourable position with a height advantage to attack the faster Germans. Up to this time, however, the

radar stations were not advanced enough to give regular practice interceptions for our fighters. Another aspect of our training now had to be
given immediate attention. It was becoming clear that we were going to
have to fly in much worse weather than in peacetime days and nights,
and so training in flying on instruments was intensified. The Gladiator
was the first fighter to be fitted with what became known as the
standard instrument flying panel. This panel grouped together in
logical layout the dials of the instruments needed for flying without
reference to outside features like the horizon. Hitherto these instruments were quite often spread around the cockpit in a haphazard
fashion, which made it very difficult for a pilot to adopt the first rule of
blind flying. This was to concentrate on continually scanning all
the blind-flying instruments together and coordinate their readings to
give a true picture of the aircraft's attitude. This needed practice and
above all concentration. If this was lost it was easy to become dis-
oriented and one was tempted to disbelieve one's instruments. I was
appointed as the Squadron Instrument Flying Instructor, and in October
was sent to North Weald for a Link trainer course. At this time I was
thrilled to get my logbook back from the squadron commander
annotated with his annual assessment of 'Exceptional as a Fighter Pilot',
a fairly rare annotation, not very often seen!

When the Link trainer arrived it was set up in the Education Section
and I was put in charge. It might be said that the Link trainer was the
first 'simulator', as it reproduced on the ground an aircraft's cockpit
with a standard instrument flying panel, flying controls and a throttle,
and it provided a means, although primitive, of training pilots to read
their instruments to maintain control of their aircraft under blind-flying
conditions The trainer could be fully enclosed and the instructor sat at
a desk where a duplicate set of instruments was displayed so that he
could monitor the pupil's performance. The instructor also had a 'crab'
connected electronically to the trainer, which marked through an inked
wheel the course followed by the trainer on a chart on the instructor's
table. There was an intercom system of communications, and blind
approaches to airfields could be practised through using the Lorenz
System. Approaches were made by flying down a beam broadcast over
the radio. A continuous note marked the desired centre-line, and dots
or dashes would sound if the aircraft was to one side or the other of the
centreline. This Lorenz System was later developed and became the
standard instrument landing system (ILS) fitted in most Air Force
aircraft and installed at many airfields. It is still in use today by both
military and civil aircraft.

When I was not flying I spent nearly all my time putting the squadron
pilots through the instrument flying routine. More and more of our

flying included practical exercises in climbing and descending through cloud, and as confidence grew aircraft were regularly taken up through the overcast in formation. As the squadron's instrument flying instructor I am ashamed to admit that on one occasion at this time I committed the worst blunder imaginable, with nearly tragic results. I had climbed up through about 5,000 feet of cloud in my Gladiator to get above the overcast and to carry out a trial on the use of a gunsight mirror in sunny conditions. After completing the trial and jotting down my notes on my knee-pad I could not resist a few loops and rolls in the lovely clear skies But in a moment of madness and disregarding all the rules that I was always impressing on my pupils, I dived straight into the cloud without a thought for checking my instruments, and forgetting that the artificial horizon would have been toppled during my aerobatics. I had no time to prepare for the concentration needed for flying on instruments before the thick fog of cloud enveloped me. From the joy and thrill of throwing the Gladiator around in the sunlight I suddenly felt the icy chill of a malevolent cockpit around me and a forboding fear that I had never experienced before. Unaccountably I then did another unforgivable thing, and trusted in my own 'seat of the pants' feelings rather my instruments. I could swear that the aircraft was diving and turning to the right, so I tried to correct this by rolling to the left. All at once the cockpit filled with dust and sand and I was hanging on my safety harness. The realization that I was completely disorientated, inverted and in a very dangerous situation unless I could regain control while still in cloud made me get a grip on myself. I concentrated on what my instruments were telling me, ignoring the artificial horizon, and gradually brought the Gladiator under control and descended gently through the cloud. With blessed thankfulness I saw horses grazing in a paddock and a newly turned ploughed field opened up below me. Once again the friendly, familar cockpit seemed to wrap around me reassuringly, and the landing back at Hawkinge was as confident as always. But it was a very chastened 'exceptional' fighter pilot who contemplated what had happened, and I admit I have never let on to anyone before now that moment of folly and its scary consequences.

CHAPTER SEVEN

Gladiators to Blenheims

September 1938 to July 1939

On 26 September 1938 all RAF personnel were recalled from leave, and the next day No. 25 Squadron moved by air to its war location at RAF Northolt. The situation in Europe was now critical, and in Britain the Territorials, Observer Corps, Coastal Defences and auxiliary squadrons were called up, and in the USA President Roosevelt sent a 500-word telegram to Hitler urging him to hold back from further demands in Europe. Russia and Britain undertook to support France if Czechoslovakia was invaded. At Northolt my squadron's fighters were dispersed around the periphery of the airfield, and we were standing by with guns loaded and at constant readiness. Around us the airfield was being camouflaged with tar roads across it and green and brown paint patterns applied to hangars and buildings. The next day the Prime Minister announced another meeting with Hitler. Daladier from France and Mussolini were also to be present. We watched with interest as three Imperial Airways airliners were positioned at Northolt and during the afternoon took off for Munich. The next day, 30 September, Chamberlain landed back at Heston waving that infamous piece of paper with Hitler's signature on it. But surely the Prime Minister did not really believe any more than the rest of us that he had achieved any real guarantee of peace? That night our Gladiators carried out continuous night patrols until the dawn of 1 October, my 22nd birthday.

The scare over, the squadron returned to Hawkinge a week later, and apart from the now usual interception exercises things got back almost to normal There were rugby matches against the Royal Engineers at Shorncliffe and against Dover, both of which we won. The squadron was practising for the Sassoon Trophy, which was a pinpointing and attack competition between all fighter squadrons in the group. This took place at Northolt in early November, but 25 Squadron only came fourth.

We also played rugby against Tangmere next day and lost that as well.

Even against the background of the emerging threat of war, the RAF commanders still sought a high profile in record attempts and prestigious flights in an attempt to impress the Cabinet and the Treasury and to gain more support for funding the development of more up-to-date aircraft and equipment. As an example, on 9 November three Vickers Wellesley bombers took off from Ismailia in the Canal Zone and flew non-stop to Australia. These aircraft were of the new geodetic construction and would be developed and emerge as the Wellington bomber, an aircraft that was to prove of the utmost value in the early days of Bomber Command's attacks on German targets. Some months earlier Flt Lt Adams, flying a Bristol 138 monoplane, had raised the world height record to a remarkable 53,937 feet, and many lessons learnt on this flight would help in the design of high-altitude interceptor fighters in later years. Perhaps one of the most dramatic illustrations of this type of spin-off came as a result of Britain winning outright the Schneider Trophy high-speed series of races, and Stainforth beating the world speed record at 407.5 mph. The development of the Supermarine S.6B floatplane used for this record led to the emergence of the Spitfire and the Merlin engine. At about this time a Fairey long-range monoplane with a Napier Lion X 1A engine set up another record by flying from Cranwell to Walvis Bay in South Africa – a distance of 5,341 miles, and landing with only ten gallons of fuel remaining. This policy of continuing with record attempts despite many other priorities played important dividends as the war clouds gathered in Europe.

On 3 December a flight of the squadron was attached to Worthy Down and Lee-on-Solent to carry out affiliation exercises with the Stranraer flying-boats of No. 228 Flying-Boat Squadron. I had a very exciting ride in the tail gunner's turret in the very stern of one of the Stranraers while my squadron chums carried out close stern attacks on the flying-boat. I was in no doubt as to which aircraft I would rather be in!

On return to Hawkinge I was once more plunged into despair as the prospect of continuing as a single-seater fighter pilot was once more in jeopardy. The squadron was now told that it must give up its splendid Gladiators in exchange for Bristol Blenheims, a twin-engine medium bomber. For one dreadful moment we thought that we were going to be transferred to the bomber force, a prospect too grim to contemplate. I found it difficult to decide whether my prejudice was the moral issue of having to drop bombs indiscriminately, possibly killing civilians, or just the wrench from the fighter role. But thankfully the question did not arise, as it turned out that the Blenheims delivered to us were designated fighters by virtue of being modified with the addition of a pod of four

.303 Vickers machine-guns slung under the bomb bay. The upper turret was retained with a Vickers 'K' magazine machine-gun. I was going to be very grateful for this armament when the shooting started! It was not yet clear what the squadron's role was to be with this aeroplane, although it was soon to be revealed.

But first I was sent off to No. 82 Bomber Squadron at Cranfield to undergo a conversion course. The Blenheim squadrons of Bomber Command at this time were in a state of low morale as they had suffered the loss of a number of aircraft and crews because of failures of the Bristol Mercury engines. However, Sgt Watkins seemed quite confident as an instructor, and after two dual flights I went solo on the Blenheim. I remembered that morning well, for there had been a very heavy frost the previous night and the rutted ground around the apron was as hard as iron. As I taxied out I was concerned at the battering that the Blenheim's undercarriage was taking, so I went very cautiously and it seemed to come to no harm. Back at Hawkinge there was no flying until after Christmas because of heavy snow, which drifted to a depth of six feet in the lanes around the airfield. On 5 January 1939 I took off from Hawkinge in my personal Gladiator K. 7999, and with a feeling of melancholy on this one-way ferry trip I headed north to Usworth in Northumberland, to where the aircraft was to be delivered. After landing and taxiing up to the hangar apron I switched off the Mercury IX, and in the sudden silence, broken only by the tick, tick, tick of the engine as it cooled, I climbed down from the cockpit. I couldn't resist a loving slap on the aircraft's side before tearing myself away with a deep sigh of regret and walking across the tarmac to where Miley was waiting in a Blenheim to take me back to Hawkinge. As we taxied out I gave a final appraising look at this last of the splendid 'silver-winged' fighters that had been such a joy to me over the preceding years. So ended another happy and exciting period of my service, but there was little time to dwell on this setback, and Miley, who had also been to Cranfield, and I set about converting the rest of the squadron pilots onto their Blenheim 'fighters'.

The Blenheim was first seen in its service form at the SBAC Show at Hatfield in 1937. It had been developed from the Bristol 142 (Britain First), designed as a high-speed transport aircraft, but its emergence as a military bomber-fighter came at a most vital time. I began to like flying the Blenheim, which, though not comparable with the single-seater fighters, had a good turn of speed and a good climb rate and was surprisingly manoeuvrable and pleasant to fly. I did not like all the perspex windows surrounding the cockpit, since although giving a good view at most times they caused all manner of reflections of any lights in or outside the cockpit. They could also mist up or freeze in cold weather, as I was to find out to my cost on a later night flight.

It took a little time to get use to the 'spectacles' type of control instead of the joystick that had come so naturally to hand in the single-seater fighters, but with the bigger and heavier aircraft it soon felt to be the right design. The Blenheim did have one serious fault, and that was that the cockpit heating was almost non-existent, and one flew around with constant cold feet. The squadron's role with the new aircraft could surely not be as long-range escort fighters, for that would mean that they would be escorting Blenheim bombers, which would not make sense. So the conclusion was that they were for employment as night-fighters, and once the squadron was operational on Blenheims by day emphasis turned to intensive night flying. Confidence in the aeroplane gradually grew and was greatly enhanced by the visit of Mr Washer, a test pilot from Bristol, who took up several of the squadron pilots and demonstrated just what the aircraft could do. When I flew with him he asked if I would like a demonstration of aerobatics, and he showed me a full range of aerobatics and finished up by a single-engine approach and landing. I was very impressed, and as I gained experience I often repeated his performance.

On nearly every flight now I was demonstrating and converting the squadron pilots to the Blenheim. With a twin-engined aircraft one soon learned the importance of 'critical speed'. With a single-engined aircraft, if the engine stopped one was left with only one problem – to find a suit-able place to land within gliding distance. With a twin it was a question of keeping the aircraft under control, and to do this it was essential to maintain a speed high enough to give directional control to compensate for the asymmetric thrust from only one engine This was the 'critical speed', and it was particularly important during the approach and landing. Misjudgement under these circumstances was the cause of many accidents to twin-engined aircraft, and I gave a good deal of time to demonstrating asymmetric approaches during my instruction to the other squadron pilots.

Hawkinge had two rugby fixtures with Dover during March, and the second one coincided with the arrival of a Spitfire at Hawkinge. The teams crowded around the lovely, sleek machine and it received many admiring glances. Unfortunately no one was allowed to fly it (it was much too precious), but it was viewed with much interest and a lot of envy. I, in particular, again got that feeling of frustration that plagued me now that the earlier promise of single-seater fighters in my career seemed to be fading inevitably into memory. With no chance of flying the Spitfire, most of us ran off to the rugby field to vent our frustration in the rough and tumble of the game. The next day I was able to borrow a Lysander from No. 2 Squadron, with whom we shared Hawkinge. It was an Army Cooperation Squadron and had recently been equipped with this remarkable STOL aircraft. It was no Spitfire, but I thoroughly enjoyed this flight and spent some time in exploring the aeroplane's low-speed handling and stalling characteristics that the full-wing slots, slats and flaps with which it was fitted made possible. This low-speed performance meant the aircraft could be landed or could take off in a very short space, making it ideally suited for the role in which it was used extensively later on, for landing and picking up agents from all sorts of fields in occupied France,

During April and May the squadron was employed on intensive night-flying training in the Blenheims. This was completed without serious mishap, which was a very good effort, as Hawkinge was a small grass airfield without very good approaches, and the emphasis was now on minimal flare-path lighting as the need for blackout on the ground became important in concealing worthwhile targets from enemy aircraft. After my flight in the Lysander when I had been able to evaluate the aircraft's stalling characteristics, I and other pilots on the airfield at the time were amazed and shocked when a No. 2 Squadron pilot managed to stall and lose control of his Lysander right over the centre of the airfield, and it flicked over and crashed in flames. It was a sad case of misjudgement, and I had already appreciated, when I flew the Lysander, that its remarkable slow-flying capabilities could easily tempt a rash pilot to take liberties with the aircraft and inadvertently induce a stall, which, although at a very low airspeed, was vicious and came without warning.

Despite the grave news of the Nazis continuing to rampage through Europe, the squadron continued to participate in traditional events in our flying calendar. Empire Air Day took place on 20 May, and Hawkinge was open to the public to come to see the Blenheims and Lysanders demonstrating their different roles. Formation flying and mock attacks on an 'enemy fort' on the airfield were carried out by the Blenheims, and formation and short landings and take-offs by the Lysanders. There was also a flypast by Sunderland and Stranraer flying-boats, and the station workshops, hangars and other facilities were open to the public. A free 'flight' in the Link trainer proved to be very popular.

Early in June a flight of three of our Blenheims was attached to Benson for affiliation wth No. 159 Squadron, which flew Fairey Battles. Interception exercises were carried out and practice attacks using camera guns for assessment of the films after landing. After returning to the mess when the day's flying was over we were all horrified to hear of the loss of the British submarine *Thetis*, which sank off Llandudno with the loss of ninety-nine lives: a tragedy for the Navy, and the war had not yet even begun.

On 14 July I flew in a formation of Blenheims, Wellingtons,

Hurricanes and Spitfires that took part in a flight over Paris in salute to Bastille Day. Nobody could guess that some of these aircraft would be returning to France in less than twelve months as part of the British AASF in a desperate effort to hold back the Nazi hordes sweeping relentlessly through that unfortunate country. On this day too came news that Alexandria had been bombed. There was no doubt in our minds now that the so called 'phoney war' was coming to an end and the serious fighting was about to begin.

At about this time I was pleased to be called in front of the CO for an interview for a commission, and I also received another annual assessment as 'Exceptional as a Fighter Pilot'. Both these were good news and helped alleviate my melancholy mood.

Among all this excitement I was concerned that Maisie had decide to take a job in Istanbul. It seemed to me to be most unwise in view of the worsening conditions abroad, but as she had already made up her mind, when she sailed out of Folkestone I took a Miles Magister from Hawkinge and flew over her ship across the Channel as an escort. She was to be a nanny to the two children of M. Monicault, *l'Ambassadore de France* in Istanbul. It was clearly going to be a worrying time, but I was heartened by the news that Gp Capt George, my old commanding officer at Hawkinge, was Air Attaché there and had agreed to keep a fatherly eye on her, and also let us correspond via the Diplomatic Bag.

CHAPTER EIGHT

First Operational Patrol

August to October 1939

The month of August 1939 brought to a conclusion all the rumours and uncertainties of the foregoing months. It was almost with a feeling of relief that at last we all knew just where we stood. It was clear that a great effort was required to speed up the rate of production of fighter aircraft, and to this end the Government called into the Cabinet the dynamic Lord Beaverbrook to take on this very responsible task. At the other end of the scale was the appointment of the Duke of Windsor as Governor of the Bahamas. The Duke had been trained as a pilot by the Royal Air Force, and a lot of servicemen had hoped that he might perhaps have been given a more demanding post in support of the war effort, in which he might have redeemed himself, but clearly most members of the Government were not prepared to forgive him his abdication. A few days later we heard with utter disbelief that a Russo-German Pact had been signed in Moscow, and my squadron was once again dispatched to its war station at Northolt, and our aircrews were at readiness in our cockpits or near our aircraft from dawn until dusk each day. Most of the crews slept in their motor cars and ate at irregular intervals from vans sent down with food from the mess. On the morning of 26 August three Imperial Airways airliners landed at Northolt, and in the afternoon took off for an unknown destination with unidentified passengers. There followed much speculation and rumour, but no information was ever released as to their mission. On the last day of August three crews of the squadron were stood down from standby to collect three Blenheim IVs (long nosed) that were being fitted out with the original primitive radar equipment. A few days later I took off in one of these aircraft to undertake one of the earliest airborne radar trials against a flying target.

These early radar sets were painstakingly assembled, and began to arrive for fitting to the Blenheim IVs. One flight of the squadron was given the task of carrying out trials and calibration of the equipment and training the radar operators. It was anticipated that the German bombers might start night attacks at any time, and a workable airborne radar was going to be essential if some at least were to be detected and brought to combat. The night-fighter crews were not at all confident at this stage that we were going to be able to achieve interceptions in the dark. So far the AI sets were primitive and untried, and the squadron had no trained operators. We were still feeling our way in this new field, and civilian scientists from the manufacturing firms often flew with us on the early trials. Each trial flight revealed new problems and frantic work on the ground followed so that the aircraft could get back in the air again. Very close contact was maintained with the manufacturers, who were of the greatest help to the squadron, and we also worked in close cooperation with Dr Watson-Watt, who was engaged in trials of a low-looking radar that it was hoped would help in the interception of the Heinkel minelayers that were operating down the east coast at this time. Flying from Martlesham Heath the squadron flew several low-level sorties out to sea from Bawdsey at the mouth of the Deben river to help in the calibration of Watson-Watt's radar.

On 1 September Germany invaded Poland, and Britain had, of course, pledged that should she be attacked we would go to her aid. General mobilization was ordered in Britain, and the evacuation of schoolchildren and the disabled was put in train. The next day the air component supporting the British Expeditionary Force left for France anticipating the declaration of war next day. At dawn on the 3rd, Royal Air Force Northolt became a frantic hive of activity. In the armoury airmen were loading up belts of .303 ammunition, our mechanics in the hangars were working flat out to finish repairs and inspections on unserviceable Blenheims, while serviceable aircraft were being taxied down to the gun butts, sights zeroed and guns fired. At 11 a.m. we were on active service, and all this noise and commotion brought home to us that from now on events were going to be for real. I remember more than anything else that the firing of our Vickers guns was the sound that announced the end of security and peace, and our world would not be the same – for how long we had no possible idea. It was only a few days before the reality was brought home to us, when, not long after midnight on 4 September, the as yet unfamiliar sound of the air-raid sirens shattered the night air and one flight of the squadron was scrambled from Northolt to intercept an unidentified aircraft detected by ground radar. Our three aircraft, led by our flight commander, with Miley and me in close formation, took off and climbed up through thick overcast. Later, we realized that this was the first night defensive patrol of the Second World War. Although the unidentified aircraft turned out to be friendly, we were kept on patrol for two and a half hours. The leader and I, after a great deal of difficulty, managed to find our way back to Northolt with no aids and almost complete blackout on the ground. With cloud base at 700 feet we were lucky to pick up the Northolt beacon (flashing NT) reflected through the cloud, particularly as for security reasons it was illuminated for only very brief periods. We managed to land both aircraft safely, and Miley, in the third aircraft, although he got separated from us in cloud, landed eventually at Hornchurch. It was the first of very many frustrating night patrols.

Before Europe had become engulfed in war British plans had envisaged a strategic air offensive against Germany by Bomber Command. Now that the stark reality was upon us it was clear that the Command had neither the capacity or efficiency to undertake the effort that would be required to have a noticeable effect on the German war effort. In response to an appeal by President Roosevelt, Britain and France announced that they would restrict bombing to targets of military importance. Surprisingly Germany followed suit after her short campaign in Poland. Thus it was that our gambit was the dropping of six million propaganda leaflets over Germany and sporadic attacks on units of the enemy fleet in Wilhelmshaven and the Schilling Roads. But it was the German response at the commencement of hostilities that was of importance to our defending fighter force.

In the first few months very few German aircraft penetrated our territory, and fighter sorties flown by the squadron were largely defensive patrols and flights for the development of the airborne radar (AI) and training of its operators. Constant reassessment of the risk of air attack and where it might fall resulted in fighter squadrons sometimes being redeployed to other bases. Accordingly, two weeks after the outbreak of war my squadron was moved to Filton to provide cover for Bristol and Avonmouth docks. Having carried out reconnaissance flights and familiarized ourselves with the approaches to Bristol and the Severn from all directions, squadron defensive night patrols continued. It was now policy for anti-aircraft defences and barrage balloons to be deployed around vital industrial establishments, particularly factories producing aircraft and aero engines. It therefore seemed appropriate that our Blenheim fighters were employed in defence of the factories in and around Filton, where our aircraft and its engines were built. Despite regular night patrols the Blenheims made no contact with enemy aircraft. There was still little air activity, but German naval units were becoming increasingly aggressive. Earlier in the month the British liner *Athenia* was torpedoed 140 miles off the Hebrides, with many Americans among the missing. Several small British ships and a French trawler were torpedoed, and the aircraft-carrier HMS *Courageous* was sunk in the Bristol Channel by a U-boat.

On a day off duty I met some of my family in Bristol, to where my brother had driven them down from Gloucester. This was the first time that we had met since the outbreak of war, and we had plenty of news to exchange. My brother, whose building firm was engaged in the construction of military facilities and airfield hangars and workshops, was in a reserved occupation and had joined the Observer Corps in Gloucester. One sister was in the Land Army and Mother was doing useful community work where they lived at Longhope, under the shadow of May Hill. My other sister was working in London at the Ministry of Information. The family brought news of the war budget: income tax at 7/6d, and 1½d on an ounce of tobacco, half a pint of beer and a packet of cigarettes! This was no great burden, but it fore-shadowed much greater hardships to come, particularly when German U-boats swarmed into the Atlantic and started their relentless attacks on ships of our Merchant Fleet carrying all manner of vital supplies to the homeland.

Early in the next month the squadron was redeployed back to Northolt, and as we took off from Filton I recalled that first visit to the Bristol Aircraft Company when mother had introduced me to the world of fighting aeroplanes, and I could again visualize in my imagination that silver-winged Bulldog fighter touching down on that very same grass from which my Blenheim now became airborne on a sterner mission. More grim news greeted us on landing back at Northolt. The battleship *Royal Oak* had been sunk by a U-boat while at anchor in Scapa Flow, with the loss of nearly 800 lives. And the first air raid on Britain had taken place when fourteen German bombers had attacked the naval dockyard at Rosythe and the Forth bridge. The next day a few bombs were reported on Scapa Flow, and there were air raid warnings sounded down the east coast. Despite all this activity around us my companions and I seemed to fit in occasional breaks for relaxation when released from duty. On one day I ferried a Blenheim IV for servicing down to St Athan, a maintenance unit in Wales, and stayed on for a mess dance at the station that night with my navigator. The next day we were collected by two friends in another Blenheim and we called in at Filton on the way home for lunch. That evening back at Northolt we went to a film in Ruislip, *Confessions of a Nazi Spy*. The next day I was invited to apply for a commission, which was approved by my station commander, and I managed to get through a local medical board without any problem. That evening we went to a station dance at Alexandra Palace to celebrate with a party of WAAF girls. Half the squadron had a stand-down the following weekend, and I met my eldest sister, who was working in

London, and we collected my mother from Paddington and went together to a film in Baker Street. The next day we went to the film *The Lion Has Wings* at Leicester Square, and then a show, *The Little Dog Laughs*, at the Palladium, followed by dinner at the Café Royal. The following day we met for lunch at the Café de l'Europe, Leicester Square, followed by the film *Black Velvet* at the Hippodrome, and finally finishing up at the Piccadilly Grill for dinner. Our leaves were short, and as can be seen we were determined to fit in as much as possible in the precious time available. Having said my goodbyes to my mother and sister, I rushed back to Northolt to be on duty at dawn next day.

The news awaiting me was not good, and this time it was a local tragedy. A pilot whom I knew well from the meteorological flight, which carried out a daily weather information-gathering, flying from Northolt in Gladiators, had crashed apparently out of control while descending through cloud and had been killed. This brought back memories of my incident when I became disorientated in cloud and so nearly lost control of my Gladiator. There was news also of a British destroyer hitting a mine off the east coast and sinking with loss of lives. A few weeks later when my squadron attacked the seaplane base from which it was believed the minelaying aircraft came I felt that perhaps that we had taken some small revenge for at least some of those who had been killed. On 21 October I had my first problem with a Blenheim when the starboard engine failed at 7,000 feet. I had no difficulty in getting back to base with all that height in hand, and landed without incident. I did not mention this episode to Captain Lord Inchquim, who was my passenger that afternoon in another Blenheim when I took him on a reconnaissance of AA sites. A further incident occurred a few weeks later with more serious consequences, which ended in my first-ever crash. I was detailed to do some night circuits and landings, and as my navigator and I walked out to our aircraft we were conscious of the very heavy frost on the ground. Strangely enough the Blenheim did not seem to be affected, and as we strapped in I could see quite clearly through the windscreen the ground-crew waiting to start the engines. Start-up was quite normal and I had no difficulty in taxiing out and lining up on the flare-path. Shortly after take-off, however, all the Perspex windows iced over, leaving me with no forward visibility. I tried to open the side window to keep the airfield lights in view, but this was firmly iced up. At this time there was no de-icing system fitted to the Blenheim, and as I realized that freezing level was obviously at ground level I could not see any way out of my dilemma. I concluded that my only option was to try and land as soon as possible. I had been flying by instruments since take-off, and it was not easy to establish my position, let alone find the flare-path on which to attempt a landing. I called ground control on the radio and reported my difficulty, and to my relief a helpful voiced answered and offered to illuminate the airfield identification beacon. Our radios at this time were not all that reliable, hence the relief to get an answer. I then asked for the landing floodlight to be switched on, as this was situated at the touchdown point on the flare-path. As these lights came on I could see their glow through the aircraft's opaque windows, which showed no sign of clearing, and I managed to set up an approximate line of approach to the landing strip. Still on instruments, with an occasional glance outside I managed to keep the blurred image of the floodlight immediately ahead and the beacon in the right relative position to starboard. I estimated my distance from the threshold and began to lose height as shown on my altimeter, and checked my heading on the compass. As I came up to the floodlight I throttled right back and checked my descent. And then the floodlight went out. Perhaps the operator thought I was already on the ground, but as it was I was plunged into a darkness so intense that I could see nothing and all I could do was just feel my way down onto the grass by instinct. The Blenheim wheels touched quite lightly, and with a gasp of relief I applied the brakes and concentrated on keeping the aircraft straight. However, my relief was premature as there was a sudden deceleration and I was thrown forward onto my safety harness as the Blenheim ploughed into the substantial grass bank at the far end of the airfield and finished up with its nose hanging over the Western Avenue, which passes alongside Northolt airfield. I managed with difficulty to get the iced-up overhead escape-hatch open with the help of a fireman who had appeared very speedily, and it was a relief to have a clear view at last as I clambered out and slid down the rather crumpled wing. The aircraft's frosted-over windows were still very evident, and I thought I was lucky to have got it down safely, even if, regrettably, not without damage, although the aircraft was flying again within a month. I was relieved to be able to put in my logbook a copy of a letter from my AOC that said, 'The icing-up of the Blenheim windows was a serious problem that had to be addressed without delay and that this accident was due to circumstances outside the control of the pilot and he was not to blame.'

After a flight to test a replacement engine in another Blenheim the next day I was called in to a briefing on a proposed operational sortie planned to take place on 26 November. This was to be a raid on the German seaplane base on the Island of Borkum, the most westerly of the Friesian Islands. The raid had two objectives: firstly to destroy or damage as many as possible of the Heinkel floatplanes known to be based there, and secondly as a propaganda exercise to support a claim that our long-range fighters were able to reach and attack the homeland of Germany itself. The floatplanes were known to be laying magnetic mines in our coastal waters, and several ships had been sunk, including a British destroyer. These aircraft had proved to be very difficult to intercept as they came in at night below radar cover, and the obvious answer was to try and catch them in their lair.

To this end nine Blenheims of 25 Squadron, led by the squadron commander with me flying as his wingman, took off from Northolt, turning east and crossing out over the coast at Great Yarmouth. We flew 250 miles to the east, low over the North Sea, but by an error of navigation failed to make a landfall, and with nothing but grim grey water in sight the formation wheeled around and returned to land at Northolt some four hours later. The failure of this enterprise was a great disappointment and happened because of a the mistake by the navigator in the lead aircraft, who had been borrowed especially from a bomber squadron. The following day four aircraft of the squadron were standing by to repeat the operation, but this was cancelled and it was not until the day after that that another attempt was to be made.

This time the six aircraft of 25 Squadron were joined by a further six Blenheims from 601 Squadron. We all rendezvoused at Bircham Newton in Norfolk for refuelling and took off in the early afternoon and flew east. All twelve Blenheims kept in fairly close formation as it was a murky winter afternoon, and we flew as before at only a few hundred feet above the dreary grey of the North Sea. An experienced and competent navigator flew with the CO in the lead aircraft, this time borrowed from a maritime reconnaissance squadron. Right on ETA the Dutch coast emerged out of the mist, and a few minutes later we were able to identify the mole, cranes and gantries of Borkum naval base. The squadrons opened out into wide echelon formation and dived down in turn, our four Vickers guns, loaded with De Wilde and incendiary ammunition, spraying the seaplanes, gun posts and installations, while our gunners joined in with their 'K' guns as we swept past and climbed away. There was some slight and inaccurate flak coming up at us, but we were too low and fast for it to be accurate and effective. There was no doubt that complete surprise had been achieved, and although it was difficult to assess at the time there must have been quite a lot of damage done. The timing of the attack was impeccable – just enough light to see the objective for our attack but gathering dusk to retreat into and re-form for the flight home. We returned westwards low over the sea in rain and gathering darkness. About an hour later all twelve aircraft landed safely at Debden after this most successful operation. A later assessment showed that the damage done at Borkum was considerable. Several seaplanes had been damaged and fires started. None of our twelve Blenheims suffered any damage, and all the crews taking part agreed that it was a few glorious minutes of strafing and beating up the Hun, giving a welcome relief from the weeks of frustrating inactivity. The Commanding Officer, Hallings Pott of 25 Squadron, was subsequently awarded the DSO, and his navigator, a sergeant, the DFM, for their leading part in the operation. The two flights that accompanied us from 601 Auxiliary Squadron were led by Max Aitken and Whitney-Straight.

While at the time the success of this raid seemed to justify the use of Blenheims as a long-range fighter, account must be taken of the fact that it was a surprise attack, the first of its kind, carried out in poor weather and at dusk. The use of the squadron's Blenheims on a similar mission but in very different circumstances a few months later was to prove the aircraft's vulnerability in a tragic way.

CHAPTER NINE

Commissioned and Shot Down

December 1939 to May 1940

At the beginning of December I had two interviews for a commission, one with my station commander, Gp Capt Orlebar of Schneider Trophy fame, and the other by my AOC. On Christmas Day the squadron remained on standby at Northolt, and in the crew room discussions ranged widely over the astounding items of news that kept coming in on our crew-room radio. In November the Russians had invaded Finland and early in December the German battleship *Graf Spee* had been scuttled in the River Plate off Montevideo and her captain had committed suicide. A fierce naval battle had preceded the scuttling of the great ship, and HMS *Ajax*, HMS *Achilles* and HMS *Exeter* had put up a great fight and suffered some damage and casualties. Apart from our raid on Borkum the squadron had seen very little action and envied the Royal Navy's opportunities to get to grips with the enemy. However, quite a lot of my friends were still in training, several of them doing their flying training in Canada under the Empire Air Training Scheme, which had just been announced in December, and the agreement signed in Ottawa was of great benefit to us as it relieved pressure on instructors in the UK who were heavily engaged in keeping the front-line squadrons manned with pilots.

Early in January No. 25 Squadron was moved to North Weald in Essex, but before we went I carried out several trials on the Holbeach ranges in the Wash of forward-facing guns in the rear turret of the Blenheim. As far as I knew these trials were not conclusive, and the guns were never adopted, which came as a surprise to me as I thought they would have given the Blenheim badly needed added firepower, particularly for attacking at night. At North Weald, besides maintaining a readiness state each night, the squadron was also tasked with providing a flight to escort the Harwich–Hook of Holland daily convoy. Our three Blenheims covered the ship half-way across the North Sea

46

and there they were relieved by twin-engined Potez fighters from the French Air Force. Our meeting in mid-channel was usually accompanied by a good-natured dogfight, which served to relieve the monotony. At this time there was much toing and froing of squadron flights between North Weald and Martlesham Heath. The flight at the latter base was employed on intensive training and air testing of the new radar equipment in the Blenheim IV, as well as keeping a night air-defence readiness state. Some night air-defence patrols were carried out from North Weald, particularly at low levels looking for the minelayers. From one of these patrols, Sgt Monk returned to base with all three blades of his starboard propeller bent up like a coathanger. He had hit the sea but by a miracle managed to retain control and recover normal flight for a return to base not a little embarrassed.

On 28 March I was required to report to the Central Medical Board of the RAF at Imperial House, Kingsway, for a full medical for my commission. The next day I was very relieved to hear that I had got through it successfully, and was told that I could go ahead and order my officer's uniform. This was an exciting time for me, of course, but depressing news from the squadron was that a new officer, Plt Off Brierly, had been killed when his Blenheim stalled after take-off at night and crashed. His radar operator, Plt Off Sword-Daniels, died later in hospital. Another tragedy happened at Martlesham when Plt Off Obelinski, the international rugby wing three-quarter, was killed when his neck was broken as his Hurricane overturned after landing, a sad loss to his squadron and a blow to international rugby. But my mood soon picked up when I set off for London in high spirits, this time to call at Fulchers of Saville Row to be measured for my uniform. As I emerged into Piccadilly the *Evening News* placards showed that Sir Samuel Hoare had been appointed as our new Air Minister. The next day I had to return to North Weald to get cleared and to hand in my rough serge sergeant's uniform, which I did with much relish. On 1 April 1940, after serving as a sergeant for three years, I received my commission. I found it quite a wrench to be leaving 25 Squadron, having served in it for most of that time. My CO provided a nice parting gesture by recording another 'exceptional' assessment in my logbook before my departure.

I was commissioned as a pilot officer and posted to No. 600 City of London Auxiliary Squadron, which was based at Northolt. I anticipated that there would be quite a change in my lifestyle, and joining an auxiliary squadron as an ex-NCO I thought might accentuate the difficulty of my being accepted into its exclusive ranks. All their pilots were what the press used to describe as weekend flyers, and were mostly wealthy financiers or their sons from the City. Even in the service they maintained a very high standard of living. Lord Lloyd was the squadron's Honorary Air Commodore, and the squadron maintained very close relations with the City's dignitaries. I was concerned that I would find them rather proud and haughty, but from the squadron commander down they were all very considerate and understanding in their acceptance of this very new member straight from the sergeant's mess with the very thin blue ring on his sleeve.

Before taking up my new posting I had a few days' leave, which I spent with my brother. After I had shown off my new uniform to the family, Leslie took me down to Bristol and we saw Tommy Trinder at the Hippodrome and then went on to Ilfracombe to stay in one of the best rooms in the Cunningham Hotel, as befitted a newly commissioned officer! We came back through Bristol to try the newly opened Mauritania Hotel, reputed to have a bar on every level of the eight-storey building. It had, and we sampled them all, but it was, after all, a special celebration of my commission. I was quite sober the next day when I joined my new squadron, which in the meantime had moved to Manston in Kent. No. 600 Squadron also flew Blenheim fighters, but they were not yet fitted with AI, and my first four flights from Manston were to calibrate the ground radar stations looking out from Kent across the Channel and to accustom us and the controllers to the interception techniques that were going to be so vital in the months to come. My next flight was a two-hour night standing patrol off the coast, which passed off without incident. That April the weather had turned out to be beautifully sunny and warm, and I well remember sitting out in front of the officers' mess after lunch with the other pilots of 600 Squadron in our shirt sleeves, drinking Kummel out of wine glasses. If this was an example of the lifestyle they were used to, I doubted whether I would be able to keep up with them for long. As we sat drinking our Kummel in the sunlight we talked of the German invasion of Norway, the bombing of Oslo and the rumour that the Nazis had landed troops in Denmark. We could only make a pathetic gesture in support when we landed a small force of British troops at Narvik. There was much speculation as to how soon the Germans would move into the Low Countries, but there was no doubt in our minds that this prospect was inevitable, and as we at Manston looked across the lawn and the well-tended flower beds of roses and marigolds, out beyond Ramsgate and Broadstairs towards the Pas de Calais, we found it hard to believe that this peace would not endure. But we were soon to learn the reality.

The warm and sunny month of May continued, and for a while the relative calm of our lives was unbroken. In the officers' mess life continued to be lavish, and the old batmen still brought us early-morning tea, ran our bath, cleaned our shoes and pressed and laid out our uniforms. After an unhurried breakfast we would set off across the airfield to the flight office to check on the day's flying programme and get our flying kit from our lockers in the crew room. There might be an air test, a radar calibration run or perhaps a convoy escort out in the Straights of Dover to be carried out before lunch. The squadron kept a flight of aircraft and crews at immediate readiness, and this duty was rotated throughout the day. So after lunch there were probably still a few officers off duty lounging and snoozing in the sun on the lawn in front of the mess. One or two of the younger officers had taken rented accommodation locally, and their wives were living near to the airfield, and so they would go to them when off duty. But even as they enjoyed this pleasant existence, German Panzer divisions were massing on the Dutch border, supported by their dive-bombers and an armada of Junkers Ju 52 troop-carriers, with a host of infantry and paratroops. Overhead, protecting this massive force, would be a fleet of single- and twin-engined fighters. At dawn on 10 May they rolled forward with relentless momentum, and the peace and tranquility of that precious corner of Kent where 600 Squadron waited was to be shattered and changed, perhaps for ever, as would the lives of those assembled to defend it.

An early German objective was the Waalhaven airfield at Rotterdam, at which they would need to land their infantry units transported in the Ju 52s. At Manston No. 600 Squadron was brought to readiness, and A Flight was warned for an operation over Holland that morning. Before a full briefing could take place, the order was cancelled and the flight could relax, although kept at immediate readiness. It was released at noon, and B Flight, my flight, came on duty, and so it was we who were briefed to carry out this operation. Six Blenheims with their crews, led by the squadron commander, Jimmy Wells, with me flying as his No. 2, took off from Manston and climbed up into that clear blue sky to 2,000 feet and circled waiting for a promised Spitfire escort. Some time passed but the sky remained clear, so the squadron commander decided not to delay our planned time on target and set course for Rotterdam. As we approached the Scheldt we climbed to 3,000 feet and changed to a loose echelon formation. Our specific task was to attack German troop-carrying aircraft and infantry on the Waalhaven airfield or airborne in the circuit, and there was no question of our engaging German fighters until that was accomplished. So all our attention was directed at the airfield, and all the Blenheims dived down and fired on the Ju 52s and other opportunity targets. Damage was done and fires started, but there was little time to assess the extent before the German fighters were upon us as we climbed away struggling for height to put us on better terms to meet the Messerschmitts. The CO's aircraft was the first to go down, crashing in flames into the outskirts of Rotterdam, quickly followed by three more Blenheims flown by the young flying officers also going down in flames. The fifth aircraft, having survived one attack, managed to evade further damage and set course for home. Unfortunately Norman, in the confusion, mistakenly turned south to make his escape instead of north, but soon realized the error and turned around. As he flew back over the same battleground he was amazed to find that there was not an aircraft in sight and the sky all around was clear. He was the only one from the flight to get back home that day, and arrived back at Manston safely but with an explosive incendiary shell lodged in a fuel tank. I, of course, was flying the remaining Blenheim, and like the others I was attacked by either an Me 109 or an Me 110 as I climbed away from attacking the Ju 52s. In the first attack by the fighter a burst of cannon shells shattered the Perspex hood above my head, grazing my helmet and destroying the instrument panel in front of me. I started to weave sharply, but the next attack stopped my port engine and riddled the port wing. With one engine out I could no longer weave, so to try and shake off the attacking fighters I dived down to low level, but the attacks persisted and yet another burst of cannon riddled my starboard wing and shot off a few feet of the starboard propeller, setting up a horrible vibration. My airspeed indicator had been shot away, but I would not have been able to read it with the severe vibration anyway, so I had no idea of my airspeed. My poor old Blenheim was now staggering along on only one engine, with a lot of surface damage hindering the airflow over the wings and tail, so I knew I must be very near to stalling and falling out of the sky. And then an extraordinary thing happened. As I struggled to maintain control of the aircraft, an Me 109 F flew alongside in close formation with my Blenheim. Either the German pilot thought we must be doomed anyway or he was out of ammunition and was just waiting for us to crash, but I was screaming at Kramer, my gunner, to shoot him down. More shouts came from the back saying his gun was jammed. 'Change the f—g magazine!' But this advice was not needed, as at that moment the gunner's 'K' gun burst into life at the sitting target. The 109 slowly fell back and was seen to disappear into the low scrub, and Kramer was sure he had hit the pilot and the aircraft had subsequently crashed. I was too busy to see what was happening astern as I nursed my badly damaged Blenheim along and tried to keep it in the air. We were rapidly losing flying speed, and my right leg was giving way under the strain of trying to keep straight against the asymmetric power with only a single engine working. I knew now that I had to try and get the aircraft down, and very quickly, before it stalled and spun in. But ahead was a line of what looked to me like the tallest trees in Holland! With the gentlest of movement of the controls I managed to lift the staggering machine over them with only a foot or two to spare, and there ahead, 'God be praised!', was mile after mile of mudbanks. I had no time or inclination to put down the flaps or wheels, but managed to put the Blenheim down fairly gently and it settled on the mud like a dying swan relieved at last of the pain of its fatal injuries. The mud quickly slowed us down, and as we slivered to a stand-still my gunner and I were able to clamber out and get onto firmer ground on the bank alongside which we had landed. We were on the Dutch island of Overflakkee, near Herkingen, and we stood on a very remote spot with only one small farmhouse in sight. As we surveyed the scene around us there was no sign of the intense air activity of a few minutes before. Nevertheless we decided that the sooner we distanced ourselves from our faithful Blenheim L. 1514 (N) the better, for it would surely never fly again. First, however, we tried to burn it, but even with the help of several Very cartridges fired into it and the fuel leaking from the wing tanks it would not oblige. We feared that further flares might draw unwelcome attention to us, as we could now see several Ju 52s not far away dropping parachute troops. With a last look at my gallant Blenheim and a prayer of gratitude for our deliverance we hurried along the bund to the small isolated farmhouse, where we were hastily ushered inside by the old man who stood at the door. Despite our protests we were sat down by the deal table in the little kitchen and given cheese and bacon and a mug of unknown beverage by his wife. We thanked the old man and his wife profusely, but not wishing to compromise them further we set off along the track pointed out to us as going to the nearest town of Oud-Beijerland. We hurried along as there was no cover on either side, and it was a relief to reach the small houses of the town. Here we were swiftly picked up by a unit of the Dutch Army, who, though initially suspicious, and who could blame them, for we had seen German paratroops falling all around, told us that they would do their best to get us to the coast and a ship back to England. Being thus assured we were content to be escorted to the Hotel de Oude Hoorn. Here we spent a very noisy night with firing and explosions going on all around, and next day we were surprised and gratified to find we were still in friendly hands. We were taken to see one of our injured aircrew in hospital nearby. Poor Hugh was badly burned and in a poor way, but we promised that we would take him with us if we possibly could. The next morning, still in Oud-Beijerland, we went in to see Hugh again. He was conscious but we were told that it would be most unwise to try and move him. Unfortunately we were whisked away at midnight when the Dutch said they were retreating. When we protested about leaving Hugh behind they said that they thought that the hospital was already in German hands. Hugh subsequently survived to become a prisoner. After we were rushed across the ferry we were escorted to the little town of Numansdorp. Here in the middle of the day we were left with a Dutch family in their large house in suburbia, with strict instructions from the Dutch militia that we must lie low until we were picked up again. The weather was very hot and cloudless, and as we waited we were invited out into the garden by the two daughters of the house and persuaded to play a game of table-tennis. It did occur to me at the time that it was a very inappropriate thing to be doing under the circumstances, and a little reminiscent of Drake and his bowls. As the game progressed we saw several Heinkels flying low overhead, and heard machine-gun fire. I persuaded the girls that we would all be safer indoors, and luckily we were picked up again by a staff car and driver soon after. We were taken to a large country house on the edge of town, where we joined a civilian party from the Philips factory at Eindhoven. Here we were accommodated in the large house, and we all slept on the floor of a huge lounge. In the morning we were given a breakfast of cold raw bacon, brown bread and margarine and cold tea before setting off in convoy out of town along a straight road into the countryside. As we marched along we were machine-gunned ineffectively by a Heinkel that flew very low overhead. Having been picked up by a Dutch Army staff car, my gunner and I were taken on a wild dash into the Hague. As we entered the city the Germans were lobbing mortar shells into the streets, and the smoke was the cause of a scare of a gas attack, which fortunately proved to be groundless but was very worrying at the time. The Dutch soldiers accompanying us in the car carried side-arms and there was one machine-gun held by the man in the front seat. I remarked that we felt a little naked without some means of defence, and the officer beside me presented me with a very neat little 9 mm Browning automatic. It wasn't much, but it gave me a little more confidence. At least it was a nice souvenir, and later, when I got home, I asked my squadron armourer to clean it and service it for me. When he reported on it he said it was just as well that I did not have to use it in a tight corner as the firing pin had been filed down to make it inoperable! Back in Holland we were still with the Dutch Army who next took us to visit another injured airman, Plt Off Savill, a Hurricane pilot from 235 Squadron, Bircham Newton. Unfortunately he was very badly injured and was not able to give us a message that we could take back to his family. We were then rushed off to the British Legation in the Hague, where we found the front door barricaded with sandbags, and so we were sent round to the back entrance. In the doorway at the foot of the stairs stood a British Tommy, tin hat, puttees and an old .303 rifle at the slope and looking just as though he had been there since 1918! After reporting in here we were passed on to the Air Attaché, who listened to our report of the action with interest. A messenger rushed in at this point, and the Air Attaché looked up from the flimsy he was reading and surprised us by offering us a chance to return to Britain by air! Apparently the Dutch troops had liberated a serviceable Heinkel at Waalhaven airfield and the Air Attaché asked if we would be prepared to fly it to the UK. After a feeling of shock I thought what a wonderful chance that would be – a bit of one-upmanship to appear in the circuit at Manston in a Heinkel bomber. Without giving it further thought we leapt at the chance, and as we were whisked off in the Air Attaché's car my gunner and I were frantically trying to work out the German for fuel, flaps and undercarriage, etc. But the excitement was shortlived, as our car was stopped further on and we were told that the airfield had been recaptured by the Germans and the Heinkel was no longer available! I did not know whether my feelings were of disappointment or relief, but it meant that that night we spent a very noisy few hours in the Hotel de Passage in the Hague, conscious of the time slipping away when we might be getting down to the coast. In the blessed quiet of the new day's dawn we were picked up by a Dutch staff car, and it was a case of a dash down to the Hook of Holland in the hope of catching a ship. There was plenty of evidence of fighting on the way, and we had to be diverted several times to avoid road blocks set up by isolated pockets of German paratroops. Arriving on the dockside at the Hook a very welcome sight greeted us: two Royal Navy frigates were tied up alongside, their white ensigns bravely waving in the fresh morning breeze. We were expeditiously ushered aboard HMS *Hereward*, with H43 painted on her hull, and surprisingly we discovered a gang of ratings busily employed in tidying the decks and polishing the brightwork on guns and bulwarks. A chief petty officer seem to be fishing with a long pole over the stern, but we were told later that he was warding off mines that the Germans had dropped higher upstream to float down to the ships moored below. After an anxious short wait with the sounds of battle getting ever nearer, there was a flurry of activity on the dockside and a cavalcade of large limousines skidded to a halt in a cloud of dust. Several distinguished ladies and gentlemen came aboard to be met with due reverence. As the last one came over the ship's side the gangway was dropped and abandoned, the warps and cables were cast off and with a surge of power the diesels gushed out a plume of black smoke as the ship cleared the inner mole, already doing some 25 knots. There was gentle panic on deck as lifejackets were handed out, and in the confusion a rather large lady, surrounded by her attendants, was struggling to get into hers. I went forward to see if I could help, but as I did so a lieutenant-commander approached with authority and said, 'I think you should come below, Your Majesty.' It was Queen Wilhelmina, and the rest of the party were members of her Court and Government. I thought it strange at the time that, although the ship had been attacked sporadically by dive-bombers during the previous night and had fired off every shell on board, no enemy aircraft came near the vulnerable ship carrying such a high prize at any time during our dash from the Hook or during our five-and-a-half-hour passage to Harwich. The Germans must have known that their most valuable hostage was escaping but seemed to do nothing to prevent it. I was much too relieved to be safely back on home ground to let it worry me further, and I went straight to the Air Ministry to report my return to the duty clerk. Then I made tracks to find a telephone to tell my family that I was safe. I did not know it then, but I had been reported missing for two days, so my call was received with great relief. But it was a sad story on which to reflect. Out of the six aircraft of No. 600 squadron that had set out on that sunny May afternoon to try and help the Dutch in a brave but forlorn effort, only one aircraft returned, six aircrew had been killed, including the squadron commander, Jimmy Wells, and his gunner, Cpl Kidd, four more were shot down, three of whom managed to get back to Britain within a few days, and the fourth was badly injured and eventually became a prisoner. It was a terrible shock for those two poor girls who had breakfasted with their husbands that morning just down the road from Manston, and now Mike and Roger were dead, shot down over the Ijsselmonde area of Rotterdam in a gallant but doomed attempt to help our Dutch friends. In November 1981 the people of Rotterdam invited members of No. 600 Squadron and the relatives of those killed in this raid to a remembrance service at their gravesides and a thanksgiving for their efforts to help them in those dark days. A young Dutchman, Hans Onderwater, has recorded in his book about the war years in his town of Barendrecht, a few miles south of Rotterdam, details of the 600 Squadron's valiant effort. He has called his book *En toen was het stil* (And then there was silence).

CHAPTER TEN

Beaufighters at Last

May 1940

Affter a few days' leave I rejoined 600 Squadron, which had now moved to Northolt to re-form and build up to operational strength. By 15 May the Dutch had capitulated, Holland was overrun and the Germans were making a strong push into Belgium. RAF aircraft were supporting our Expeditionary Force in France and Bomber Command was attacking military targets in Bremen, Hamburg and the Ruhr. It was becoming clear that the Germans would soon take airfields in France in easy range of the south-east of England and London, and they would clearly be vulnerable to air attacks in a couple of weeks. At the end of May the evacuation of our forces from France began at Dunkirk, and my squadron was kept busy on operational patrols at night, but still without any interceptions or combats. On 7 June a flight of three aircraft from the squadron was scrambled from Northolt and flew via Shoreham and Fécamp and landed at Boos, a small airfield north of Rouen. It was known that the Hun was in the vicinity of the town, but we were told that several wounded aircrew were at Boos and hoping to be airlifted home before the Germans could get there. Our three aircraft landed to find the airfield deserted, so we made enquiries at a small café on a long straight road going south to Rouen. Needless to say, we were welcomed in and plied with glasses of anis and brandy, but no one knew anything about the injured aircrew. Things were getting very friendly when a Frenchman rushed in shouting, 'Les Boches, Les Boches', and looking up this long straight road we could indeed see the Germans coming, in the shape of a column of light tanks. The retreat to our aircraft, getting engines started and taking off must have been the quickest 'scramble' ever, but we were very distressed that we had not been able to carry out our mission. It was very sad, but we never heard what had happened to our injured colleagues, though we realized that a crate of brandy that we abandoned in our haste was still sitting on top

55

of the bar in that café. On our return flight one of our aircraft was lost when the propeller sheered off the starboard engine of the Blenheim and the aircraft crashed into the sea, killing the crew. These were our first casualties since the Rotterdam raid. The pilot and gunner were both auxiliary officers of considerable experience and very well liked in the squadron. On our return to the mess that night, apart from this loss discussions were mainly about the worsening situation in France.

The Germans were already in Boulogne, the Belgium Army had capitulated on the orders of their King and the air battles began to intensify. At about this time Defiants, with their four-gun turrets, were brought into action and initially met with marked success, claiming thirty-six German fighters shot down in one day. But the *Luftwaffe* soon recognized that they were not Hurricanes, as at first thought, and attacked them from below, where the turret's guns could not be brought to bear. They suffered badly and soon had to be withdrawn from day operations and used only at night. At this time the Bristol Beaufighter began to come off production as the new night-fighter, and I went down to Filton to fly it with Bristol's chief test pilot. I was very impressed with this powerful, rugged aeroplane, and came to love flying it day or night. It never let me down throughout many operational patrols.

On the day that the French General Pétain announced that the French must stop fighting, 600 Squadron, now fully operational again, moved back to Manston. Now that the French had signed an armistice, a great area of northern France became available to the Germans for the use of existing airfields and for building new ones. This would mean firstly that a large part of Britain would come within range of their bombers, and more significantly their escorting fighters, and secondly we would have considerably less warning time of approaching raids. It was now clear that our airfields in Kent were most vulnerable and could expect to be attacked soon.

Before going on to describe my part in the forthcoming battle I should explain my feelings as a result of my being inveigled out of my chosen role as a single-seater fighter pilot and finishing up in a night-fighter squadron, in which I now found myself. I admit that I never took naturally to flying at night and was full of envy for the day-fighter boys. But not for me was there the thrill of a dashing scramble, leaping into a Spitfire's cockpit, the engine already running, swinging into wind and taking off with the rest of my flight close around me. In broad daylight I would have climbed into a clear sky and been able to see all around and plan my tactics as the enemy aircraft approached. Action such as this demanded a special sort of courage and endurance and produced many heroes and aces. But the night scenario was very different. To take an example of a typical night's operation, the night-fighter crew, having done a night-flying air test earlier in the day, would come to immediate readiness at nightfall. In the crew room we would sit, fully kitted-out in flying gear, with dark glasses on to keep adapted to the dark outside. As with the day-fighters we would get the heart-stopping ring of the operations phone ordering a scramble. But from then on things would be very different. Firstly, the controlling radars could normally handle only one fighter at a time at night, and so we would go alone. Secondly, the rush to get airborne meant groping through the dark to find our aircraft, dazzled by many pin-pricks of lights from the torches waved by our ground crews trying to be helpful. Finally scrambling up the wing to settle down in the cockpit, adjusting the inadequate cockpit lighting and a final check around with our little hand-held torches before a flash outside to the ground crew for starting engines. Once both were running and warming up, a check on temperatures and pressures before feeling around for the right radio button to call ground control for taxi clearance. Then brakes off and taxiing out, sticking very carefully to the dimly lit taxiway to the end of the flare-path. A quick magneto check on both engines and then opening up both and peering ahead to try and pick out the faintly glowing Glim lamps that marked the runway ahead. As the flare-path lights fell away under the wing, propelled into the pitch-black void by the powerful thrust of the twin Mercury engines, there was nothing ahead but a dark unfriendly sky with no visual reference points, necessitating immediate reference to the blind-flying instruments dimly glowing in the cockpit. Having established a safe rate of climb one could then concentrate on following directions from the ground controller on the radio at the ground radar station, hoping that he would be able to bring us close enough to a raider for us to pick it up on our own radar – in the early days, unfortunately, a rare event. So for another hour or two we would probe every dark corner of the night sky in the hope of sighting a hostile aircraft, but it was a vast place of mystery and menace at night. Occasionally a combat would ensue, and this would alleviate our hours of frustration and be of tremendous boost to our morale. Whatever the outcome of our sortie, we still had to cope with finding our way back to base. Our airfield being located near London, the balloon barrage was always a constant threat and our own anti-aircraft guns a menace if we approached within the trigger-happy gunners' range. After what would probably have been an exhausting sortie we were finally faced with making a safe landing, often in bad weather but always in the darkness of the blackout, on an airfield with the absolute minimum of lighting.

So far from the 'gung-ho' enthusiasm needed to make up the character of the day-fighter guy, I, his night counterpart, had to have endless patience, the ability to work very closely with our radar operator and the radar controller on the ground, and of course to be highly able and skilled in flying at night. I, on my own admission, was impatient and impulsive, so it was not easy for me to settle down happily to my role even though I was always eager and anxious to make a success of any tasks I was given. But in those early days the odds were stacked heavily in favour of the night intruder, and there was an overall feeling of total frustration among the night-fighter crews.

Later, after the Battle was won, quite rightly, the greatest praise and approbation was showered on the day fighter pilots and whilst not for a moment belittling their splendid courage I was disappointed that the night fighter crews received little or no recognition.

There were seven squadrons of night fighter Blenheims operating in the same skies and often from the same airfields as the Spits and Hurricanes and they flew some thousand operational sorties during the period. Although these were at night and they may not have faced the same risk of interception by German Fighters, the hazards of night flying in "black-out" condition and poor airfield lighting were always present and there was very seldom any reward as night combats were very rare at this time. Many hours were flown by the pilots and gunners of these Blenheims, not without casualties, and I think when recalling the Battle of Britain, more recognition should be given to them and the splendid ground crews who serviced the Blenheims, often under attack.

Manston was now very much in the firing line, and it was not long before the sirens sounded and 600 Squadron's aircrews, caught on our way to the flights, were diving for cover in a nearby air raid shelter. We spent a very uncomfortable few minutes waiting in nervous silence for something to happen, and when the crumps and bangs came from exploding bombs outside there were looks of disbelief, together with grins of bravado. The shelter became full of choking Kent chalk dust, and when we emerged on the 'all clear' we all looked as white as millers and there was much laughter, but mostly from the feeling of relief that all was quiet again. But all around was not a pretty sight, and the idea of glasses of Kummel on the immaculate lawn in front of the mess was but a fading memory, as bomb craters had straddled the lawn and churned up the flower beds, as well as falling on the airfield itself. I admitted that cowering in that shelter I was terrified and vowed that I would never go underground again in an air raid, and never thereafter did so.

Hurricane and Spitfire squadrons were also based at Manston, and so my squadron was always very much aware of their activities. Their scrambles to meet incoming raids engendered in us a feeling of envy, but tinged with apprehension because we knew that there was a good chance that the very raid that the fighters had gone after would shortly be bombing us at Manston. Towards the end of June there were a lot of hit-and-run raids by German fighters, as well as their bombers. These fighters would come in very low over the sea, pull up over Ramsgate or Broadstairs and almost immediately would be in a position to attack Manston without warning. The journey from our quarters to the flights was across the open airfield, and was most perilous if one was caught midway, as happened from time to time, with nothing higher than a tuft of grass to shelter behind. There was now a constant threat of enemy intrusion into the south-east corner of the home counties and the surrounding sea areas. On 9 July there was a heavy bombing raid on a convoy off Margate, and shipping around the South Foreland and ships off Dover were constantly under attack. All the forward airfields like Manston, Hawkinge, Detling and Eastchurch were bombed regularly, and with all this hostile activity going on there was naturally a good deal of nervous tension among crews flying in the area. On one occasion I was engaged on an RDF trial out to sea from Rye when my Blenheim was intercepted by a flight of Hurricanes that closed in on my aircraft in a menacing fashion and made it clear that I should not delay in landing at Manston. On another occasion some of the squadron crews who had just landed were outside our crew room awaiting the last crew to land when we saw his Blenheim approaching the airfield from the east. Even as we watched we saw an Me 109 climb from sea level just behind him and fire a long burst of cannon fire into the Blenheim. It all happened so quickly that the crew did not stand a chance, and the aircraft rolled over and dived down with smoke coming from it and hit the sea beyond Broadstairs. We stood in helpless and horrified silence for a moment, and then our flight commander rushed into the office to call the air-sea-rescue unit at Ramsgate, which had already seen the incident, and a high-speed launch was already on its way. But we knew that there was not a chance that the crew could have survived. It was quite sickening to see our two friends killed in such a way when just for the sake of getting back a minute or two earlier they might well have been with us now, returning to the mess for tea. The Spitfire squadrons had had a successful operation over the Dover Straits at the time, and the leader was very upset when they landed back at Manston to hear that a German fighter had got through to shoot down one of their fellow squadron's night-fighters. The squadron's crews were now vulnerable whenever flying in daylight, and even when carrying out our essential night-flying tests we were often recalled if ground radar detected hostile aircraft approaching. This feeling of constantly running for cover made us realize how very ineffective we were, and added to the frustration of our lack of success at night. Our morale was suffering badly and we could only watch the day-fighter boys with envy and admiration. On the 'glorious' 12 August it was not only the grouse who were under attack: Some 250 bombs were dropped on Manston and at least two of our Blenheims were set on fire and several more damaged, and the hangars also were badly hit. The squadron's beloved Tiger Moth was also destroyed, and it would be a long time before the Germans would be forgiven for that. After several more raids Manston was no longer tenable for a night squadron, and 600 retreated to Hornchurch. Although this move gave us some respite from the hit-and-run raiders, Hornchurch was subject to constant bombing raids. To make matters worse the squadron crews were accommodated in flimsy caravans offering no protection whatsoever, and within a few hundred yards was a battery of French 88 mm anti-aircraft guns. The racket from those when they opened fire was worse than the exploding bombs, and the shrapnel from their shells that fell around us was just as lethal.

I, at least, had a few days' rest when I was invited to an investiture at Buckingham Palace to receive my medal from King George VI. Both Kramer and I had been awarded the DFC for our escapade in Holland and this was a very proud moment; we were almost overwhelmed with the splendour of the occasion and the magnificence of the palace. My mother and youngest sister were also invited to be present at the investiture and were able to share this thrill. The King's handshake was very firm, but I remembered my brief, that one should not grip His Majesty's hand too enthusiastically in return. He said one or two very kind words of congatulations that I appreciated.

Afterwards, Mother and my sister, and numerous friends and relations, joined us for a celebratory lunch at Simpsons in the Strand. A few days later Buckingham Palace was hit by a bomb and I could not resist saying with a grin, 'They are determined to get me!'

Despite the poor morale in the squadron we still vigorously tackled the task of improving the performance of our AI sets and the capability of our radar operators. Operational patrols were flown every night and occasional contacts were made, but the enemy bombers always seemed to be able to evade us. The squadron crews liked to feel that perhaps they were at least turning some of them back to drop their bombs harmlessly into the sea. On moonlit nights some day-fighters were also used on 'fighter nights', when aircraft were stacked at different heights in a gaggle across the line of approach of a raid. Some success was achieved, but the bright moonlight favoured the hunted as much as the hunters, and once visual contact was lost it was surprisingly difficult to pick up a twisting, diving and turning aircraft desperate to escape. Trials were also being carried out at this time with the night-fighters working closely with the searchlights, with the idea of putting more fighters into the air and keeping them under control by patrol lines within designated 'boxes'. Each box would be marked by a coloured searchlight and one fighter was designated to each. On the approach of a raid each searchlight beam would be depressed on the bearing of the raid and the fighter would follow the beam until, hopefully, there would be a cone of searchlights on the bomber. It rarely worked, as searchlights were not definitive enough to bring the fighters into range of our AI, but trials continued and efforts to improve our night defences were never relaxed. On 7 September some 1,000 enemy aircraft flew up the Thames Estuary and attacked oil refineries, docks and the East End of London, starting many fires, which continued to burn through the night and into the next day. The air attacks on London continued, but the threat to the fighter stations was at last alleviated, much to the relief of the AOC, Fighter Command. In a final retreat from the holocaust, 600 Squadron was moved west to the small grass airfield at Redhill, where we continued our night operations. At last the replacement for our ancient Blenheims arrived, and I flew the first Beaufighter from Redhill on 17 September. After a few days' leave I returned to Redhill, only to be nearly hit by a bomb! I had been scrambled for a night patrol in a Beaufighter, and as my aircraft was accelerating down the flare-path a stick of bombs was dropped down the length of the airfield, the last one falling only a few yards in front of me. The blast stopped both engines of the Beaufighter, blew in the two clear-vision panels of the windscreen and left the aircraft teetering on the edge of a large crater. A most upsetting experience, and followed the next night by a heavy attack of incendiary bombs on the airfield, which had all the crews rushing around with shovels and buckets of sand to try and save some of the wooden buildings that made up our mess and flight crew rooms. In this activity the squadron commander, David Clarke, unfortunately became the first casualty when he fell into a trench in the dark and broke his leg.

CHAPTER ELEVEN

Resting in Scotland

October 1940 to July 1941

B y the beginning of October the air battle against the *Luftwaffe* was showing signs of easing off and the immediate fight for air superiority was won. I think the following poem, written many years before, surely predicted this modern battle:

> The time will come when thou shalt lift thine eyes
> To see a long drawn battle in the skies,
> While aged peasants too amazed for words
> Stare at the flying fleets of wondrous birds.
> England, so long mistress of the sea
> Where wind and waves caress their sovereignty.
> Her ancient triumphs yet on high shall bear
> And reign the sovereign of the conquered air.

On 12 October the AOC judged that No. 600 Squadron had had enough and had earned a rest, and so we were moved up north to Acklington in Northumberland. Unfortunately, much to my regret, we had to leave our Beaufighters behind and we flew up in our ageing Blenheims. Ten days later one flight was moved further north to Drem, and I joined them there when I flew up in a Miles Magister. Drem was a few miles east of Edinburgh on the Firth of Forth, and the station was commanded by one of the Atcherly brothers. Both brothers were known to be scatty, but Batchie was the wilder of the two, and serving under him there was seldom a dull moment. After the traumas of the south, Drem was a rest indeed, although the squadron brought with them a bit of excitement. On our arrival the resident squadron had organized a guest dining-in night of welcome, and we all sat down to dinner in a happy and relaxed mood. The dinner over, the port was being passed around when the unmistakeable drone of German Mercedes-Benz aero engines was heard, followed shortly by the whistle and swish of falling bombs. On one side of the table there was no movement, but on the other, as one man, the pilots of 600 Squadron were struggling to get the best place under the table. Our hosts looked with wide-eyed astonishment at all their guests lying prone on the floor. Even the crump, crump of exploding bombs did not immediately register with the hosts, but luckily no serious damage was done. These were the first and the last bombs to fall on Drem, and again I couldn't resist the joke that I thought that the Boche were still determined to get me!

Although our flight continued to carry out night patrols over the Firth of Forth areas and provide targets for gunnery practice for the Royal Navy ships in harbour, life was much more relaxed and we began to feel the benefit of the change.

Between our duties the local Scots were extremely hospitable, and on several occasions squadron aircrews were invited to Lord Tweeddale's estate for grouse shooting and lunch at Yester. North Berwick was near, with several golf clubs that were open to us, and Norman Hayes in particular made good use of them. Several lady guests soon appeared for drinks in the mess with reciprocal invitations to local houses.

The battleship *King George V* was at anchor in the Forth off Rosyth, and I did several night patrols in cooperation with the ship for her gunnery trials There was always a slight feeling of apprehension as the Navy were using live ammunition, but they assured me that they had a system of a ten-second delay in the gun laying, which ensured that shells would pass 200 metres behind the aircraft. Even so! But months later I felt I might have contributed in a small way to the sinking of the *Bismarck* in the memorable engagement with the *Hood* and *King George V*. The latter ship's shooting was decisive, but sadly not in time to save HMS *Hood*, which was blown up by a direct hit from *Bismarck's* fourteen-inch guns before she was sunk. The most exciting moments at Drem for the aircrews was being driven by Batchie in his large Humber to Edinburgh. He had a preference for driving over the moors, avoiding the roads as far as possible. We spent our time either hanging on or leaping in and out of the car, opening and closing farm gates.

In our northern hideaway we felt a bit cut off from the war, but we heard of the Italians attacking Greece, Roosevelt voted in for his third term in the White House and the sinking of the *Empress of Britain*, and we followed with great interest the news of the air battles that were still being courageously fought down south. On a flying visit to Catterick we met several old Blenheim friends from earlier times and during lunch exchanged views and news. I was very sorry to learn that one of my oldest sergeant friends from 25 Squadron days had been killed in a Beaufighter crash. Remember Sgt Monk, with the bent Blenheim propellers? We all returned in time for a Christmas party in our crew room at Drem at which great rivalry ensued around the dartboard and the table-tennis table. Wives and girl friends participated and Francis Day was the judge.

On the last day of the year Maisie arrived back in Britain after an amazing and hazardous journey by ship from Basra. It was a great relief to know that she was safely back, and we became engaged. On my return to Drem I found that 600 Squadron was being split up, with one flight sent down to Catterick while I was temporarily left in charge of the other flight at Drem. I heard that David Clarke was forming a new squadron, and I pulled a few strings so that I could join him as one of his flight commanders. Before I went, however, I was invited to Yester House, where I met and fell in love with a beautiful redhead. This was Rebecca, the best of a litter of three cocker spaniels, who was to be my faithful and constant companion, flying with me on many non-operational flights for the rest of the war. After another day's shooting at Yester and a final night patrol, we left Drem in flight formation, and after a gentle 'beat-up' of the girlfriends' houses we flew down to Catterick.

So it was that I finally left No. 600 (City of London) Auxiliary Squadron after a flying tour full of interest, excitement and some frustration. I was promoted to flight lieutenant, having skipped the rank of flying officer, and took over B Flight of the new No. 68 Squadron. The arrival of our Blenheims coincided with heavy snow, and flying was curtailed for some days. I took this opportunity to catch the train down to Gloucester and marry Maisie at Churcham church where the two families foregathered. The wedding was made notable by the bride and groom being driven off for their honeymoon in a taxi with a huge gas balloon on its roof – a wartime economy measure that added a measure of merriment to the memorable occasion! In retrospect I think I came to realize that it was rather a marriage of desperation, for with the inevitable wartime conditions there was little prospect of our being able to live a normal married life, and I knew that our future was going to be difficult. At least we were able to fit in a short honeymoon.

During February and March back at Catterick 68 Squadron was air-testing Blenheims, training aircrews and getting the squadron into operational shape. One great improvement was that we were now receiving trained radar operators. I was very pleased with the sergeant allotted to me and we got on well as a team. There was an added advantage in that Jack loved Becky, my dog, and whenever she flew with us on non-operational flights Jack would see that she was happily snuggled up on a flying jacket at his feet. Training was going well until the end of the month when one of our sergeant pilots went missing on a night-flying training exercise. I set off in a Magister accompanied by several other aircraft to carry out a search, but the wreck was not found until the next day, burnt out on one of the highest points of the Pentland Hills. On 6 April I was carrying out a night test of formation lights on the Blenheim when Jack and I were caught out in a heavy snowstorm and were lucky to get back into Catterick in one piece. There had been several local blizzards in the previous few days, and it seemed probable that the sergeant pilot had been caught out when descending through such a storm and flew into the Pentland Hills while in cloud. During the month I had the opportunity to borrow a Miles Master trainer and a much loved Gladiator to throw around the sky in a brief few moments of enthusiasm. But then back to the routine of Blenheim preparation, where guns were tested by live firing out to sea from Whitby and AI calibration runs were carried out by day and night.

On 17 April 68 Squadron took off from Catterick and flew in formation down to a new airfield, High Ercall, in the shadow of the Wrekin in Shropshire. It had a splendid runway but the accommodation was far from ready, and a lot of improvisation was called for in the first few weeks. There was no water and no lights, but the clerk of works did promise that they would do their best to have the roof on the mess by the end of the week! Aircrews were flying on reconnaissance flights round the new sector, exercising with the local GCI radar unit and getting familiar with the new airfield lighting and the relative position of the Wrekin on their airfield circuit, as it was 1,000 feet high. When the mess had its roof on and conditions at High Ercall were improved, two Beaufighters arrived for the squadron, so once again I was involved in converting a squadron to the new type. By this time Max Aitken had taken over as CO of the squadron, but we did not see much of him at first as he had made himself comfortable in a local country mansion. Later on, when the squadron moved to Coltishall, enemy activity on the east coast was considerably more, and 68 Squadron amassed a very creditable total of enemy aircraft destroyed under Max's command and his personal score earned him a DSO. Despite his squadron's great efforts, the city of Norwich suffered a very heavy air raid at this time.

Meantime 68 Squadron at High Ercall continued with the conversion to the Beaufighter and build-up to operational status on the new type. On 17 June our efforts were rewarded when Flt Lt Paine shot down an He 111 near Bath. The squadron maintained constant night readiness with regular night patrols, but there was little hostile activity and it was November before they achieved another victory, by which time I had been posted to a staff job. Before leaving I did two more night operational patrols in the Beaufighter and had another interesting flight that brought back recollections of my Holland experience. On a visit to the Enemy Aircraft Evaluation Unit I flew with their pilot, Sqn Ldr Smith, in a Heinkel III Mk IV. I felt that I could have flown that Heinkel from Rotterdam without any trouble, but persuading the Spitfire pilots from Manston that I was friendly might have been another problem.

My new post was to be on the night operations staff of Headquarters No. 9 Group at Preston. This was my first staff job and I did not have any idea what would be involved, but I hated the idea of being off flying. However, Headquarters seemed quite agreeable to my keeping in flying practice, so I was quickly in contact with the group communications squadron at the local airfield at Samlesbury. To my delight I was able to get airborne regularly, and during my six months' tour I was able to fly twelve new types of aircraft. However, I did not get away to a very good start, as when I arrived in my sporty but ancient SS 100 car I found that the headquarters was accommodated in the very grand Barton Hall, and without thinking I parked the car immediately under the imposing columns of the portico. As I got out a gentleman dressed in smart country tweeds and trilby hat came by and gave me a haughty look. 'Nice car', he managed to grunt. 'Would you like to make me an offer?' said I, but the gent walked on with another haughty look over his shoulder. The next day, when I was ushered in to meet the AOC, I got another glare and he said, 'I don't want to buy that dreadful car of yours and I hope that you have now parked it round the back like the rest of the staff!' However, he did give me a friendly grin as I went out. On 12 July I drove up to Blackburn and sat as a member of a selection board for VR commissions in the Training Branch, and the next day was able to borrow a Hurricane from Squires Gate and indulge in my favourite sport of aerobatics. Although my AOC didn't want my SS 100, I soon managed to sell it. The next day on a cross-country to Pershore in a Miles Mentor to clinch the deal I had to force-land at Tern Hill with a cutting engine. The following day Maisie's brother Eddie, an airman armourer, arrived by hitch-hiking from Cornwall, and I flew him up to Wrexham and back in a Magister to see the family. I then had to drive up to Lancaster to give a lecture to the Royal Observer Corps, but two days later I was able to take Eddie down to High Ercall in a Mentor and arrange for a Blenheim to take him on to Halton, where he was under training. I took a train to London to attend a Fighter Command conference, where I met several old squadron friends, including my erstwhile squadron commander, who took me out to lunch at Scott's. While in London I took the opportunity to look for another car, and eventually bought an old but good-condition Riley Kestrel from Rowland Smith, which I drove back to Preston. I was welcomed with the good news that I had been promoted to squadron leader, but this was tempered with tragic news of the death of one of my pilot officer friends from 600 Squadron with whom I had shared so much fun at Drem. The worst of it was that the crash happened when he was shooting-up his home at St Albans in full view of his family. In early September I heard about the Royal Air Force Expeditionary Force landing in Russia under the command of an old friend, Ramsbottom-Isherwood. I envied them the Gladiators that they took with them. October was a good flying month, when I got airborne in a Hurricane and a Defiant at Squires Gate. I also flew a Beaufighter at Duxford, an Oxford and a Hornet Moth from Samlesbury and ferried a Lysander to the target-towing flight at Valley, on Anglesey. Several of my flights had the purpose of taking officers around to the group stations on their staff visits. On 20 October I flew the AOC and his SASO on a staff visit to Andreas, where they were flying ground-controlled pilotless gliders to act as targets on the air-firing ranges. One of the group captains on the staff at Group Headquarters wanted to renew his twin-engine rating, so I gave him several dual flights in the Oxford, on which I was becoming quite proficient. Finally I flew up to Wrexham in a Hornet Moth with Becky, as I had been told that there was a Wellington III bomber requiring an air test after having extensive repairs done to it after a forced landing some weeks previously. I had never flown a Wellington before, or any aircraft quite so big as this one, and I spent some time studying the cockpit layout, all the dials and levers and reading the Pilot's Notes, which I found in a pocket in the cockpit. When I felt confident that I had taken in all the important dos and don'ts, and in the absence of any volunteers, I climbed in and took the left-hand seat in the cockpit on my own. Start-up and take-off were no problem and all seemed to be functioning well. I felt a bit strange flying around in this huge and strange beast, but in fact I found it remarkably pleasant to fly, although very heavy after the fighter types or light communication aircraft that I had become used to. After exploring some of the Wellington's performance abilities I brought it into land and taxied in feeling well pleased and quite a guy as I took my flying gear from the large aircraft. My pride was seriously dented the next day when the Wellington was collected and flown away by a slender blond girl of the ATA. On one of my last flights from Samlesbury I took two Army colonels on a reconnaissance of their ack-ack gun sites at Preston, Southport and Blackburn, a flight only remarkable for the perfection of the day and visibility that ranged from the Ribble northwards to the wide expanse of the sands of Morecambe Bay.

On my last evening at Barton Hall, as I slumped into one of the comfortable leather arm chairs in the beautiful lounge of this old Georgian mansion where we were quartered, surrounded by valuable old paintings hanging on most of the walls I was very conscious of the all-pervading peace and tranquillity around me, and thought what a contrast it was to the grim war news. The USA had repealed its Neutrality Act and was arming her merchant ships. The German armies in the East were still being held by the Russians before Moscow and Leningrad, but they had made advances in the Crimea and were outside Sebastopol and Kerch. The *Ark Royal* had been sunk in the Mediterranean by a submarine, and great tank battles were being fought in Libya between the Afrika Korps under Rommel and the British Eighth Army.

And then on the radio came the most astonishing news of all. The Japanese had attacked the United States' Pacific Fleet in Pearl Harbor with a series of bomb and torpedo attacks launched from aircraft-carriers, several battleships had been sunk or damaged and there had been many American casualties in the naval ranks. Rumours were spreading that Japanese ground forces had landed on the east coast of Malaya and a further force was threatening Hong Kong. Surely the United States would now join the Allied forces in the war? But the spreading of the struggle to the Far East would now stretch our forces even more thinly on the ground and in the air. With Singapore, Hong Kong and Burma at risk, even India could be threatened. With these sobering thoughts I went up to my room and started to pack my kit and prepare for my next posting. I would be joining another operational squadron, which would bring me a bit closer to the war, but regrettably still on night-fighters.

CHAPTER TWELVE

First Command –
Defiants and Hurricanes

January to November 1942

M y new posting was as Commanding Officer of No. 96 Squadron, which was equipped with Defiants and stationed at Wrexham, and while I was disappointed that it was not a Beaufighter squadron it was my first command and I was very excited about that. With the dawning of the new year 1942, I was settling in at Wrexham, getting to know my flight commanders and aircrews and becoming aware for the first time of my responsibility for some two hundred NCOs and airmen as well.

The Defiant was designed as a day- and night-fighter. In the former role it had been successful in attacking a bomber stream, but when faced with fighters of superior performance it was very vulnerable, particularly after the Germans became aware of their initial mistake of misidentifying the Defiant as a Hurricane, whose silhouette was similar. Thereafter it was only employed in the night-fighter role. The Boulton and Paul gun turret with which it was fitted, although of ingenious design and very effective with its four .303 machine-guns, was very heavy, and when ready for action the aircraft weighed 20% heavier than the Hurricane and had a slightly smaller wing area. Therefore its performance was not very brilliant, and from a pilot's point of view one had to start thinking in abstract terms as to how best to manoeuvre the aircraft in a scrap to give one's gunner the best attacking position to bring his guns to bear. This was a departure from the pilot's normal leading role in an attack, and it meant that pilots and gunners must work very closely together to decide on their tactics. I now teamed up with a regular gunner, Flt Lt Bob Smith, and we got on well together, but I also flew with other gunners to monitor their training.

No. 96 Squadron formed originally with Hurricanes, and in the latter part of 1941 had been able to destroy quite a few hostile aircraft when operating in defence of Liverpool. As luck would have it, when I took over the squadron there was a marked falling-off of enemy action in our area, caused, perhaps, by the Germans moving a considerable portion of their bomber force to the Russian front. I still had several Hurricanes left in the squadron and would fly these from time to time. If the truth be known I very much preferred these flights than in the Defiant, but I was, of course, duty bound to primarily operate the Defiant as it was the squadron's role aircraft.

The squadron now began to receive the replacement Defiant Mk 2, which had an uprated Merlin engine and was fitted with Mk 3 AI radar. Unlike the Blenheims and Beaufighters the radar screen of the Mk 3 was situated on the pilot's instrument panel, and so it was he who was solely responsible for interpreting its display. This at least put the pilot back in control of radar interceptions, but the set was largely in the experimental stage and had a poor performance in picking up other aircraft as its range was short and its field was restricted. However, it was excellent for homing on navigation beacons set up at night-flying airfields, and I took advantage of it often and could achieve approaches and landings in very much worse weather conditions than before it was available. At this time there was very little hostile air activity, and flying was mostly confined to training and air exercises. On one such exercise the squadron provided a Defiant escort to six Beaufighters of No. 68 Squadron led by Max Aitken flying over Crewe, followed by a simulated bomber attack on targets in the vicinity of the city for the benefit of Army ack-ack gun regiments. At the end of February the squadron moved into new offices and crew rooms dispersed on the perimeter of the airfield. We had a small party to mark the occasion, and afterwards we all sat around in the crew room discussing the latest news. There was incredulity at the large loss of Allied aircraft, mostly Royal Navy Swordfish torpedo-bombers, suffered at the hands of the *Scharnhorst*, *Gneisenau* and *Prince Eugen* when the German ships made a courageous break down the English Channel. We were amazed too that the ships had managed to get so far without being detected. When they were eventually spotted, it seemed that our response was ill considered and inadequate. At the time there was general belief that the escape of these major units of the German fleet was due to a belated response by our forces, but later there was a rumour that Churchill had a hand in the planning of the operation, as he was concerned that had the ships remained in ports in the West they would have been a direct threat to the advance guard of American troops then nearing the UK crammed aboard the liner *Queen Elizabeth*. But whatever the truth, the German ships were now bottled up in their home ports, from where they took no further part in the war at sea. We were concerned to hear reports from the Far East that were of an even greater calamity. As early as 1920 it had been decided that the main British base in the Far East should be Singapore, and its defence was planned to depend on coastal artillery and locally based torpedo-bombers. When the Japanese invasion was deemed imminent, the war in other theatres was going so badly that the Chiefs of Staff were obliged to abandon any prospects of reinforcement for Singapore. The only air defence that was available was quite inadequate, and the only fighters available were fairly ancient American Buffaloes, which had been rejected as unsuitable for operations in Europe and were hopelessly outclassed by the Japanese Zero fighters. Despite a desperate, courageous defence, we heard with dismay that Singapore had surrendered, with many Allied soldiers taken prisoner. AVM Pulford, the Air Commander, managed to escape by small boat to a little island south of Singapore, where he later died still trying to evade capture.

In the Middle East Rommel was still moving towards Alexandria in Cyrenaica, seemingly unstoppable, although the Hurricanes of the Desert Air Force were beginning to impose an increasing threat to the Panzer tanks with remorseless and ferocious rocket attacks. Despite all this depressing news, we had plenty to take our minds off it and were kept busy on our day-to-day duties. We also had our own tragedy and were mourning the loss of two of our aircrew who had been killed in the crash of a Defiant at Sealand. These were Plt Off Potter-Smith and AC Steed. The cause was obscure and never satisfactorily explained.

The weather in March started off with days of fog and mist, which curtailed most of the flying. We were still evaluating the operational capabilities of the Defiant II, and when the weather improved I did several flights with my gunner and we tried out varying tactics in attacks on an accompanying target aircraft. On the odd days when the fog returned I made good use of the radar homer, which gave me great confidence in returning to base in marginal weather conditions. On one occasion I was scrambled to search for a missing Hampden bomber that was overdue, but after an hour's fruitless search I was recalled when the Hampden was discovered on a Welsh mountainside, where it had crashed in cloud. On non-flying days the crews sometimes bussed down to Wrexham baths to practise our dinghy drills. News of these visits seemed to have reached the ears of a certain Welsh coracle maker in Llangollen, who got in touch with me and said that he would be prepared to demonstrate to us how to paddle our little dinghies with only one paddle. We were mindful of how difficult it was to make any headway with a one-man dinghy and guessed that the old man would like to feel that he was doing his bit for the war effort, and so he was invited along to the baths. This little, wizened old Welshman, without hesitation, jumped into the water and clambered into one of our dinghies, and with his short little paddle over the stern proceeded to rush up and down the length of the pool as though propelled by an outboard motor. The watching crews were most impressed, and I thanked him profusely and presented him with a squadron badge, which he took away with obvious pride, no doubt to go on display in his coracle workshop, marking his valuable war effort.

April began like March with poor flying weather. The 1st was a very rough day with showers and violent winds strong enough to damage one of our aircraft, although it was securely picketed down in the lee of the hangar. Repairs were put in hand at once and I was able to test-fly the aircraft by the following week. In the middle of the month on a visit to Group Headquarters I was told by the AOC that my squadron would soon be re-equipping with Beaufighters in place of our Defiants. On my return to Wrexham I found out that the final Defiant II had arrived for the squadron but at the same time a twin-engined Oxford was delivered. Before our Defiants went, the squadron took part in another form of operation in a further effort to improve on the existing number of night interceptions achieved against the German raiders. This was the 'fighter night' which concentrated a large number of fighters on moonlit nights over one possible target. On this occasion twelve aircraft from 96 Squadron were joined by eighteen from two other night-fighter squadrons, and we were concentrated over Liverpool. It was an interesting exercise, the sky was full of eager fighter crews, doing their best to avoid collisions, but no German raiders turned up. At the end of the month eight of our gunners were posted to flying units in Bomber Command, so it was clear that the Beaufighters would be arriving soon, as they needed a radar operator in the second seat, and not a gunner. On the strength of this I flew down to High Ercall to visit No. 255 Squadron, which was already equipped with Beaufighters, to refresh my memory and get the latest 'gen' on the aircraft.

In early May I was pleased to welcome the arrival of the first two Beaufighters but disappointed to be told that it was policy for twin-engined aircraft squadrons to be commanded by an officer of wing commander rank. As I was a fairly junior squadron leader and therefore could not be promoted to fill the post, a wing commander was posted in to command the squadron and I became a flight commander. Nevertheless the task of converting the whole squadron of single-engine pilots to fly twins fell to me, and the training was begun in earnest as I and the new CO were anxious to get the squadron fully operational on Beaufighters as soon as possible. This was the third occasion that I had been faced with this responsibility, and I was getting to be a leading exponent on the Beaufighter. But this time it was different in two respects. Firstly, I was the only twin-engined-trained pilot on the squadron and would have to give dual instruction to my own squadron commander, and secondly, the aircraft we received were Beaufighter Mk IIs. These differed from the other Beaufighters in being fitted with Rolls-Royce Merlin engines in place of the Bristol radials, and while the Mk II was very smooth and pleasant to fly under normal conditions, its single-engined performance was more tricky for an inexperienced pilot. On take-off considerable concentration had to be applied to anticipate what could be a vicious swing if allowed to develop. A twin-engined Oxford trainer had already arrived for the squadron, and a dual Blenheim followed, and I gave priority for training to my two flight commanders, so that they would be able to help with the conversion of the remaining pilots when they had reached an advanced stage. In due course, after a total of 1,844 hours, all of them became fully operational on the Beaufighter without any serious incident or accident. Very gratifying for me, and I was later Mentioned in Dispatches for my efforts.

Flying in the one or two of the Defiants left, the squadron continued with training exercises and cooperation with units of the Army. On one of the latter exercises, while beating-up an Army post, one of our pilots in a Defiant, Plt Off Bowan, made a gross error in judging his height, and pulling out too low he crashed into the ground and was killed. His gunner, Plt Off Cadman, survived the crash but died later in hospital. Some days later a sergeant flying a Blenheim lost one of his propellers in flight but with commendable skill managed to land the aircraft safely on one engine. I was reminded of a similar incident when one of the pilots from No. 600 Squadron had suffered the loss of a propeller on a return flight from Boos in Normandy, but he had crashed into the sea and he and his gunner had been lost.

I was thoroughly enjoying my Beaufighter flying now that conversion training was completed, and on 15 June I was attached to Rolls-Royce Derby for a detailed engine-handling course on the Merlin. It turned out to be an excellent course technically, and needless to say I and the other students were lavishly entertained when out of the classroom. While there we learnt that the company had approached a well-known artist to produce a stained-glass window depicting aircraft and aircrew of the Battle of Britain, which they were proposing to erect in the main hall of the Derby works, dedicated to the Few. I was invited to attend the unveiling of the window, which was designed by Hugh Easton and which was revealed by Lord Tedder at a ceremony on 11 January. The dedication read, 'Tribute to the Few', and the window is remarkably stirring and well worth seeing, and represents a generous gesture by the Rolls-Royce Company. When I got back from the engine course I was tasked with a reconnaissance of several local landing fields to assess their suitability for operating Beaufighters at night. These included Rednal, Montford Bridge, Condover and Bratten. They were all grass airfields and presented quite difficult approach and landing conditions in daylight, let alone at night. They had obstructions on the approaches, some of which could perhaps be cleared, but most of them had nearby rising ground that made them quite unsuitable. It was clear that Command Headquarters was getting pretty desperate for more bases from which to operate its night-fighters. I had another look at a grass airfield when I was invited to liaise with No. 70 Field Force Brigade, which was based at Shobdon. On arrival overhead in my Beaufighter I could see that the field was covered in a vast flock of sheep, and I wondered if the 'pongos' hoped to have a good laugh at my discomfiture. But without further ado I set about herding the animals up in my Beaufighter, with one wingtip almost touching the ground as I did steep turns around the field, and in a very short time had the flock cowering in the far corner of the field. As I was landing I saw a Hurricane arrive overhead, and this followed me in to land as the pilot was also visiting the brigade. We had a successful liaison visit, neither side commenting on the sheep, and after an al fresco lunch I was about to taxi out to take off when the Hurricane pilot indicated that he could not get his aircraft to start, so he clambered aboard the Beaufighter and settled down sitting on the cannon, after being introduced to Becky, for a lift back to his base. There were several more Army liaison exercises in the next few days, including simulated ground strafing and low-level attacks on Army targets, and these made a welcome change to the constant frustrating night patrols undertaken by the Beaufighters without conclusive results at that time. In the middle of August I flew a Beaufighter to Wittering, of fond training school memory, where I was to undergo a four-day blind-flying course flying Master IIs. Instrument flying was of great importance still, for we were fast becoming an all-weather squadron, with radar aids and ground control making it possible and necessary to fly in much lower weather limitations. It should never be forgotten that our role of night-fighter differed markedly from the day boys, who very seldom had to fly on instruments for any length of time and usually had bright clear skies as their medium.

I was hardly back from Wittering with my updated instrument rating than I was off to Henleaze, near Filton, another airfield of happy associations, where I was to do a Bristol engine-handling course. This was a clear indication that the squadron would shortly be re-equipping with the Beaufighter VI, which was fitted with a pair of Bristol Hercules engines. This was good news, as the VI was a much more manageable and reliable aeroplane than the previous mark with Rolls-Royce Merlins.

At the beginning of September my flight was moved south to Honiley, an airfield south of Coventry. I led the formation of Beau-fighters taking off one after another in a stream from Wrexham. As soon as I was airborne my navigator came through on the intercom and reported that the last Beaufighter had swung badly on take-off and had crashed just outside the perimeter of the airfield. On landing at Honiley I was horrified to learn that both the pilot, Plt Off Birkbeck, and his radar operator had been killed in the crash at Wrexham. This was the first fatal accident that any of my squadron had suffered during the conversion to Beaufighters and since becoming operational, and I was very distressed over this tragic loss of two well-liked crew members. On the first two nights after arriving at Honiley, George, my new operator, and I were scrambled on operational patrols under the control of Comberton radar. Several contacts were followed but no visual contact was made, although one was chased for half an hour and we only turned back when recalled, as at that stage we were not allowed to take the radar sets too far over enemy-occupied territory. The following week I flew several of my officers and Becky in an Oxford up to Wrexham to attend the funeral of our two colleagues.

In October the remainder of the squadron moved down from Wrexham and the last Beaufighters IIs were withdrawn. Within a month the squadron was operational on the Bristol-engined Beaufighters, which were also fitted with updated AI. Few raiders came the way of the West Midlands, however, so we had little opportunity to prove their worth against a German target. For the rest of the year we consolidated our interception training, and off duty I had the opportunity to take up playing rugby again. After getting into training and a practice match to mould a team into reasonable shape, the station team had a tough away match with Coventry and got badly beaten, and it was clear that more training was required. I arranged a nightly gym session for all aircrews not on duty, and a semblance of a rugby team gradually emerged.

I was still very busy back at the squadron air-testing the new Beaufighters and the AI equipment and getting my crews into a high state of operational readiness, and so it was some time before I had any spare time.

During standby in the crew room at dispersal we relieved the boredom by discussing the war situation in the other theatres. In Egypt the Eighth Army had at last managed to reverse its fortunes and it now had a good chance of securing Tunisia. It had terrific air support, particularly from the cannon-mounted Hurricanes that were creating havoc among Rommel's tanks. American troops had been landed at Algiers, Oran and Casablanca and were advancing under their own air umbrella. The attitude of the French in Tunisia was interesting in that the resident commanders adopted an attitude of passive resistance to both sides and kept out of sight as far as possible, although they did attempt to blockade the ports. The Russians were now counter-attacking between the Volga and the Don and scoring considerable gains, and the Germans were beginning to wonder just what they had taken on.

At home things were fairly quiet, and although operational patrols were maintained no contact was made with the *Luftwaffe*. With the squadron crews the chief excitement was the forthcoming dance at Comberton, the radar station that controlled our aircraft when on operations or interception practices. All off-duty personnel had been invited, and happily there were a number of WRAF girls around to act as partners. The day after the dance George Evans, my radar operator, and I were air-testing a Beaufighter when a cylinder blew off the starboard Hercules sleeve-valve engine and caused a lot of damage. I set up a single-engine approach and landed without any hassle, and was just in time to take a telephone call from Wrexham with the splendid news that my daughter had just been safely brought into the world and mother and daughter were both well. Champagne miraculously appeared at dispersal, and toasts were drunk to the new baby and her dad's successful single-engine landing, not forgetting poor George, who had an anxious ride in the back seat grimly holding on to Becky, who was quite oblivious of any problem.

CHAPTER THIRTEEN

North Africa

December 1942 to May 1943

On 2 December, No. 96 Squadron was withdrawn from operations and was to receive special training. What this was to consist of was not clear, but rumour had it that we were destined for overseas. Our first task was to strip the black paint off our Beaufighters, a job that all the aircrews had to put their hands to. The aircraft were then sprayed with desert brown and grey camouflage paint, which seemed to confirm our future location as being somewhere in the desert.

While I was being kitted out with tropical gear Becky had been sent up to Wrexham in anticipation of a happy event. I flew up there for a day, only to discover that Becky had produced just one puppy, which sadly died after only a few days. Back at Honiley the squadron crews were being given armed combat, ground defence and weapons training and lectures on tropical medicine and desert diseases. I was able to fly up and spend Christmas Day with the family at Wrexham, but unfortunately was marooned there on Boxing Day by fog and only managed to fly back for duty on the 27th and over the New Year holiday. In the New Year I organized a party for my flight at the Phantom Coach Inn near Coventry, where 1943 was celebrated in fine style, as was the AOC's signal of congratulations on my Mention in Dispatches. The next day all the squadron aircrews attended what was called a Battle Inoculation course on an Army range near Warwick, where we were required to keep our heads down in slit trenches while tanks were driven over the top, followed by a fusillade of live Bren gun bullets fired a few inches over our heads. We were then given live hand-grenades and told to remove the safety-pin, wait five seconds and then throw the grenade out as far away as possible and duck down into the trench. It sounded pretty easy, but it was surprising how nervous one suddenly was of fumbling with the lethal thing. Luckily no one did fumble, as they really went off with a horrible bang.

After a week or two the squadron's warning for overseas seemed to have been postponed, and with some renewed enemy bombing of London we were once more required to have aircraft on operational readiness each night. On one night George and I were scrambled and I was flying my new Beaufighter with the modified dihedral tailplane. This made the aircraft a steadier gun platform, and I thought perhaps on this flight he might at last have a chance to prove it by having something hostile at which to shoot. The Comberton controller gave us a good interception steer, and George picked up a contact on his radar at a range of four miles. We closed in rapidly with hopeful anticipation, only for me to get a visual on two Lancasters. My fingers still hovered over the firing button but I resisted the temptation. On 9 February I took to my bed with a violent dose of flu, but I was up the next day because I received the distressing news that my deputy flight commander had been killed in a flying accident. Two days later my other flight managed to crash a Beaufighter on the runway, where it burst into flames. I happened to be on hand, and grabbing a fire extinguisher almost managed to douse the flames before the fire truck arrived, but unfortunately the aircraft was subsequently a write-off.

On 20 February I led a formation of five Beaufighters and three Spitfires over Birmingham to celebrate, of all things, Red Army Day. The Spitfires were from Castle Bromwich, and were led by the Rolls-Royce test pilot, Alex Henshaw, who had flown more Spitfires than any other pilot at the time. He subsequently wrote a delightful book called *Sigh for a Merlin*. At the time we were full of admiration for the bravery of the Russian troops who were fighting with incredible courage before Stalingrad and Moscow, and so our salute over Castle Bromwich was not entirely inappropriate.

At the beginning of March I took my flight on detachment to Tangmere for Exercise Spartan. Night interception exercises were carried out with a mobile radar unit, and night operational patrols with searchlights were tried, but on this occasion too many friendly fighters saturated the night sky, and identification became impossible. After leading my flight back from Tangmere and landing at Honiley after the exercise, I received a signal posting me to a staff job at Fighter Command Bentley Priory. The next day I packed up my kit, stuffed it into the Riley and set off south to Bentley Priory and another non-flying post, but even then I was determined to keep in flying practice. As it turned out, I got in as much flying as I would have done on a squadron, and in several different types of aircraft.

Bentley Priory was, of course, the very centre of all Fighter Command activities, and several of my colleagues were there on the Air Staff, and most of the fighter squadron commanders gravitated there from time to time on visits and conferences, so my staff job would have its compensations. The Communication Squadron was based at Northolt, and I did not waste time in making contact with its commanding officer. There were quite a few different types of aircraft on the squadron, and after a few days to settle into the office I took a Spitfire from Northolt to visit my old squadron at Honiley. I had a flight lieutenant radar operator on my staff, and we usually went together on visits to squadrons, so it was not often that a Spitfire was appropriate. Consequently, on the next visit to Church Fenton, Usworth, Cranfield and Twinwood Farm, to accommodate my colleague I took a Vega Gull, which was a small low-wing cabin aircraft with four seats and reasonable blind-flying instruments, a useful little communications aircraft that I used quite often. The following week I flew my group captain boss in an Oxford on a staff visit to three more fighter stations. On 27 April I heard the sad news that Eddie, Maisie's brother, had been killed in North Africa. He was an armourer, and was apparently one of a party of airmen loading a Blenheim with 500 lb bombs when there was a premature explosion. There was considerable pressure on the ground crews servicing the bombers and fighters supporting the Eighth Army in the Desert, which was now advancing at great speed, and the Air Force units were also having to move to advance landing grounds at short notice and quite often having to improvise on the use of equipment and methods, thereby increasing the possibility of accidents. Eddie's death was a very sad loss, particularly at that time, when his father had been taken ill at Newbury, where they had rented a house.

The Night Operations Training Unit was due for a visit, so I flew up to Charter Hall in a Spitfire a few days later. The unit was still suffering from a bad record of flying accidents. Charter Hall was just north of the Tweed, and until then night training for pilots had been initially on the Oxford. And then after a flying demonstration by an instructor on the Beaufighter II they would be sent solo in this type.

The Oxford was a comparatively light and docile aircraft, but as I have already mentioned, the Beaufighter II was a much more rugged and heavy aircraft that could be quite a handful on one engine, even for an experienced pilot. The accident rate at the OTU had become unacceptably high, and the object of my visit was to fly and evaluate the Bristol Beaufort as a step in the training programme. The Beaufort was designed and used as a torpedo-bomber and was very similar to the Beaufighter – in fact its rear half came from the same jigs. I thought the aircraft handled well, and that when fitted with dual controls it should prove to be a good transitional trainer. Its Bristol engines were more reliable than the Beaufighter's Rolls-Royces and the aircraft was easier to handle. Their great advantage was, of course, that they were fitted with dual controls.

The de Havilland Mosquito was now coming into service with the night-fighter squadrons, and I considered that as a good staff officer I should familiarize myself with the new aircraft being flown by the Command's night-fighter squadrons. I therefore took the Vega Gull to Cranfield and borrowed a Mosquito III for an hour's trial flight. The fighter version of the Mosquito was fitted with the one-handed control column, which was a temptation to try some gentle aerobatics, which I did, but I was conscious of the seat beside me and was resigned to the thought that this was no single-seater, although it handled like one. It was with great reluctance that after a glorious hour and a half I had to land and return to my humble Vega Gull.

In the next week or two I was busy carrying out staff visits to the fighter squadrons in either the Spitfire or Vega Gull. On 29 May I flew the Spitfire to Predannack in Cornwall and met my brother at the Caerthillion Hotel at the the Lizard. The next day, while walking on the beach of extensive sands, by a strange coincidence we met, walking on her own, miles from anywhere, a WAAF officer with whom I worked at Headquarters 9 Group, where she was the assistant adjutant.

On the way back from Predannack I landed at Colerne to visit my old squadron commander, who was now commanding a Mosquito night-fighter squadron, and took the opportunity of quizzing him on night operations in the Mossie. On 9 June I flew some staff officers to Honiley and while there was able to borrow a Leopard Moth for a trial flight. On return to Fighter Command HQ I was told that I had been selected to fly to North Africa to carry out a liaison visit to the night-fighter squadrons operating with the Middle East Air Force. Arrangements were made for me to fly out with the Americans, so to get to their base in Scotland I took an Oxford from Bovingdon to Ayr and thence by road to Prestwick. The next day aboard an American DC-4 Skymaster we took off at dusk heading south-east over Ireland until we reached 12° West and thence South, making landfall in Morocco at 07.30 and landing at Marrakesh after ten hours' flying from Prestwick.

Then I boarded an American DC-3 Dakota and flew to Casablanca and on to Oran. The intention was to reach Algiers that night, but bad weather over the Atlas Mountains made us turn back to Oran. The following day the weather improved, and we landed at Algiers (Maison Blanche) in time for lunch. I visited the headquarters of Coastal Air Force for a presentation and went on to see the night-fighter squadron at Maison Blanche. The next day I met General Pete Quesada of the USAF in North Africa and went on to visit the American squadron at its airfield at Reghaia. The following night I had dinner at the AOC's villa outside Algiers with several senior officers and COs of the squadrons, and then some of us met up at the Coastal Club. After a bleary start the next morning I visited another squadron and met George, my old radar operator and Becky's friend.

We all assembled at the Rest House at Secouf on the beach and had a party, followed by a bathe in the Mediterranean and a night spent in a tent on the shore. The next day I borrowed a Hurricane from the local squadron and flew eastwards to Constantine to give another presentation of night-fighter tactics and operating methods. At this time the squadrons under the African Coastal Air Force were already operating well to the east of Bone and were having very good results with their Beaufighters. My old squadron, No. 600 City of London, had already amassed a total of fifty-five enemy aircraft destroyed, and when Rommel had eventually been driven out of Africa and the squadron moved, first to Malta, then Sicily and finally Italy itself, its score exceeded a century. As well as Junkers and Heinkels, their victories also included several Piaggios, Savoias and other Italian aircraft. After discussions with SASO, General Spatz, and other staff about the squadrons' operations, I returned to Maison Blanche in the Hurricane via Reghaia. Before landing I could not resist the temptation to carry out a few aerobatics, but quickly regretted it as when I was inverted during a slow roll a great deal of sand from the cockpit floor enveloped me and took time to settle before I could see clearly. However, the landing at Algiers was without further incident. After being seen off by AOC Coastal Air Force, I was given a car to Maison Blanche and boarded an American DC-3 for Gibraltar via Blida and Oran. I then took the right-hand seat and flew as second pilot in a British Dakota flown by a Czech pilot from Gibraltar to Hendon.

I reported to Headquarters Fighter Command at Bentley Priory at ten o'clock the next morning to learn that I had been posted to No. 54 Operational Training Unit. This was the night-fighter training station at Charter Hall just north of the Tweed near to Coldstream, which I knew quite well, having visited it when a staff officer, and I was to be Wing Commander Flying. I barely had time to complete my report on my North Africa visit when I was winging my way in an Oxford northwards once more to Scotland.

CHAPTER FOURTEEN

No. 9 Group Headquarters

June 1943

harter Hall airfield was situated in the lovely Tweed valley with
rising ground to the north that was not ideal from the flying
point of view. The aircraft that we were operating were
the Beaufighters with Rolls-Royce engines, which were certainly not the
most satisfactory type for sending off solo inexperienced student pilots.
The Beaufighter II was a very good, rugged aircraft, and the Rolls-Royce
Merlin was an excellent aero engine, but when married together the
result was a bit of a disaster. The single-engine performance was not as
good as it should have been, and the aircraft suffered from this tendency
to swing on take-off, which could be dangerous if not anticipated in
time. As a consequence the first solo flights of pupils were always
moments of some anxiety both for the pupils concerned and for the
watching instructing staff. Several fatal accidents had been witnessed
by them on or near the airfield, and it was a relief when the Beaufighter
IIs were replaced by the more amenable Beaufighter with Bristol
Hercules engines. It was not possible to fit dual control to the
Beaufighters because of the cockpit design, which was, in fact, ideal for
a single pilot, so the question of an interim dual aircraft was still an
urgent need. It may be remembered that when I was a staff officer at
Headquarters Fighter Command I had visited Charter Hall to fly a
Bristol Beaufort to assess the type for its suitability for the purpose. I was
now gratified to see that Beauforts fitted with dual control were now
available and flying as an interim training type before the pupils went
solo on the Beaufighter. There was good reason to believe that accident
rates at the OTU might well improve. I was responsible for organizing
the training programme and supervising its execution. It was intensive
and difficult at times as weather quite often prevented flying and even
greater efforts were needed as a result. However, I was lucky in having
a very good and pleasant station commander and efficient training staff,

and time could usually be found for relaxation in amusing and friendly company. As I had learnt on my previous posting to a unit north of the Border, the local Scots people were always hospitable and generous, and Fitzgerald, our senior air traffic controller, was an old hand in the area and was well in with several of our neighbours. He and I spent many happy hours shooting on several of the local estates or at drinks or dinner parties at their invitation It was always a marvel to me that they should all be so friendly and kind when they were subjected to the screaming of our Beaufighter engines day and night over their farms and houses. My responsibilities also ranged to the satellite airfield at Winfield, a few miles to the east, and I had to pay regular visits there, which gave me a welcome excuse to fly backwards and forwards in any type of aircraft I could get my hands on, often accompanied by Fitz and Becky. On 10 and 11 July I took a Martinet and a Beaufort, and later in the week a Dominie, to get to Winfield and back for my regular weekly visits. On the 19th, I flew the Dominie on a sea search for a missing Barracuda from the Royal Navy. After landing I rushed down to Berwick-on-Tweed and joined the crew of the air-sea rescue launch to continue the search. But after a fruitless hour's patrol we returned to port and no trace was ever found of the Barracuda or its crew.

When an invitation arrived to a dance at Headquarters No. 9 Group Preston, another wing commander from the staff and I flew down to Samlesbury in a Beaufighter. We were pleased to meet several old Battle of Britain cronies, including Freddie Rosier and Pete Brothers, and the beautiful old mansion of Barton Hall resounded to the jollifications and ribaldry until the early hours.

A day or two later, back at Charter Hall, Fitz and I flew up to the Orkneys in a Beaufighter II with Becky to carry out take-off and landing trials at RNAS Twatt, to assess its suitability for the operation of Beaufighters day and night. I reported that the airfield and its approaches were suitable, but that an upgrade of the air traffic facilities would be necessary. The next day I took a visiting staff officer to Grangemouth in the Dominie, and returned in very bad weather, and Fitz had to work hard to talk me down to a safe landing. He always did.

At the beginning of August I managed to get a few days' leave to go down and see my sister at her home in Longhope, near Gloucester. I had a good reason to get back to Charter Hall, so I got a lift to Honiley, where I had arranged to be picked up. Unfortunately and unexpectedly, the Beaufighter that arrived burst a tyre on landing and the swing resulted in a collapsed undercarriage and a wrecked aircraft. My old chum the station commander very kindly then offered to lend me his Martinet, and I was able to continue on my way, only to have to land at Scorton because of bad weather. I eventually landed at Charter Hall after dusk, and the Martinet had to return to Honiley next day. The following weekend I was invited with Fitz to shoot at Lord Craigmyle's estate on Peel Moor, Galashiels, and enjoyed a very productive day's sport and a splendid picnic lunch, with cold Scotch salmon and sparkling wine. The shooting after lunch was a bit haphazard, to say the least.

I was able to get my hands on a Miles Magister, and carried out an exercise of aerobatics and low flying, and finally earned Fitz's disapproval by landing on the perimeter track alongside his control tower. However, he soon recovered his customary cheerful good mood the next day when we went to visit one of his ladies at Kimmergham, a beautiful house and garden, not to mention the lady concerned. Perhaps it should be mentioned that Fitz was small and dapper and an example of one of Britain's perfect gentlemen, as well as being a very fine air traffic controller. When I returned to Charter Hall I took the opportunity to fly a Beaufighter VI powered with Hercules engines and the added safety feature of fully feathering airscrews. I couldn't resist making my final landing with one engine stopped and feathered, accompanied by Fitz's 'show-off' remark from the tower.

A Wellington III C that had force-landed with engine trouble some days before was now fitted with a replacement engine and was ready for air test, so I and my chief flying instructor, with Pilot's Notes in hand, flew it on air test, and after an hour in the air landed and declared it serviceable and ready for collection by the bomber squadron to which it belonged. The next day I had to take a Beaufighter VI on another air-sea rescue search, this time for wreckage and a dinghy twenty-five miles out to sea from Boulmer. I landed at Winfield at dusk after an unsuccessful three-hour search. On 16 September a visiting staff officer flew in with a Spitfire, and I persuaded him to let me borrow it for a short flight to practise my rather neglected aerobatics. I was enjoying the flight until the Spitfire developed very severe and frightening vibration on top of a loop and the engine nearly stopped, so I made hasty tracks for home. The staff officer said he had not suffered any problem but admitted he had only flown the Spitfire straight and level during his various visits. To be on the safe side the Spitfire went into the servicing flight for investigation, and I flew the pilot to Ayr in the Dominie, and took the opportunity to visit my old squadron at Drem to discuss the training of Beaufighter pilots for the night-fighter role.

On 1 October, my 27th birthday, I was working on the next training schedule, and in the afternoon played in the first rugby match of the season. It was a bit chaotic and no one was very fit, but there was some promise for the future with a little effort on everyone's part. The supervision of training at Charter Hall continued, with the occasional drama, such as the time when I and my senior QFI had to take the Magister and look for the wreck of a Beaufighter that had crashed up in the hills to the north on the previous night. Three days later Fitz and I had a day's shooting at Kimmergham, followed by another half day's shoot around the airfield on the following Saturday. One Monday morning when the station commander and I were discussing the future training programme in my office, the phone rang and air traffic was on to tell the station commander that a pilot under training was in trouble in a Beaufighter, apparently with an engine failure. We both dashed outside, scrambled into his car and tore down the hill towards the airfield. We could see that there was a senior training officer already in the control tower talking over the radio to the pupil, who was only on his second solo, and as we leapt from the car we could see the aircraft clearly on only one engine, flying very slowly over the centre of the airfield. Even as we watched with bated breath, the student pilot could no longer hold the pressure on the rudder bar to keep the aircraft straight, and it veered towards the dead engine, seemed to shudder in the air, rolled over and crashed into the runway with a sickening thump. For a moment all was silent, and then, almost leisurely at first, flames began to creep up around the wreck. The fire crew was there almost at once and sprayed foam on the burning aircraft, and an asbestos-suited fireman walked into the flames, but all in vain as the pilot would doubtless have been killed on impact. The station commander, clearly shaken, asked me to drive him back to his office, where he called in all the senior training staff immediately to examine all the possible reasons for the accident, for it was essential to lose no time in assessing the cause so as to avoid unhelpful speculation among the trainees. In the meantime flying training continued without a break, as was customary.

On the 18th, I took a Beaufighter down to Thelthorpe and picked up Flt Lt Lister, Maisie's other brother, to take him to Greenham Common to see his father, who was now dangerously ill in Newbury hospital. The next day I flew Eric back to his bomber squadron at Thelthorpe. Seven weeks later Eric was posted missing on a bombing mission over Germany, but his father never heard the sad news, as he had already died.

At the end of October there was a party at my old station at Honiley, and George, who was just back from Africa, and I flew down there in a Beaufighter and met up with old squadron friends. In the middle of November flying was held up by bad weather, and quite a lot of snow had to be cleared from the runway and taxiways. On the 18th, I did a weather and runway check in a Beaufighter, and flying was able to resume. The next day I took the Dominie to Drem with several staff officers to visit the radar station at Direlton. Not long afterwards a new wing commander was posted in to take over command of the satellite airfield of Winfield, and Fitz and I flew over in a Martinet to welcome him and brief him on the stage of training of the senior course now based there. On the return journey I made a bet with Fitz that I would fly him back to Charter Hall below ground level! With a scornful laugh Fitz said, 'You're on!' But he lost the bet: there the Tweed runs in a valley, and I followed the twists and turns of the river a few feet above the water all the way up it to just south of the airfield, where I lowered the under-carriage and pulled up to runway height and landed before anyone knew I was there. On Christmas Eve we all went to a dance and a party at Winfield. On Christmas Day there was a dining-in night at Charter Hall for all officers after they had served the airmen with their Christmas dinner.

On the 28th I received a signal to report to AOC 11 Group, so after travelling down to Bentley Priory by the night train I reported to the AOC's PA and had an interview with the AVM in the morning. I was delighted to be told that I was to command No. 488 New Zealand Squadron, which was equipped with Mosquito night-fighters.

CHAPTER FIFTEEN

New Zealand Squadron Mosquitos

January to July 1944

Having received the good news about my new command, I returned to Charter Hall by train on 31 December and arrived in time to celebrate at the New Year's Eve Party. It would be quite a wrench to leave the OTU, for I had made many friends and got on very well with Rupert, the charming and good-natured station commander. We had enjoyed many good times together and shared a lot of the grief for all too many fatal crashes. Somehow I felt I was letting him and the rest of the loyal staff down at a crucial time by leaving to enjoy flying the more benign Mosquito. I soon had a rude awakening, however! No. 488 Squadron was based at Bradwell Bay on the south side of the Blackwater estuary opposite Mersea Island. More than half of the squadron aircrews were New Zealanders, including two Maoris, and they were mostly inexperienced. I would have one British and one New Zealand flight commander, both of whom were fairly experienced at the game. So it was with high hopes that I cleared from Charter Hall during the first two days of January 1944 and flew down in a Beaufighter VI to Bradwell, taking Becky with me. She was to get a surprise, as the squadron already had a mascot, a huge Great Dane. But subsequently they got on well, with never a cross word between them, although it was rather a case of the giant and the dwarf.

On the 5th I flew the retiring CO of the squadron up to Ouston, the station he was taking over on his promotion to group captain. On the return, flying the Mosquito solo, I was thoroughly enjoying the flight during the pleasant evening of a sunny day, and called Bradwell on the radio, giving my ETA and not bothering to ask for a weather update. But Bradwell came back to say a thick 'smog' was moving eastwards from London and that the visibility at Bradwell was already down to 1,000 yards. But now I was only ten minutes from the airfield, and I said I would continue and take a look at the conditions on reaching the base. There was an inversion, and the fog had settled on the ground with the top at about 1,000 feet. With an easterly drift the approach to the runway in use was going to be directly into the setting sun, which was by now low on the horizon, and I found that I could see nothing on that approach. It was at this point that I made one of the worst decisions that I had made in the whole of my flying career. Bradwell tower gave me the option of several alternative airfields where the weather was better, and clearly I should have diverted while I had sufficient fuel, but I decided to see what the approach was like from the other direction with the sun behind me. Although it was still poor, I thought the visibility was better, and determined not to be denied a landing at my new base I told the tower of my intentions. I realized that I would be landing with a tail-wind, but it was only slight, and by now the tower had switched on the 'FIDO' in the hope that this would help. This was a method of dispersing fog by lighting petrol burners all the way down either side of the runway. This was a fearsome sight at the best of times and an appalling waste of fuel, and in this case quite ineffective as this was not fog but heavy industrial haze. I did a trial run and was then given a radio-directed talk down, which put me in a position to see the runway ahead through the murk. I lowered the wheels and the last of the flap, closed the throttles and landed smoothly on the runway, calling the tower to say I was down. My relief turned to horror when I suddenly became aware that I had touched down a long way down the runway: through the murk emerged the far end of it and the solid hut containing the runway approach beacon, and beyond that I knew the sea wall awaited. I was still travelling at a rate of knots, with no hope of stopping, even with full braking, so I made the split-second decision, released the over-ride and retracted the undercarriage. The Mosquito slithered to a stop on its belly a few yards short of the obstruction ahead. As I sat there in bewilderment that moment would haunt me for a long time in the future and I was furious with myself for such a gross error of judgement, which resulted in serious damage to an aircraft. I did not enjoy relating this incident, and I was pretty upset by it, but the reaction of my New Zealand aircrew, which I had dreaded, was much better than I deserved. Firstly they were mildly sympathetic, and then they kept ribbing me about it; this treatment I applauded, and it endeared them to me, for it lightened the load of my shame.

The rest of January was taken up with night-flying tests and AI practice runs with my new AI operator Pete Bowman, and we had nightly stand-bys for operations. On the 13th I flew to North Weald in my new Mosquito XIII to visit the controllers at the nearby sector operations room, where I met Paul Raymond, the actor, who was a wing commander controller there. Pete and I went on from there to Trimley Heath, which was our controlling radar station. On 20 January I was invited to visit the de Havilland Aircraft factory at Hatfield. I was very pleased to accept, particularly as I was now flying the de Havilland

Mosquito, and I looked forward to discussing the aircraft with the experts. On arrival I was introduced to the major and Peter de Havilland, and invited to join them for lunch. After lunch we were all ushered outside to see the Vampire fighter flying over. The whistling screech was a new sound in the air and one with which I would become very familiar in the future.

On the night of the 21st the squadron shot down two Huns – a Dornier Do 217 and a Junkers Ju 88. After congratulating the two crews concerned and marking up their score on the crew-room score-card, I flew down to Greenham Common to attend Capt Lister's funeral, and then returned to Bradwell without delay as the squadron was very busy with regular night interceptions. On 28 January the staff of 11 Group Headquarters threw a party at Uxbridge, and many of my friends were there, including several whom I had met recently in North Africa during my visit to the Coastal Air Force. The festivities went on well into the early hours, so I spent what remained of the night in the Chequers at Uxbridge. On 5 February my Dutch crew shot down a Dornier Do 217, and Pete and I were scrambled to patrol in cooperation with the search-lights, but made no interceptions. The next night we were scrambled to patrol under Trimley radar control, and chased after a searchlight 'canopy', but no visual was obtained so we had to return empty-handed. Bradwell was one of the best-equipped and largest runways in the south of England, and being close to the continent it was often host to returning bombers that might be short of fuel or with other trouble after a raid. On the 5th Pete and I were diverted from our night-flying test to lead in a B-17 bomber that had made a distress call to the tower. We were homed onto the American aircraft, which was clearly badly damaged and staggering along on only two engines, barely maintaining height. We flew alongside and synchronized speed, and then took the lead, aiming with radar help to take the bomber in on a direct approach to the runway in use. I called the tower to clear the circuit and give priority for landing to the crippled bomber, and provided them with an accurate time of our arrival. The bomber's radio seemed intermittent, but we kept up a running commentary on our position in case they could receive it. With a mile to go we told the B-17 to look ahead for the runway and were relieved to see its undercarriage being lowered. As our Mosquito flew ahead, the bomber landed safely and came to a halt on the side of the runway. This was one of the many B-17s to creep into Bradwell with damage, and sometimes they made crash-landings and remained ominously still while the crash tenders and ambulances rushed to their aid. Sometimes members of the crew had been injured or killed, and the rescue team were faced with the dreadful sight of the aircraft dripping blood onto the runway. The US bomber force on daylight raids suffered dreadful casualties, and no one at Bradwell envied them their job. It was a great relief to the Fortresses when their long-range Mustang fighter began to become available and could escort the bombers for a great deal of their route.

Pete and I flew three operational patrols at the beginning of the month without success. In between night sorties I managed to get a day or two off, and on the 12th we had an evening in London, where we had dinner at the Liaison Club and danced until the small hours at the Cabaret Club. On my return to Bradwell, Pete and I flew four more operational patrols, either with the searchlights or under control of Trimley radar, but without contacts, although on one chase we were baffled by a good deal of 'window'. This was bunches of aluminium strips dropped by both sides to clutter up the radar. Some of the other crews of the squadron, however, were more successful, and shot down a Junkers Ju 88 and a Dornier Do 217.

March continued with a good deal of enemy activity, and on the 18th Nigel Bunting shot down a Junkers Ju 188, which crashed locally. The next morning Nigel and his operator, the AOC of 11 Group and I were all photographed by the press in front of a huge hole in the ground, with Nigel pointing down at the carnage below, which thankfully was not visible in the picture. On the 21st Pete and I got a good contact while on patrol with Trimley radar, and chased it, following violent evasive action, all the way to the French coast, when we were recalled, as we were not allowed at that time to take our radar, which was still secret, over enemy territory. That night the squadron shot down two more Huns under radar control and three more in conjunction with the searchlights – a great night's work.

The fact that Pete and I had not yet 'broken our duck', as it were, was galling and frustrating, particularly as Pete was a very good operator, but there was no doubt that a great amount of luck was involved in bringing to a satisfactory conclusion the picking up of a contact, following it on the aircraft's radar, getting into visual range and identifying a target as hostile so that it could be shot down. On the other hand the experience and expertise of some of my aircrews was now beginning to tell, and some individuals were becoming highly skilled when given a target. Perhaps it should be appreciated that I had twenty-eight crews flying on operational patrols regularly, and what enemy trade there was had to be spread out between them. Despite my personal frustration it was very gratifying that the squadron's score was beginning to mount up, and morale was high.

On 30 March I was able to welcome the New Zealand Deputy Prime Minister, who visited the squadron with the AOC of the Royal New Zealand Air Force. Clearly, they too were delighted to meet the

Bristol Bulldog.

Mother and father.

First solo in a Gipsy Moth, 1935.

Sergeant's stripes and coveted Wings.

Hawker Fury.

Right: Squadron fighter pilot.

Middle: Furies at Hendon.

Bottom: Hart on the approach to Hawkinge.

Gloster Gladiator.

Battle of Britain pilot.

Bristol Blenheim

Right: Return to duty after escaping from Holland 1940.

Middle: Hawker Hurricane, No.96 Squadron.

Bottom: That awful car.

Blenheim IV Night Fighter.

Defiant Night Fighter.

Beaufighter Night Fighter.

'Air dog' Becky.

Top: Mosquito Night Fighter with A.I Mk.8 Radome.

Nigel Bunting's Junkers 88.

Below: Junkers 188 crashed on runway at Bradwell. Crew captured.

Kai Tak, 1945.

Officer Commanding R.A.F. Kai Tak. Take-over parade.

Pilots of the Air Fighting Development Squadron. Central Fighter Establishment, West Raynham.

An early Meteor III

A Royal Party visits West Raynham.

No.6 Squadron Venoms start-up on departure from Iraq.

Venom formation.

Venoms operating from desert airfield Mafraq, Jordon.

My Venom.

The Crown Prince of Iraq. A regular vistor to Habbanya Officers' Club.

Dubai 1955, awaiting development.

Station Headquarters staff, R.A.F. Habbaniya

At Akrotiri, Cyprus with Andrew Humphrey, later Air Chief Marshal Sir Andrew Humphrey, Chief of Defence Staff.

A.O.C.'s Inspection by A. V. M. Boyce with Group Captain Hughie Edwards, VC.

Meeting and greeting at Edinburgh airport: Monti with General Murray.

Javelin squadron at Turnhouse.

Greeting Princess Alexandra.

Handing out awards to airmen.

A 'gaggle' of Group Captain Battle of Britain pilots. Twelve were chosen to provide an escort at Churchill's funeral.

A.O.C.'s Inspection of Hastings aircrews of Bomber Command Bombing School.

Hastings of B.C.B.S. showing H2S radar scanner.

Reviewing Officer at Air Cadets Passing-out Parade.

Retirement to Suffolk.

squadron aircrews and ground crews who were making such a splendid contribution to the war effort. At the beginning of April Pete asked me if we could have a change from daily night-flying tests and do a cross-country exercise to give him some practice in straight navigation. This seemed a good idea, so I left him to work out a flight plan, with turning points at known airfields where let-downs and radar approaches could be practised. This was always valuable exercise for air traffic controllers as well as pilots, as the former rarely got enough aircraft with which to practise. I did a check of Pete's flight plan and we set off from Bradwell, climbing through cloud, and set course for St Mawgan in Cornwall, Pete busy with his stopwatch and CSC. On ETA I called St Mawgan tower and asked for a let-down and radar approach to their runway. This they did gladly, and the Mosquito broke cloud at 450 feet on the glide path and on the centre line, with the runway dead ahead, making a roller landing a simple matter. Having taken off from the roller and started my climb up through cloud, I congratulated and thanked the St Mawgan controller for a faultless approach and set the next course that Pete gave me. We followed the same procedure at Valley in Anglesey and at Honiley. In the latter case we had to break off our approach as we were still in cloud at 400 feet, so we climbed up through the cloud again without seeing the ground. We landed back at Bradwell having done our night-flying test en route.

Life at Bradwell was pretty hectic at this time, with a good deal of enemy activity at night. But I managed to get an odd night off immediate duty when I could invite local friends into the officers' mess for an evening's drink and discussion. These became quite popular, and several local characters were made honorary members of the mess.

Notable among these guests was a certain Tom Driberg, who lived locally and brought several cronies with him, and in retrospect I hoped that our discussions were not on sensitive matters, in view of his later reputation as being very Left Wing. But it was always an amusing evening. There was not a great deal of enemy activity in the next few days, although operational patrols were flown. While I was at stand-by one night in the crew room the chaps told me an interesting story, which I had never appreciated before. When I was sitting in the crew room at readiness, Becky would lie at my feet, and as soon as I went out to fly she would hop up onto my chair and there she would sit, without stirring. Quite suddenly she would get down, go to the door and sit outside. The chaps naturally thought that I was just about to walk in, but in fact I had only just called the tower from some miles away for landing. She always seemed to know when I was overhead, and whenever she left my chair the chaps would say, 'The boss is back', knowing that I was just about to land. But how did she know? She never made a mistake. If

I was diverted they found it very difficult to get her to leave my chair and persuade her to go back with someone else to the mess.

It so happened that one night Pete and I had just landed from a patrol and were walking to the crew room to greet Becky when we heard an aircraft low overhead, obviously in trouble. As it turned and began to descend onto the runway, Pete and I jumped into my Jeep and drove out onto the airfield. The aircraft crashed onto the runway with its wheels retracted, and slithered to a halt. As we drove up and the lights of the Jeep illuminated the aircraft, we were astonished to see the German markings on its side and wings, and recognized it as a Ju 88. Four figures emerged from the wreck, gesticulating and demanding in halting French to know where they were. Pete in his immaculate French replied that they were in 'Angleterre and you are our prisoners'. They made a half-hearted attempt to draw their side-guns, but as the ambulance drove up and came to a screeching halt Pete and I rounded them up and herded them into the ambulance with vague but forceful threats. As soon as they were all inside, the doors of the ambulance were slammed and, escorted by the Jeep, they were whisked off to the guardroom. It was only then that I realized that Pete was locked in the ambulance as well as the Germans, and I was very relieved to see him descend in good order as the four prisoners were led away by the service policemen for interrogation. When we got back to dispersal and were welcomed, at last, by Becky and several of the crews, I couldn't resist an aside to Nigel, 'You may have shot down more Huns than us, but Pete and I are well ahead of you on capturing prisoners!'

Over the next few nights there was considerable activity from enemy raiders, and the squadron was very successful and shot down a further six Germans. We were pleased to receive a very nice signal from the C-in-C ADGB sending 'Congratulations on the outstanding success and brilliant night's work'. And a similar signal from C-in-C Headquarters No. 10 Group was received.

Pete and I took a Mosquito down to Zeals in Wiltshire to assess its suitability as an airfield to operate Mosquitos from at night, as there were plans afoot to move the squadron there. The airfield itself was acceptable, although it only had grass runways and few facilities were available as yet, and so pending these being completed the squadron would operate from Colerne on the hill south of Bath. Much to our regrets we moved down there on 5 May, sorry to leave Bradwell, where the squadron had been so successful. In the absence of proper accommodation we were accommodated in a tented camp on the east side of the Colerne airfield.

On 11 May we started night-flying from Zeals, and on the 14th Pete and I were scrambled for a patrol in association with the searchlights.

After following searchlight indications we intercepted and fired on a Ju 88, but lost it after violent evasive action. It was probably damaged, but no confirmation could be obtained as it was over the sea. On 20 May the AOC of No. 85 Group presented No. 488 NZ Squadron with a squadron crest at a formal parade on the airfield. The next day Nigel and his operator were awarded a bar to their DFCs, and another crew, John Hall and Jock Cairns, received a DFC each, having shot down the squadron's fiftieth enemy aircraft. After the war John became a respected barrister, studying at Trinity Cambridge, and was called to the Bar at the Inner Temple.

It was becoming more and more obvious that the invasion of the continent was only a few days away, but before the news broke I managed to get a few days' leave and arranged to rent a tiny thatched cottage in a charming village in Suffolk where I settled Maisie and daughter Sue before returning to the frantic activity back at base. On 3 June I went to Middle Wallop to collect some very important documents, which were to be guarded like the Crown Jewels and not opened until authorized. On 4 June I was summoned to Headquarters No. 10 Group for briefing by the AOC and his intelligence officer, one Rex Harrison. At a final conference the next day at Tangmere it was announced that 'D' Day was on the morrow, and the squadron commanders received their briefing regarding their flying operations required over the beachhead.

The day broke fine and clear, but the forecast for the next few days was not too good. After our usual night-flying tests the squadron provided maximum effort on regular patrols over Normandy and the beachhead after nightfall. We had at least four night-fighter Mosquitos in the air every night under close control of our radar stations – some on the south coast, but one already at sea with the invading forces. Pete and I flew at least once every night, as did most of the other crews, and we maintained a very high flying intensity. I should mention that our servicing crews worked all hours to keep the Mosquitos flying. They did a marvellous job, and deserve the highest praise for their considerable part in the squadron's success. On 13 and 14 June the squadron shot down five more Huns, and Peter and I did five more operational patrols without success. But by the end of the month the squadron had shot down a further three aircraft. As the ground forces were overrunning more occupied territory, plans could be made to establish forward radar control stations in Normandy. On 27 June I flew an Oxford with another squadron commander and some radar controllers to an advanced landing ground AI at St Pierre De Mont, and then we were taken by Jeep to a 21 Sector radar unit that had been established near Cherbourg. Here we were shown around the site recently deserted by the Germans, and the temporary buildings housing the control room. We then spent our time getting to know the controllers and discussing interception techniques with them, as these were the guys who would hopefully be bringing our fighters to successful interceptions and kills. We flew back to Zeals with German souvenirs and a crate or two of brandy.

At the beginning of July I did a navigation trip down to Aston Down to take an airman on compassionate leave. I took the opportunity to take my brother, in his capacity as an Observer Corps officer, on a flight in the Mosquito. On my return to Zeals, Pete and I flew two more patrols, one when we were sent off chasing flying bombs, which unfortunately we were unable to catch, although twice we had the jet flame in sight but were unable to get closer. During the other patrol we made two interceptions, but on Stirling bombers that were dropping window. On 30 July I was temporarily away from the base when I received a message to say that Nigel was missing on a Lone Ranger patrol over France. Without losing a moment I rushed back to Zeals, full of remorse and a feeling of guilt. I must admit that I did leave the base fairly often when off duty, and I made a pledge that I would not leave it again if I could possibly help it.

I was devastated to lose a flight commander and a friend, and not being with the squadron at the time made it even worse. It is doubtful whether my presence would have made any difference, and the chaps had done everything possible to find out what had happened to Nigel. As soon as I got back to the squadron I got authority to fly two sorties over the area where he was last plotted, in the hope that we might pick up a clue. But nothing was discovered, and his loss was still unaccounted for when I left the squadron, despite all our efforts to arrive at the reason for his disappearance. I later heard that Nigel had been shot down by enemy flak and is buried in France.

CHAPTER SIXTEEN

The Destruction of Two
Junkers Bombers

August 1944 to July 1945

B y the beginning of August my squadron's victories had amounted
to 41 German aircraft destroyed. On the night of the 4th while on
my 112th operational patrol, Pete and I were flying over the
beachhead when ground control warned us of an unidentified aircraft
six miles ahead and crossing from port to starboard. Pete picked up a
contact on our radar and was able to put us in a perfect position to
identify the aircraft as a Ju 88. I closed in to 200 yards and opened fire
with the aircraft firmly in my sights. A two-second burst of the four
cannon was devastating and started a fire in the port engine of the
Junkers, and pieces began to fly off it and whistle over our heads. It then
turned slowly to port and dived steeply down, and we saw it explode
on the ground east of Vire in Normandy. Ground control soon put us
onto another contact that we chased after, but in the end had to abandon,
as we ran into heavy flak from Allied ships. Not surprisingly the Navy
gunners were a bit trigger happy at this time, and it was unwise to
provoke them.

On landing back at Zeals my ground crew gave a cheer as we taxied in
and they spotted that I had fired my cannon because the fabric patches
that covered the cannon mouths were in tatters. The next night we flew
two more patrols, but all was quiet. On the 9th, during another patrol,
we had a visual sighting of a Ju 88 but could not get into firing range
when it took violent evasive action. After two more rather dull operational patrols over Le Havre and the beachhead, we had a far from dull
patrol on the 26th. It was a bright moonlit night and we were given a
patrol line that we followed for some time without incident. After an
hour our controller called to say that we had a friendly aircraft in our
vicinity that was showing an undue interest, and advised us to do a
quick turnaround to shake it off. So I pulled around into a steep turn,

and after straightening up we came under attack, with a burst of cannon shells hitting the Mosquito in the fuselage behind the cockpit. A bit shaken, and not knowing what damage we had suffered, I called up Colerne and reported the action and requested an emergency landing either at an airfield en route or back at base. I advised Pete to put on his parachute and be ready to jettison the escape hatch, even though everything seemed to be behaving normally. We stayed on course for Colerne for twenty minutes, and with the airfield in sight I began to relax and we landed without any trouble. It transpired that the culprit was an American Black Widow night-fighter pilot who misidentified the Mosquito as a Ju 88. On inspection after landing, our servicing crew found several 20 mm cannon shells lodged in the dinghy pack a few inches behind Pete's head! We were both very lucky to have escaped more serious damage, but no apology was ever received from the American pilot or his unit. A subsequent board of enquiry by the Americans found he was not to blame, and he was promoted to major and sent back to the States. I heard later that when he was questioned about not identifying the aircraft that he fired at as a Mosquito his answer was that he thought it was 'a small Ju 88'! I wondered at the time what would have happened if the attack had been successful. Anyway, the day after the incident, Paris was liberated, which served to take our minds off the affair.

On 1 September Pete and I had another success while patrolling south of Caen. He got a good radar contact and I followed his instructions until I got a visual. The long, tapered wings of a Ju 188 were unmistakeable, and I closed in and after a sustained burst of cannon fire it crashed in flames west of Le Havre. After the combat, we returned to Colerne to land in heavy rain, with a cloud base of 400 feet. The local controller gave me an excellent talk-down, which made the landing straightforward despite the rain and low ceiling. We were again treated to a cheer from our ground crew as we taxied in with clear evidence that we had fired our cannon again. The next day, as our night patrols continued, came the good news that Brussels had been liberated and the Dutch border crossed by our troops in several places. The reoccupation of European territory continued to go well. In the middle of all this action the squadron was re-equipping with Mosquito XXXs, which were fitted with the new AI Mk 10 SCR 720, the new American radar system. This was a great improvement on previous marks, as regards both range and its resistance to Window interference. On 9 September I had my last flight in my faithful steed, the Mosquito Mk XIII MM566, and Pete and I air-tested my new Mk XXX MM 818 with AI Mk 10. For the rest of the month flying was mostly taken up with conversion training for Pete and the other operators on the new radar, which was substantially different from the old mark.

Then rumour had it that the squadron was to move to Hunsdon early in October, as other squadrons started moving to the continent. Clearly 488 would go over soon, and so on 2 October Pete and I in the Mosquito XXX flew over to take a look at the airfields coming into use in France. We landed at Amiens Glise, then on to Brussels Melsbroek, where we had a stopover and a chance to savour the nightspots of Brussels. The next day we went to Ghent by road and returned, and then flew back to Colerne. A couple of days later on a flight in an Oxford to Sudbury with Pete and Becky, I had to force-land at Lyneham when a piece of the port propeller flew off in flight, causing very severe vibration. On the 9th I led a squadron formation from Colerne to Hunsdon on the squadron redeployment, and we started operational patrols from there without delay, although things seemed rather quiet and we felt that the squadron had been taken out of the front line temporarily, pending a move to the continent. On the 19th I flew to Lille Vendeville via Le Treport, and a day or two later to Ghent (St Denis-Westrem) to where No. 85 Group HQ had been moved. There was a party for the Belgians at the Hôtel de la Poste that evening, where there was a large gathering of officers from most of the British squadrons then in Belgium, and good relationships were built up with our Belgian visitors.

At the end of the month, much to my disappointment I was posted onto the staff of 85 Group, pending the formation of a wing headquarters, to take two squadrons to France when an airfield was available. As there was no immediate job for me, I asked to be attached to the Group Forward Repair Unit as its test pilot to test operational aircraft after repair or inspection and return them to operational squadrons. The unit was based at Odiham, but before reporting there I flew a Mosquito to Hunsdon to attend No. 488 Squadron's farewell party, where I was well and truly 'dined out'. I was very sad to leave the squadron that had been so successful and where I had made so many New Zealand friends. Not least of all, I was very sorry to have to say goodbye to Pete, who had been my splendid radar operator for some hundred flights, and I was very pleased that before splitting up we managed to shoot down two German aircraft together. I think that he stayed with the squadron for a while, but I regret that I lost touch with him.

On arrival at Odiham I soon settled into my new job, and on my second day I air-tested a Mustang III, a Mosquito XIII, and another Mosquito. This was the first time that I had flown a Mustang, and I found it a delight to fly, with a comfortable and roomy cockpit to make its long range and endurance tolerable for long hours at the controls.

The locking tailwheel for take-off was an innovation I had not come across before. The next day I flew a Mustang and a Typhoon, the latter type being new to me, and this too I found was a very rugged fighter, but pleasant to fly. It had a much bigger, heavier feel to it after the Mustang and the Spitfire, but it was a really aggressive and pugnacious machine in which to go to war, as was proved by its reputation as a 'tank buster'. I also tested a Mosquito and then ferried it to Lille and was flown in an Oxford by a Canadian pilot to Amiens Glisy, together with the indomitable Jimmy Rawnsley DSO, John Cunningham's radar operator. There was a resident night-fighter squadron at Amiens, and we took the opportunity to exchange views and experiences of the night-fighting game. The following day I flew as second pilot in a Dakota back to Hawkinge to pick up a Proctor, and took it back to Odiham. For the next week I was kept busy air-testing Mosquitos and Mustangs. After some time I managed to get in a game of rugger at Odiham, but there was little enthusiasm among the participants and, it must be admitted, not a lot of talent. However, I felt fitter after the game. Over the last few months I had been making efforts to obtain a posting to the Empire test pilots' course at Farnborough, but I had heard nothing in response to my formal application, so after an air test I took a Mustang to Boscombe Down to make enquiries from the commandant, whom I knew. I was told that the prospects did not look good! The following day I tried to deliver a Mosquito to Ghent, but the weather was bad and I had to post-pone the trip. I finally spent a day in Ghent, the capital of East Flanders, and was surprised to learn that it was the second largest port in Belgium, even though miles from the sea. At the confluence of the Scheldt and Leie rivers, it has access to the sea, not only by the rivers but also by several canals. In the city the shopping was very expensive, but it was full of the most beautiful buildings, the most splendid of all being the cathedral of St Bavon, the construction of which was started in the tenth century. I was sorry to have to leave, but work was building up at Odiham and I flew back there via Courtrai and Lille. After a short break I flew the Proctor back to Odiham and arrived in time to air-test a Spitfire IX. The next day, before taking the Proctor to West Hampnett and Middle Wallop, carrying delivery pilots, I air-tested a Typhoon. The following day I had another delivery flight, this time in the Oxford, to Cowley and Reading, and returned in time to air-test a Tempest and a Spitfire XIV. Before the end of the month I was asked to demonstrate a Beaufighter to a group staff officer, so I flew him on an hour's handling flight. In December there were several delivery flights to the continent, including Ghent, Amiens and Courtrai. While in Courtrai I was asked if I would fly an American B-25 Mitchell back to the UK on a delivery flight. I hadn't flown anything similar before, so it was a bit of a challenge. A plucky corporal who was keen to get back home agreed to come with me, and it was useful to have him in the right-hand seat turning to the right page in the Pilot's Notes, as I needed to refer to them. The Mitchell turned out to be a very pleasant and straightforward aircraft to fly, with a spacious and well-laid-out cockpit, the flight only being spoilt by deteriorating weather, which made it necessary for us to creep into Manston under low overcast. However, it soon cleared, and after another easy take-off I landed back at Odiham with a feeling of great satisfaction, and, I guessed, some relief in the case of my passenger.

Three days later I was back at Ghent and taken by staff car to Ath to sit as president of a district court martial that lasted for two whole days. On my return to the UK I heard that my posting to command No. 147 Wing had come through. The wing was forming at Odiham and would shortly be proceeding to an airfield on the continent to accommodate a Mosquito and a Typhoon squadron. On the first day of the New Year I returned to Odiham to take over the new wing, and heard the startling news from No. 85 Group that the *Luftwaffe* had made a last desperate effort to try and counter our air superiority by launching about 300 Fw 190s against our fighter airfields in Belgium and France. About half their force was shot down, but the Allies suffered considerable losses of aircraft caught on the ground. A salutary lesson. The day after testing a Spitfire XIV I flew to Ursel and on to No. 85 Group HQ for briefing on my new wing.

On 10 January I was attached to Hatfield to do a course on de Havilland propellers, which was a very nice rest and a few days of relax-ation. The members of the course were accommodated in the Mayfair Hotel, and on the first night after dinner at the Hungarian Restaurant we were taken to a show at the Lyric Theatre. During the next two days we attended lectures and demonstrations, and after a delightful lunch at Brentwood visited Stag Lane, and were given a tour round the factory, finishing up later with another dinner at the Hungarian Restaurant. We finally visited Hatfield, where I met my old friend John Cunningham, who had been taken on by his old firm de Havilland as a test pilot after his very distinguished career as a night-fighter pilot. We were then given an aerial demonstration of the new Hornet fighter, which looked most impressive, and after taxiing in we were intrigued to see the contra-rotating propellers as the engines were shut down. After lunch at Brentwood the course dispersed and we went back to our various units. On the 16th I had to go to Ath once more to finalize the courts martial as president. This time my journey was not as convenient as the last time when I had flown most of the way. Now I first drove to Dover, where I went aboard an air-sea rescue launch to Ostend, and took a train to Ghent and then a staff car to Ath. I tied up the findings of my court after two days and was picked up by an Oxford and returned to Odiham. I was very disappointed to hear that my application for the test pilots' course had been turned down, as wing commanders were no longer eligible. I flew to Northolt and went in to the Air Ministry to see if I could persuade the Postings Branch to find me a flying job. In early February I heard that the wing would shortly be moving to Ibsley, so I flew down there in an Oxford to find suitable accommodation for the troops. The next day, back at Odiham, I air-tested two Spitfires and arranged for their delivery back to their squadron. Two days later I heard that our move to Ibsley was to be on the following day, so I managed to get in air tests on two more Spitfires and a Tempest after an engine change before I had to leave. I flew down to Ibsley in an Oxford and the rest of the personnel went down by road. We were to be phased in to move to Ghent in the following week, and I went to Hornchurch to arrange a motor transport column to pick up personnel and stores according to the plan I had prepared. On the 21st I took the Oxford to Ghent to arrange for the reception of the wing and accommodation for its personnel, and flew back to Odiham. I air-tested a Typhoon 1B the next day and then flew down to Ibsley in the Oxford. While I was down there I took the opportunity to visit the Central Fighter Establishment commandant and senior staff at Tangmere in the hope that I could persuade them to give me a flying post, as I knew that when I had moved 147 Wing to Belgium I would be out of a job. I also went to see my old rugby friend, Tom Morgan, who was a staff officer at Tactical Air Force HQ, on a similar mission. When I got back to Ibsley there was an American pilot visiting who offered me the chance to fly his Vengeance aircraft in exchange for a trip in my Oxford. I think I got the better part of the deal. On 3 March No. 147 Wing convoy moved off from Ibsley at 06.00 hrs, with me in the lead driving a large Humber shooting brake and the remainder following in three-ton lorries or coaches. We arrived at Hornchurch exactly on schedule and were accommodated for the night. The next day we moved down to Tilbury and started embarking at 0830 in a tank landing craft. We sailed at 13.30 hours and lay off Southend until midnight. At 01.00 the TLC sailed from Southend and docked in Ostend at 17.00 hrs. Having rapidly offloaded troops and stores in our vehicles, we set out on the road to Ghent, where the convoy arrived safely and intact at 21.00 hrs. On the following day the wing was settled in and ready to receive our flying element of a squadron of Mosquitos and a squadron of Typhoons. These duly flew in during the afternoon, and I was able to hand over command to the resident airfield commander, and flew back to Ibsley, still without prospects of further useful employment. On 15 March I delivered an aircraft to Ghent and spent the afternoon at Ghent golf course contemplating my chances of landing a flying job. The prospects were not very bright, as I had only recently relinquished command of No. 488 Mosquito Squadron, but on my return to Ibsley there was a signal from SASO No. 12 Group saying he wanted me to take over command of Winfield, the satellite airfield to No. 54 OTU at Charter Hall. I was delighted to be going back to my old post in Scotland, and a flying job! On the 18th I reported to Charter Hall, and the next day I flew down to Turnhouse in a Mosquito IV with Mike Maxwell, the Wing Commander, Flying, at Charter Hall, and we had tea with his family in Edinburgh. In the evening we had a party at the De Guise to celebrate Isobel's birthday (I think she was Mike's girlfriend, but I never found out!). I took a Beaufighter 6 and flew down to B.61 Airfield Ghent to clear my desk at No. 85 Group, and left the Tactical Air Force and the war in Europe for the last time.

Once settled in at Winfield, I called a meeting of all my officers, who gave me a briefing on the workings of the station and the senior course of the Night Operational Training Unit who were based there. As I had served at the OTU before, it was all fairly familiar, and I could not see the necessity for any immediate changes. The great difference on the flying side, however, was that they were now operating Mosquitos instead of Beaufighters, and this made the life of the instructors much less stressful and easier for the pupils. The Mosquito was an aircraft of superior performance, more docile and pleasant and easy to fly. Some of the aircraft had the added advantage of being fitted with dual controls, so the conversion to flying them solo was a much safer operation. I was soon enjoying the kind hospitality of the local Scots people again, and before Easter I was invited to Caldra for tennis and tea. I discovered that Isobel was my partner on the tennis court. I don't remember where Mike was.

During the Easter break that followed I took the opportunity of a Navex (navigation exercise) and flew south to Aston Down to visit my brother and my mother in Cheltenham. On 3 April I was busy again when the next course began flying, and there was a good party in the Charter Hall mess to welcome in the new course members. My friends down south soon learnt that I was a good source of Scotch salmon from the Tweed, and often my Mosquito was loaded with fish on my navigation exercises and liaison visits to the other OTUs in the south. Cranfield was one where Johnny Topham was in charge, and a regular customer.

The early days of May brought great news of the German collapse, and it was reported that Himmler had offered surrender to the Allies but not to Russia. The Huns in Italy had surrendered, and Berlin was about to be taken by the Russians. Rumour had it that Hitler and Goebbels had committed suicide and that Admiral Doenitz, the new Führer, said they would fight on. In Burma the 14th Army had entered Rangoon, and the Huns in north-west Germany and Denmark had surrendered. Among all this shattering news I was posted to Charter Hall as chief instructor, and there was a mess party at Winfield to see me on my way. The next night there was a mess party at Charter Hall to welcome me there. On the following day, 8 May, the Prime Minister and the King made a broadcast announcing the unconditional surrender of the Germans at midnight. Needless to say, there was yet another party in the mess, preceded by a celebration with the NCOs and airmen. The following day was an ordinary working day, but all aircraft were kept under strict guard to prevent any over-enthusiastic celebrations in the air, which might well have ended in tragedy. I, however, did a restrained flight in a Mosquito that was overdue for an air test, but only to land and hear that I was on the move again. This time I was posted to command the Spitfire OTU at Eshott, which un-fortunately was due to close down. I flew down to the new station in a Mosquito to talk over the handover arrangements with the Group Captain Commanding, and next day I set about packing all my kit into the Anson and flew down to Eshot. On the Friday evening I flew a Spitfire back to Charter Hall for the weekend. Several of us were invited to tennis at Caldra, and as usual Isobel was my partner. She was a lovely girl, but with a permanent air of melancholy that I found hard to fathom. She was on sick leave from the Royal Navy, being a WREN, but I was never able to find out more about her or her illness. I found it difficult to make her relax and she did not smile very often. But we had some very happy times together and often went for long walks down the lovely Blackadder valley with her sister Alex and a friend, and she seemed to enjoy that. Isobel regularly came to mess parties and joined in happily, but seldom left my side or danced with anyone else.

What with my constant moves and the great news of the end of the war in Europe, there were constant parties at the several stations, and I seemed to spend my time flying backwards and forwards in a Dominie that I had inherited from Eshott. But I found time to contemplate the way ahead, as there seemed to be no plans for my future employment. Over the previous few months, because of a fairly active time, I had been able to see very little of Maisie and Sue, and now I earnestly hoped that perhaps I might be posted to some station where I might have my family with me after the months of separation. But that problem was to be dramatically solved for me when I was told to report to Headquarters Transport Command, Bushey Park, where I learnt that my next posting was as SOA to Headquarters No. 302 Wing forming at Ibsley and proceeding as soon as possible to the Pacific theatre.

Perhaps it came as a feeling of relief, for clearly I was going to be frantically busy and faced with a most interesting and challenging posting that would take up all my time and thoughts. More separation from my family was going to be most regrettable, but now inevitable, and the question of any reconciliation with my wife must now await events in the future. For me there was still the Pacific war, and that problem had to be addressed first.

On the 12th I took the Anson down to Ibsley, having reduced my personal kit down to the minimum, as no doubt we would be fitted out with tropical gear at some point. While waiting to be called forward for embarkation I had an interesting flight that certainly served to concentrate the mind. I joined a few more daring fellow pilots and clambered into a Hadrian glider. This was a very basic glider designed to carry about ten armed infantrymen and light machine-guns, to be released from a towing Dakota over the battlefield. But this flight was a test to see if the glider could be snatched from the ground by a Dakota trailing a hook, with the intention of picking up a long length of bungee rubber cable suspended between two poles and attached to the front of the glider. Clearly this would require great skill on the Dakota pilot's part, and steady nerve and skill by the glider pilot, who in this instance was a sergeant from the Army Air Corps. We could see the Dakota circling around, but when it came up astern it disappeared out of sight. However, a character posted in front of the glider was gesticulating wildly, and obviously something was about to happen. Although my fellow passengers and I were thrown into an undignified heap as the bungee rubber rope took up the strain, the acceleration was surprisingly smooth, and in no time Sgt Fielding was settled into normal towed flight behind the Dakota. The glider was released over the airfield and we were soon safely down on the ground, all smiles of relief and slaps on the back for the sergeant, who seemed to take it very calmly as if it was an everyday experience, although he told us that this was the first time that the snatch had been done with a load of passengers.

On the last day of June I reported to RAF West Kirby, the nearest unit to our port of embarkation, Liverpool. There were still a few days before the ship sailed, and I was invited up to Caldra to stay with Isobel and her mother. We talked long into the night about prospects for the future for everyone, and the next day we had another long walk down the Blackadder. When we came to say goodbye, Isobel, surprisingly, put her arm around my shoulders and held me close as we walked together to my taxi. There, as I turned, she kissed me in a way she had never done before, and gave me a most lovely smile, which made her look even more attractive. Involuntarily I hugged her close for a moment, and as I was driven away it was I who was sad and regretted our parting. Looking through my diary, I found an entry there which said, 'Left Coco with Pip for Isobel'. I never saw or heard from Isobel again, but regretted it, if only so that I might have learnt who Pip was, and who or what Coco was. I never forgot Isobel, but had no recollection of the others.

On 4 July, with my headquarters staff and about 3,000 troops I went aboard the 'four-stacker' ship *Empress of Australia*, one of the largest liners afloat at the time, as she lay massively alongside Liverpool dock. The next evening, shepherded by four fussy tugs, she felt her way out of the Mersey and set her prow to the west, bound for Panama and I thought to who knew what perils. The troops aboard were mostly airfield construction engineers and other tradesmen, with a few RAF Regiment officers and men. I was very pleased to have the latter when things got a bit strained later in the voyage. I was SOA and my colleague Freddie Chadwick was SASO, and we shared command of the whole force, since the designated commanding officer, a group captain, although he came aboard, retired to his cabin and was not seen again until he was taken ashore some weeks later, a sick man.

Tiger Force, so called, was intended to sail to Okinawa, a large group of islands that were still being fiercely fought over by Japs and US forces, and to set up airfields from which Lancasters and Lincoln bombers would carry out intensive bombing raids on mainland Japan in an attempt to shorten the war. Little did we know then that our plan would be pre-empted by a far more dramatic event that would hit Hiroshima and Nagasaki.

As can be imagined, morale on board was not good, and would gradually worsen. The majority of men aboard were disgruntled at being uprooted from families and friends just as peace was declared at home, and the prospect of a long boring sea voyage terminating with the thought of facing up to the Japs was far from alluring. But from time to time there were interesting events aboard to keep them quiet. Some relief came when we arrived at Colon, Panama, after an uneventful crossing of the Atlantic. Troops in parties were allowed ashore on the dockside at Christobel to marvel at the huge lock-gates marking the Atlantic end of the Panama Canal. Fifty miles long and averaging 150 metres wide, the canal was built by the American Corps of Engineers between 1904 and 1914. The Americans retained control of the canal and the land immediately bordering it, but the Panamanians have now taken over the administration of the area, having guaranteed its neutrality. General Bradley came aboard to welcome the troops before the ship started her ponderous way through the numerous locks and the fresh-water lake en route. At night we were all excited to see the shining eyes of black panthers prowling through the jungle within a few yards of the ship's starboard side as we glided along at little more than walking pace. On the evening of 21 July we sailed past Panama City to the north and Balboa and entered the Pacific.

Far from living up to its name, the ocean was very rough, and our escorting American destroyer had a hard time. There were many flying fish that leapt out of the water, some even flying as high as the ship's open decks. The ship's captain would not allow any alcohol to be handed out to the troops, although we carried the whole of the NAAFI's stocks of beers and spirits down in the holds. There was strong resentment, and I tried to get the issue of a small ration from time to time, but the skipper was adamant. If the truth be known I think he was really scared of the mass of troops on his ship when he was only used to a relatively few fare-paying and docile passengers. The only entertainment we had was one film, which nearly drove me crazy, as it was shown every night in the main saloon. Unfortunately Freddie's and my cabin opened out onto the gallery around the saloon, and even with cotton wool in our ears it was constant torture. It was a pleasant change when early in the evening Freddie, who was an accomplished pianist, would sit at the piano and play a selection of popular classics. For a while 'Clair de Lune' and 'The Warsaw Concerto' would have ascendancy over that other ghastly moon tune. During this time there was a worrying sign of rebellion among the troops aboard, particularly those quartered on 'F' Deck, where the accommodation was truly dreadful, particularly in the rough weather that seemed to predominate. The ship was overcrowded and there was very little that could be done, but the other ranks' letters home showed a growing bitter resentment of the contrast between their treatment and that of the officers. As their mail was censored it was clear that they were exaggerating the situation and causing unnecessary anxiety at home, but I clearly recognized that a careful watch had to be kept on events.

I called a conference of all the unit commanders and warned them to keep a very close eye on the situation and also to call a meeting of all the troops in their units to hear their moans and try to alleviate the situation where we could. I also formed the RAF Regiment into flights of Military Police to detect and deal with any ringleaders who might emerge. I then had a public address system set up in the main ballroom and spoke to the whole force. I promised them that in a week's time the ship would be docking in Honolulu, where they would be given shore leave, and I took the opportunity to warn them that their behaviour ashore must be exemplary, as they would be the first large force of Britishers to arrive *en masse* at Hawaii. I left the meeting with my fingers crossed because at that time it was by no means certain that they would, in fact, be allowed ashore.

CHAPTER SEVENTEEN

West Through Panama to Hong Kong

August 1945 to February 1946

I t was very hot at the beginning of August when we arrived at Honolulu, but happily my promise of shore leave was realized and the troops were allowed ashore in parties and were given the most cordial welcome by the Americans and the people of Hawaii.

Freddie and I went ashore and were invited by a Mrs Macropolis to her lovely bungalow overlooking Waikiki. The next day we went bathing at the Outrigger Club in Waikiki, where my lasting impression was of sparkling clear surf and sand too hot to walk on with bare feet. We were invited to drinks at the Hawaii Hotel on the American Base at Hickham Field, and we had lunch at the Mowana Hotel with the Hawaiian Chief of Police, who made us both honorary members of the Hawaiian Police Force. I have my membership card to this day, just in case it should be needed! On 6 August a conference was called ashore, followed by a party with a group of charming and welcoming American nurses. All too soon they were all recalled aboard to be told of the 'Little Boy', the American nuclear device that had just been dropped on the South Honshu city of Hiroshima. Although it was a centre of industry and military supply bases, it was horrific news, with an estimate of some 150,000 people killed at one stroke. The significance of this dreadful event for all people on earth was not lost on the members of Shield Force, who were so near to it, and, no doubt, by most thinking people. Another nuclear attack four days later on Nagasaki convinced the Japanese that they had no course open to them but to surrender, which they did on 15 August 1945.

After another day of rather subdued festivities ashore at Waikiki, the force sailed in the *Empress of Australia* for Eniwetac, a small island of the Lesser Marshall Islands. En route we crossed the International Date Line and thus missed the day of 12 August. On the 16th we arrived at Eniwetac, no more than a coral strip, but the Americans had established an officers' club of some comfort where we spent a few hours bathing and relaxing. The troops were also allowed ashore, but after only a day or two our ship set sail again, this time for a unknown destination. Our course was now taking us north of New Guinea into the Bismark Archipelago. Here we anchored off the Island of Manus, and the group captain aboard appeared from his cabin at last and was taken ashore to be casevacked by air to the Philippines, while I was appointed officially in command of Shield Force aboard the ship. The next day I went ashore to the shore establishment, which was extensive and included a large Royal Navy base and dockyard. I was briefed by the SBNO that our destination was Hong Kong, and that the whole force would probably be put ashore there to help rehabilitate the Colony. Thus the remainder of our voyage was to be used in preparing for this task, and Freddie and I set about putting this in hand. Duty done, I went to a party aboard HMS *Vengeance* (the first of many), and the next day, having lunched aboard our four-stacker with Tiger Force, I went ashore again to see a Gang Show at the officers' club. On the 27th I had a further briefing from the SBNO, followed by drinks and lunch aboard HMS *Montclare*, where I met Admiral Fisher. It was a good lunch, and as always the Navy was most hospitable, to the extent that I nearly missed my ship, which was already moving out of harbour as I was escorted down the gangway. Luckily there was a 'Skimmer' to hand, and I was whisked out to the liner, which was already moving at about eight knots. A rope ladder had been dangled down its cliff-like side, but the climb aboard was formidable, and when I was finally dragged aboard at the top my arrival bore little of the dignity that the newly appointed Officer Commanding Troops should have shown.

Now that our destination was known, our morale improved, and Shield Force personnel all joined in the planning and training for the rehabilitation of Hong Kong with enthusiasm. But our troubles were not yet over, and on 31 August the ship ran into a typhoon and conditions on board became extremely uncomfortable. The captain had told me that if the ship rolled more than 28° there was a real danger that she might capsize. During the night she rolled to 34°! We had to reduce speed considerably and let our escorting American frigate lie in the big ship's lee as she was on the point of foundering. Thus the *Empress of Australia* was delayed in joining the Royal Naval Task Force under Rear Admiral Harcourt, which now lay off Hong Kong. The Admiral had sent an Avenger aircraft escorted by Hellcats into Kai Tak to pick up the Japanese commander and return him to HMS *Indomitable* to discuss terms for the British takeover. The Admiral demanded to know details of offshore minefields guarding approaches to the harbour, and information on the possible use of Japanese suicide boats still known to be sheltering off Lamma Island. The following day the Admiral transferred his flag to HMS *Swiftsure*, and having received all the necessary navigational information, entered the harbour with an air escort. This precaution turned out to be a wise move, as three suicide boats did in fact leave their lair and were sunk by aircraft from HMS *Indomitable*.

Thus, on 30 August the Royal Navy, through the Fleet Air Arm, re-established a British air presence in the Colony. Originally the Fleet Air Arm base had been built at Kai Tak some twenty years previously, precisely to meet the need for a base in the Far East.

Because of the delay caused by the typhoon, Shield Force entered Hong Kong aboard the *Empress of Australia* on 3 September, by which time Admiral Harcourt had taken over as Military Governor. The ship docked alongside the go-downs on Kowloon Dock, and I have never forgotten the impressions of that moment as I looked across the busy waters to Hong Kong Island and the beautiful panorama that lay before me. The great harbour itself was dominated now by five large Royal Navy warships dwarfing the countless junks and sampans already criss-crossing around them. The Hong Kong Peak formed an impressive towering background, with houses and bungalows dotted among the trees right up to the summit. To the west I could see countless small islands, with a dim outline of the largest, Lanthau, dominating the western approaches. Looking north, over Stonecutters Island, the highest peak around the Colony, Tai Mo Shan, was a formidable obstruction to Kai Tak, but even nearer to the runway was Lion Rock, which in later years made approaches to the runway by the big jetliners an exciting experience. The next day, when I went out to Kai Tak, I could see how it nestled at the base of the surrounding hills, the only level ground before the sea. At the other end of the runway was more rising ground, and to the right the Lymun Gap leading out into Mirs Bay and the open sea. From Kowloon the Hong Kong waterfront looked a jumble of wharves and go-downs, and a handful of modern buildings clustered around the Hong Kong and Shanghai Bank, then a modest six storeys high. This was the first time I had ventured far abroad, and I found it immensely exciting: at that moment, standing on the upper deck of the huge liner, now sitting docilely at its moorings, with the permeating smell of the tropics in my nose, I was entranced with the unforgettable experience.

Ashore the romantic dreaming was soon dispelled, and I found that the Japanese had looted and despoiled nearly everything within the Colony. Latterly, bombing by the USAF had done great damage in the docks area and the airfield, but nothing could compare with the Chinese widespread looting and ravaging of property and murderous attacks on the Japanese since the declaration of surrender and before the British had time to have troops on the streets. The joyful but painful business of releasing prisoners and seeing to their welfare was an urgent priority, and Freddie's and my first duty was to visit the prison camps at Shamshuipo and Argyle Street. It was a moving experience, but to our surprise the ex-prisoners' main needs were not material things as much as news of home and what had been happening in the world outside their prison walls. However, a few hours later, when Freddie and I returned to the Peninsula Hotel, where we were billeted, the smart salute that we received from the naval guard was acknowledged by two very bedraggled officers deprived of most of their uniform and personal effects gratefully handed over to the ex-prisoners. Our hotel accommodation in the recently 'liberated' hotel was spacious but sparsely furnished, and when Freddie complained of the dirty rust stains in the bath he was told by the manager that it was not rust but the blood of a disgraced Japanese colonel who had previously occupied the room and had committed the only recorded act of 'Hara-Kiri' in Hong Kong. We asked for another room, and one was found for us, but accommodation was a minor matter and our duties that lay outside were far more urgent. Clearly there was going to be a great deal to do, and my first duty on being posted to command Kai Tak immediately on getting ashore was to get the airfield serviceable and capable of receiving aircraft. On 4 September I was established on the airfield with a nucleus staff, and the RAF Regiment Squadron was deployed around the perimeter, mainly to prevent looting by the Hong Kong Chinese. There had been sporadic firing from the hills behind the airfield during the night, and there were still quite a lot of armed Japanese skulking around, so on 6 September No. 201 Staging Post was established on the station, and I organized a small parade and took the salute when the Union flag was raised to mark the taking-over of command of Kai Tak by the Royal Air Force after nearly four years of occupation by the Japanese. The next day the first Dakota landed at Kai Tak, having flown over 'the hump' from Burma, and the following day it took off, outward bound, with urgent dispatches, while another Dakota landed to uplift casualties.

Soon Dakotas were coming in regularly, bringing administrative personnel and urgent stores, and after turn-round returning to Burma with ex-prisoners in need of urgent medical attention.

Transport was one of my big difficulties, but the MT Section managed to make an old motorcycle serviceable, and I rode this across the airfield to visit the Royal Navy MONAB that had then been established there. This was a Mobile Operational Naval Air Base, whose task was to carry out major servicing of Navy aircraft flown ashore from aircraft-carriers. I lost no time in getting to know the Commander Flying of HMS

Knabcatcher, as it was called, and on the following day I managed to borrow a Navy Corsair to obtain experience of all the airfield approaches and to carry out a reconnaissance of the local area. The Corsair was the first American fighter with a radial engine that I had flown, and I found it a delight to fly, without any vices once one had remembered to unfold the wings and make sure they were locked before take-off. I flew the Corsair the next day and went nearly as far as Canton on a reconnaissance flight.

The motorcycle soon packed up and my adjutant produced a horse for me to ride on my airfield inspections. Poor animal, it was so thin that its saddle was in danger of slipping off, and after one slow amble across the airfield through the sensuous mimosa which covered the area between the runways I returned it for what I hoped would be a happy retirement. Finally a twelve-year-old American Pontiac saloon was produced, which the Japanese had acquired and done their best to wreck. The clutch did not work and it was permanently in second gear, which made it dodgy to drive. Luckily American Jeeps were not long in arriving in the Colony.

I was just settling down and getting Kai Tak organized when I was very disappointed when a wing commander from the UK was posted in to command Kai Tak, and I had to return to staff duties with 302 Wing on Hong Kong Island. This meant living in the Gloster Hotel and working in an office in the Hong Kong Shanghai Bank. This did not prevent me from getting the odd flight, and on 23 September I went across to Kai Tak and flew an American L.5 Sentinel light aircraft on a reconnaissance of the Colony and the New Territories. No. 302 Wing was soon absorbed into Air Headquarters Hong Kong, and I was attached to fill a post on the C-in-C's staff as Air Adviser. Admiral Harcourt was now, of course, Military Governor and living in Government House, but his offices were situated in the Hong Kong Shanghai Bank. On my birthday I flew a Spitfire XIV on an anti-piracy patrol around the islands. Piracy in the South China Seas had always been endemic, but it was a major problem now that goods of all sorts were being poured into Hong Kong, and the rich pickings were well worth the risk. Air patrols might be a deterrent but needed to be co-ordinated with naval units to be really effective. Cdr Gick RN (later Admiral Sir Percy Gick) was the anti-piracy coordinator, and as well as flying on air patrols he also operated a 'Q' junk with a powerful diesel engine and twin Oerlikon cannon under covers on the foredeck. This was a most effective unit and had considerable success in catching pirate junks, in cooperation with air patrols. Late in September I went out on an anti-piracy patrol in the RAF high-speed launch, accompanied by several other officers, including Lt Col Tim Evill of No.

1 Commando, who was later to become a good friend. On 4 October No. 132 (Bombay) Fighter Squadron arrived on board HMS *Smiter*. Its Spitfire XIVs were ferried ashore on lighters, as the runways at Kai Tak were still in need of further repair. Accommodation was becoming a major problem, and the old officers' mess was still quite uninhabitable, so a convent belonging to the Little Sisters of the Poor on the Clear Water Bay road was taken over as an officers' mess, and shared with the Sisters, who benefited with more generous rations than those they had been used to. Later in October No. 681 Squadron, also with Spitfires, arrived in the Colony on SS *Highland Monarch*. There was a large shortage of Spitfire spares at this time, and No. 681 Squadron never became operational while in the Colony, but moved to Kuala Lumpur at the end of the year.

By 13 October there were four squadrons sharing Kai Tak. As well as the two Spitfire squadrons, No. 209 Squadron flew in three Sunderland flying-boats from Koggala in Ceylon, and No. 96 Squadron with Dakotas was established at Kai Tak. However, I was kept busy on the C-in-C's staff, and only managed to get in the occasional flight in a Corsair or Spitfire on anti-piracy patrols or a reconnaissance in a Sentinel. But on 2 November an interesting flight came my way when I was asked to fly a certain Portuguese gentleman called Dr Lobo across to Macau. At that time there was no recognized airfield on the Portuguese colony, so I flew him in the small L.5 Sentinel and landed on the rather boggy padang on the sea front. It was only on my return that I was told that Dr Lobo came from one of the richest families in the Far East, and owned a very large percentage of the gold in the area; and I never even asked him for the taxi fare!

On the 27th I was invited aboard HMS *Vengeance*, and the ship sailed out into Mirs Bay for exercises with a submarine. At the conclusion of the operations I flew off the carrier in a Barracuda and landed back at Kai Tak. In December I again managed to borrow a Spitfire, and also flew a Barracuda on two separate sorties a few days later.

With at least seven Royal Navy ships in harbour there was never any lack of parties, and WRENS and WRAF girls were beginning to arrive in the Colony, so partners were becoming available to add to the fun. I was very lucky to be on the Admiral's staff, as most of the others on his staff were naval officers with whom I got on very well and made a lot of friends. Admiral Harcourt was a charming and delightful man to work for, and always willing to join in any of the many festivities that his staff thought up. One of the happiest occasions was at Christmas, when the Admiral invited several of the staff, including me, to join him in Government House over the holiday. The celebrations started on the 22nd with a dance at Government House, and lunch aboard HMS

Vengeance the next day. In the evening there was a WRAF party, followed by all the crowd going out for Chinese chow. Back at Government House we had lunch and played crazy games until we all went out to a party at the Peninsula Hotel. On Christmas Day we all went down to Big Wave Bay for a swim and lunch back in Government House. Christmas dinner was a wonderful occasion, followed by a riotous evening of ingenious games and 'in-house' entertainment. On Boxing Day the whole gang went swimming, and then back to Government House for a musical evening and dinner. So ended a really wonderful holiday, where many friendships were made.

On the 28th I flew up to Kiangwan airfield at Shanghai with Charles Little, an officer from Intelligence, to look at the prospect of establishing an RAF staging post there. We dined with the Naval Attaché, and also there was General Carton de Wiart. That night Charles and I were accommodated in the China Club, but when we went up to our room it was so cold and the bedclothes so inadequate that we had to pull down the long heavy curtains from the windows and sleep under them to try and get warm. The next day we drove around Shanghai, Bubbling Wells Road, along the Bund, and then treated ourselves to vodka cocktails at the Long Bar (100 feet). We had both received an invitation that evening to a cocktail party at the Russian Consulate, but had an urgent signal from Command that on no account were we to attend. We thought it was a pity, but Charles reckoned that our Command HVQs were worried that the Russians might try and compromise us. We subsequently heard that the party was awash with beautiful White Russian girls. The next day, after a visit to Whangpo and the International Settlement, we returned to Kai Tak.

Early in January Percy Gick and I took off in two Corsairs, accompanied by two Spitfires, and intercepted several pirate junks off Ping Chan. A high-speed launch was led to intercept them, several were captured and the crews arrested, and after a thorough search their junks were burnt on the spot. On 21 January I was delighted to be posted back to Kai Tak as Wing Commander Flying under Jackie Horner as the new station commander, with prospects of more regular flying. On the 24th I flew down to Seletar (Singapore) in a Sunderland for an interview with the C-in-C ACSEA. Freddie and I had a very comfortable stay at the Raffles Hotel, where we met a naval officer friend who introduced us to two WREN officers, and that evening we took them out to dinner at the Johore Club. The next day we flew in a Sunderland to Labuan (Borneo), where we found it extremely hot, but we were put off swimming by the sight of sharks cruising off shore. We returned to Kai Tak the next day in the Sunderland in very bad weather with low overcast, but luckily the sea was calm so we were able to land on the sea some distance out and taxi for the rest of the way into Hong Kong harbour under the overcast.

Maisie and I had now been separated for nearly two years, and though we had kept in touch and I had had regular news of Sue's progress, it had become clear that there was now no prospect of saving our marriage. We were divorced soon after I returned to England from the Far East.

On 4 February I did a further reconnaissance of the Colony's coastal waters in a Sentinel, and this time I was accompanied by a girl, Eve, from Military Intelligence as observer. She proved to be a very attractive and useful member of the crew, and two years later in England we were married.

CHAPTER EIGHTEEN

Kai Tak

February 1946 to January 1947

On 10 February I borrowed a Spitfire XIV from No. 132 Squadron to carry out bad-weather approaches to provide practice for the air traffic controllers in Kai Tak tower. In mid-February I set off for Burma to collect three Beaufighters allotted to Kai Tak. I went in a Dakota that was routed via Tan Sun Nhut (Saigon) and Don Muang (Bangkok), to Mingaladon (Rangoon). Having collected the aircraft from the latter airfield the following day, I flew a Beaufighter X on the reverse route, with two other Beaufighters in formation. Unfortunately one crashed on landing at Tan Sun Nhut, but after 4 hours 20 minutes of flying I landed Beaufighter X RD.157, accompanied by the one other, at Kai Tak, the first ever to do so. I thoroughly enjoyed flying the Beaufighter again, not having done so since the night-fighter operations in 1942/3. It had always been one of my favourite aeroplanes, and it had lost none of its magic. Back at Kai Tak on the 19th I air-tested a Tiger Moth that had come out in a crate from the UK for the formation of a Hong Kong auxiliary squadron and had been erected in the Technical Wing's hangar. At the end of the month I air-tested a Beaufighter that had been fitted with modified anti-balance tabs on the elevators, which were designed to improve the aircraft's stability. It was true that the Beaufighter tended to oscillate in the vertical plane at high speeds, and I found that the tabs certainly seem to dampen these down.

On 9 March I took a Spitfire to investigate a burning ship in the typhoon anchorage, and I went on to provide an escort for the Dakota carrying Charles Little on his leaving the Colony. Two days later I air-tested a Corsair and afterwards carried out a reconnaissance of the proposed Air Gunnery Ranges in Mirs Bay and reported on their suitability. On the 19th I was scrambled in early-morning fog for a sea search for a Corsair pilot. I found no sign at this time, but the following day I did another search in a Corsair, and the pilot was found and picked up from his dinghy by a Sea Otter of the Fleet Air Arm.

On the 25th I carried out a relative speed trial with a Mosquito and a Beaufighter at sea-level, and to my surprise found the Beaufighter was marginally faster than the Mosquito. On the following day the air traffic controller called me in his office to say that a Dakota was missing on the approach to the airfield, and an immediate search was organized. I took off in a Sentinel and retraced the approach route probably taken by the Dakota. After an hour searching the sea, as a last effort I went further afield and circled Lantau Island, where I discovered the crashed aircraft near the summit at 1,800 feet. While I hurried back to land at Kai Tak to report the position of the crashed aircraft, a high-speed launch was organized with a rescue party. I rushed down to the quay and joined the launch crew, and we discussed a plan of action on the way out to Lantau. A landing was made on the beach and we climbed our way up to the wreck. When we arrived it was clear that the aircraft had run into the peak without warning when it was in cloud, and all five crew had been killed instantly.

On the 29th I flew a handling flight of a Navy Firefly FR 1 with a seaman as passenger, and the next day a radio test was carried out on a Sentinel in case it should be needed for a rescue search again.

At the beginning of April a Navy Vengeance crashed into the harbour after overshooting the runway, and the next day another Vengeance crashed on the airfield, but happily without serious injury. On the 9th I took the air controllers one after another for a demonstration of airfield approaches in the Sentinel. After several flights in the Beaufighter on radio tests, single-engine flying and let-downs, I took the AOC for a demonstration flight prior to his going solo, which he did a few days later, carrying out several take-offs and landings and clearly enjoying flying the Beaufighter.

Over Easter a party was assembled at Star Ferry Pier, and we set off for Macau in a high-speed launch. We lay off Lantau for a swim and picnic lunch on a sandy beach before sailing on to the Portugese colony for the night. We visited the incredible gambling joints that proliferated in every street of the colony, but did not dare join the obsessed gamblers who scrambled and fought to make their bets in the Fan Tan halls. The next day we embarked on our return voyage, breaking our journey to swim from another Lantau beach. I arrived back at Kai Tak to hear that a Sea Otter had crashed in the sea the day before, but without serious casualty. On the 26th I did a low-level search over Mirs Bay in a Firefly, and two days later I led three Corsairs in a formation to escort the new Governor, Sir Mark Young, on his arrival in the Colony. Later in the day I flew over the reception ceremony at Queen's Pier in an Oxford for official photographers to cover the Governor's arrival.

On 1 May Vice-Admiral Sir Cecil Harcourt, the past Military Governor, departed from Hong Kong aboard HMS *Argonaut*. He had been the principal author presiding over the remarkable recovery that had been achieved in the Colony under his wise stewardship. He was admired and respected by all the service people under his command, and we all felt that he should have a fitting departure. Consequently his air escort, which I led in a Corsair, consisted of three Corsairs, a Beaufighter, a Vengeance, two Dakotas, a Sunderland, an Oxford, a Sentinel and a Tiger Moth. The whole formation flew low over *Argonaut* and peeled off one at a time in salute, as she sailed out through the narrows. The next day it was the turn of *Vengeance*, bound for Colombo, the ship in which I had found so much camaraderie and enjoyment and made many friends. For her escort I did several low fly-overs in a Beaufighter, and also teased the Navy by making an approach to the flight deck with wheels down as though I was going to land aboard. I got a frantic wave-off from the flag man! For the rest of the month I flew several sorties of Sentinel, Oxford, and Dakota, and also a Corsair sortie to escort HMS *Apollo* out of harbour. On the 27th, No. 201 Staging Post at Kai Tak threw a party to celebrate the handling of its 1,000th aircraft since the airfield had reopened. Congratulatory telegrams came pouring in, particularly from the Dakota squadrons whose aircraft had come flying in and out during the whole period. On 10 June I and several other senior officers were invited to the Governor's Box to view the Victory Parade on the racecourse at Happy Valley, and on the 13th a similar parade was held to celebrate the King's Birthday. At the end of the month the AOC left the Colony by Sunderland flying-boat.

On 17 June a typhoon warning was received, and as many aircraft as possible were flown out to safe diversions away from the path of the storm. The wind picked up to severe gale a few days later, and all remaining aircraft were picketed down as securely as possible and marine craft were moved to the typhoon anchorage. There was a shortage of qualified skippers to move them all, and I volunteered to take a 62-foot air-sea rescue launch, with only an airman engineer as crew, round to the other side of the Kowloon Peninsula where the shelter was situated. It was an exciting trip, particularly as the wind had already whipped up a choppy sea, but the launch was wonderfully manoeuvrable with its three individually controlled Napier engines. The next day the full force of the storm hit the Colony, and Kai Tak suffered very heavy damage despite the precautions that we were able to take. The majority of our Dakotas were flown out to places of safety, as were several Sunderlands, but seven Dakotas and two Sunderlands were wrenched from their picketing ropes and concrete blocks and were badly damaged. At one point I saw a Sunderland that had been pulled up on the slipway almost completely clear of the ground, with all four propellers turning by the strength of the wind. Needless to say, all the temporary tents and wooden huts were swept away, and fuel drums and wreckage that was hurtling across the airfield made it dangerous to venture out. In twelve hours the typhoon had passed on up the coast, and there was an uncanny calm hanging over the Colony.

The huge task of clearing up, rehousing the troops and getting the aircraft back from where they had been dispersed was put in hand at once. The two Sunderlands that had flown south had run into head-winds and been force-landed on the southern shore of Hainan, at Sama. At Hong Kong the Royal Navy Sloop *Black Swan* was prepared for sea, to sail down and rescue them. She sailed out of the harbour in the gather-ing dusk with an RAF technical team and me aboard, and went south. We arrived off Sama at dawn to find that one Sunderland had beached successfully, but the other had run up hard, broken its back and was clearly a write-off. Preparation were put in hand to tow the serviceable aircraft out into deep water, a task more easily said than done, as it was firmly embedded in the sand. There was some damage to the hull, so concrete was laid along the damage to strengthen it and hopefully to stop any leaks. The first attempt to drag the aircraft off was un-successful, as the cable laid from the ship was too weak, and a heavy swell had developed that necessitated putting further attempts off until the next day. In the morning conditions had improved, and with a heavier cable and the ship's winch churning at full power, the Sunderland very slowly gave up its grip in the sand and slid gracefully down the beach out to deeper water. After refuelling from *Black Swan* and a thorough inspection and engine test, she was flown back to Kai Tak, where a safe landing was made. *Black Swan*, after this very successful salvage job, returned to Hong Kong, but not before also salvaging the four engines and other useful gear from the other Sunderland. The whole operation was undertaken with a certain amount of trepidation, as the beach and sand dunes were overlooked by armed Chinese Communist troops who clearly lacked a leader and didn't seem to know what to do in the circumstances. Luckily they only glowered at the working party, and did not try to interfere.

At the beginning of August I was detailed to escort Dr Ba Mawr, the Burmese 'Quisling', down to Singapore after a war crimes trial in Japan. We flew down in a Sunderland to Seletar, and the doctor was duly handed over to the authorities after signing my logbook.

After an interview with Freddie Guest at Headquarters ACFE, I returned to Kai Tak in a Dakota. The interview confirmed my worst fears when I was told that I had to relinquish my acting rank on posting to a staff job on the Air Staff at HQ at Changi. I knew that this was always a possibility, but it came as a deep disappointment, as I had held my wing commander rank for over four years, including five command posts. On the other hand I had been very lucky in rising from sergeant to wing commander in only three years. There followed periods of depression and lack of enthusiasm, but luckily I had a very understanding immediate boss, who was also a very keen flyer, and we managed to get away from our staff duties from time to time to get airborne. I also took up sailing, and from this small beginning it became second only to flying among my favourite interests. Before going to Changi and losing my acting rank I was sent up to Shanghai to take over command of No. 200 Staging Post at Lungwha. To assess my responsibilities for the air route north I flew up to Iwakuni in a Dakota and did a reconnaisance as far as Hiroshima. On returning to Kai Tak at the end of the month my posting to Changi came through, but I did not go before I had another flight in my favourite Corsair, and my lads at Kai Tak were entertained to a quarter of an hour's aerobatic show as my farewell. I flew down as a comfortable passenger in 'Hotspur' the BOAC Hythe flying-boat. We landed on the river at Bangkok the next day and flew on to Singapore, alighting at Kallang and reaching Changi by road late in the day, where, as usual, I was not expected and nobody bothered to meet me – a depressing beginning that reflected the gloom of the following months. I found the large Temple Hill officers' mess dull and entirely uninspiring, but I soon started to spend a good deal of time down at the sailing club when I was off duty, and took to sailing as readily as I had to flying.

Two days after my birthday I went over to visit No. 84 Squadron at Seletar and air-tested one of its Mosquito VIs after a tailplane change. A few days later I flew an Auster from the Station Flight at Changi to reconnoitre the beautiful sailing waters around Changi. On the 16th I accompanied the C-in-C, Sir George Pirie, on an inspection tour of some of the stations in the command. We flew in a Dakota, and our first stop was at Medan, where we were dined by the Sultan of Deli, Sumatra. The next day we flew on to Butterworth (Penang), where we had lunch at Government House and stayed the night at Fort Aukrie Rest Camp. We returned to Seletar to inspect the squadrons there, and then flew on to Kuala Lumpur and Tengah, and thence back to Changi, to complete the C-in-C's tour of inspection. The next day Richard (my boss) and I flew an Auster over to Seletar to collect a Mosquito. On the return flight Richard flew the Mosquito and we had a dogfight, which I was deemed to have won as the Mosquito was quite unable to get its sights on the small, highly manoeuvrable Auster that I was flying.

In the middle of November I had a few days' leave and flew up to Hong Kong, via Saigon, in a Dakota. On the 18th I managed to borrow a Seafire from the Navy MONAB, and enjoyed an hour's aerobatics and a look around the coast of the Colony again. I returned before the end of the month and sailed nearly every evening, practising for the races due shortly at Changi. In December I had two flights in the Auster, and on Christmas Eve I borrowed a Spitfire XIV from Port Swettenham for a local reconnaissance and airfield inspection. January was a quiet month and I only managed three sorties in the Auster to keep in flying practice. Off duty I sailed a lot and began to do well in the pram dinghy races. February and March were also quiet, and in April I flew in a Sunderland as an observer on a search-and-rescue exercise off Penang. Later in the month I had another flight in a Spitfire XIV, doing an air test for No. 390 Maintenance Unit at Seletar.

The beginning of May was fruitful as far as flying was concerned, and I managed to get away from my staff duties to fly a Spitfire XVIII of No. 60 Squadron at Tengah, a Mosquito VI on an air test and a Spitfire XIV. In the middle of the month I had the good news that I had been selected to attend the Day Fighter Convention at the Central Fighter Establishment at West Raynham in the UK. In due course I set off in a York of Transport Command, arriving at Negombo (Ceylon) on 16 May. During the next three days we flew to Mauripur (Karachi), Habbaniyah (Iraq) and Luqa (Malta), finally touching down at Lyneham on a glorious spring evening. I reported to the CFE a few days before the convention was due to begin and was delighted to meet some of my old fighter friends again. I did my best to persuade them to use their influence to try and get me posted to the Air Fighting Development Squadron to join them on my next posting. And persuade them I did, for I heard that I was to be posted to the Air Fighting Development Squadron at CFE in the following January. During the convention I had the opportunity to fly several new types, including the new turbine-powered aircraft. I flew the Meteor III with two jet engines first, and the next day the de Havilland Hornet, the single-seater fighter version of the Mosquito. I flew the Meteor III again the day after testing the performance of the Seafire 46 with the Griffon engine. I then visited Odiham and flew a Vampire I, and did staff visits to the Gloster Aircraft Company at Moreton Valence and the Bristol Aircraft Company at Filton, where I was allowed to fly the larger and heavier version of the Beaufighter, the Brigand TFI, a powerful aircraft full of menace, though it never went into general service. On the way to Lyneham I called in at Hullavington and flew a Vickers Viking with a test pilot doing stalls and dive tests. On the 19th I flew back to Changi in a York, following the reverse route as the flight out.

Shortly after arriving at Changi, Richard and I did a very-early-morning trip in a Harvard to Tengah, where a Meteor IV was waiting for us to try out. Richard flew it first and came down bursting with praise and enthusiasm. After refuelling with the unfamiliar Avtur (virtually paraffin), I took it on a thorough handling test. It was so much more powerful than the Mk III, and performance was dazzling in comparison. At sea level I clocked up 585 mph, and climb and descent performance were equally outstanding, and yet the approach and landing were docile and easy. Not surprisingly the Harvard on the flight back felt lifeless and dull, although it could be landed in a small field at 60 mph. After two more Harvard flights, one checking longitudinal stability, Ron Cooper and I took an Anson up to Kuala Lumpur with passengers, and after a visit to the races the next day returned with our passengers to Changi. On an Auster flight to Tengah after an overhaul, I found the elevator controls very slack, but after picking up a passenger for the return flight they seemed to be quite normal. An investigation at Changi revealed that the flimsy passenger seat had partially collapsed, and with the weight of a passenger it was pressing down on the elevator control cables that passed underneath, acting as an effective tensioner.

I started off November with an hour and a half's instrument-training flight in the Anson, and later flew a Spitfire XIX for an hour on performance-handling and aerobatics. Later I had a very rough flight in climbing up through a cumulo-nimbus storm cloud in a Harvard to gain experience of instrument flying in a storm cloud, which I did not enjoy very much. The time was approaching when I soon would be tour expired and returning to the UK, so I volunteered to fly a Dakota back there. After a dual flight with an instructor I took a category test and did a few hours' solo flying in the Dakota, including single-engine handling, approaches and landings. Two further flights both ended in engine trouble, and I became aware that Dakotas were going through a particularly bad patch of these failures at the time. So when the time came for my return to the UK I took up an offer of a flight back in a Sunderland flying-boat, as I was not keen on ending up somewhere en route with a single-engined Dakota! Before finally leaving Changi I took part in the sailing regatta, and not only won several races but carried off the Battle of Britain Challenge Cup for racing dinghies, much to my satisfaction. I packed up my kit after the weekend and got a lift to Seletar and put it aboard Sunderland RN. 297. We flew in the large flying-boat from Seletar to Koggala (Ceylon) and then via Korangi Creek (Karachi) to Bahrein, where we had a champagne party with friends who were also going home. The next day we flew to Fanara (Fayid, in the Canal Zone), and on to Kalafrana (Malta). After a day's stop-over in Valetta, the take-off the following day was very scary, as the swell was fierce and the first attempt was aborted because the flying-boat was being badly battered by the large waves before flying speed could be attained.

Finally the take-off had to be abandoned here, and we taxied round to the inner harbour, where the sea was calmer, but there was only just room to get airborne, and the climb-out over the buildings of Kalafrana was very exciting but too close for comfort! There was a lot of low cloud and snow over France, and we landed at Calshot in a typical English drizzle, but I was glad to be back home again after two and a half years away.

CHAPTER NINETEEN

Air Testing Jet Fighters

January 1948 to May 1949

My posting to the Central Fighter Establishment was confirmed, and I reported to West Raynham on 19 January, and was delighted to hear that my immediate boss was to be a Battle of Britain survivor Ras Berry, who soon became a firm friend. It did not take me long to get into the routine of an RAF station at home, with a 'dining-in' night in the mess at regular intervals, a parade on Saturday mornings, a weekend holiday each month and occasionally a long weekend. I was soon flying every day, and I started my tour in the Air Fighter Development Squadron (AFDS) with two more flights in the Meteor III before starting regular flights in the Meteor IV. The project assigned to me was an assessment of the aircraft as an interceptor fighter, with wide-ranging trials on optimum climbs to altitude, fuel consumption at all levels, flying for best range and radius of action at variable power settings, general handling under different configurations and loadings, and finally carrying out trials to ascertain the best tactics for intercepting and attacking heavy bombers with cannon, as represented by American B-29s. As can be imagined, this was quite a demanding task, involving a good deal of accurate and meticulous flying and the preparation of a comprehensive report at the end of the programme. The former I revelled in, but the report writing I found a tedious chore, though this came much later, when most of the flying was done.

Even though I was doing two or three Meteor sorties a day when weather permitted, I still found time to fly other types, of which there was a wide choice at West Raynham. In the first month, as well as the Meteor IV I had flights in the Auster, Hornet I, Vampires I and III and the Oxford, the latter for instrument-flying practice.

In my second and third month the emphasis was on formation tactical trials, often involving my leading a finger-four formation of Meteors through cloud up to 40,000 feet – their highest practical altitude for air fighting. Flying trials also involved maximum-rate turns at various altitudes and Mach numbers, and these were done at that time without the benefit of pressure suits, which had not yet come into use. On 7 May I flew Meteor EE 549 down to its birthplace at Glosters, Moreton Valence, for repainting and generally tarting up. This aircraft had previously held the speed record, for which it had been specially prepared and had been painted royal blue. When it was returned to West Raynham I had flown it as a demonstration aircraft on several occasions. On the 8th I took several passengers down to Hendon in the Anson for a weekend in London.

At this time my painful divorce proceedings were concluded, and Maisie and I parted company. To my deep regret she was given custody of our daughter Sue, whom I had not seen since she was four years old, and it was still some years before we met again. But that is another story, and an unusual and happy one.

The CFE Annual Tactical Convention began on 25 May, and many old friends assembled at West Raynham. On the second day the air display took place with demonstrations of new aircraft by their company test pilots. John Cunningham flew the Ghost-engined Vampire in which he shortly was to beat the world altitude record when he reached a few feet short of 60,000 feet. The DH 108 delta-wing research aircraft with an uprated Goblin engine was then flown by John Derry. The previous month this aircraft and pilot had been in the news with a world air speed record of 605 mph. John was the first British pilot to fly faster than sound, and he was later to be killed when demonstrating a Mach 1 dive over Farnborough. Mike Lithgow then flew the Attacker, and Paddy Lynch flew in the rear seat of a modified Meteor to demonstrate the Martin Baker ejection seat. A Lancaster was also demonstrated with a Rolls-Royce Nene jet engine fitted in its bomb bay. This gave an impressive flypast, with the Nene gently throttled back and all four Merlins feathered, and only the windscreen wipers visibly working!

At the beginning of June, although the loss of my acting wing commander rank still rankled, I was pleased to hear that I had been granted a permanent commission. Several of my squadron leader friends and I were now studying madly for the newly introduced promotion exams, and the anxiety of these hanging over us made it feel like schooldays again. It was difficult for me to give these studies much priority when my trials report took up most of the time when I was not flying. I was doing night-flying practice in Meteors at the end of the month, and on an instrument training exercise I had an engine failure in the Oxford, necessitating an emergency landing. The following week I had to take my green card instrument rating test in the same Oxford after engine repairs, and all went well. On the 20th I flew a Spitfire XXIV on a camera recorder trial, and finished the month with more Meteor sorties on fuel-consumption trials.

In August AFDS started simulated attacks on B-29 bombers of the US Air Force as part of our air fighting trials with the Meteor. After some tentative attacks from the quarters and astern, it was decided to try the feasibility of head-on attacks, using ground radar controllers to turn the fighters onto our targets far enough ahead to give us time to line up, get our sights on and fire an effective burst of cannon. Head-on attacks could be very effective, as the bombers were very vulnerable from this direction, but they presented only a very small target. Quite a lot of practice was needed, both for the radar operators at the ground radar stations and for the fighter pilots. With a closing speed of some 900 knots, some very accurate flying was called for, and camera gun films showed that only about a three-second burst of cannon fire was possible. The attacks were fun for us Meteor boys, but pretty frightening for the bomber crews, and recorder cameras showed our Meteors were passing only about twelve feet above the high fins and rudders of the B-29s as we broke away after each attack. Not a popular exercise for the Yanks, but they stood up to it well and kept coming back for more as the trials progressed.

Early in September AFDS pilots were called on to provide a small fighter force of Vampires and Meteors for Exercise Dagger. On returning from the first scramble, and after intercepting four B-29 bombers at 32,000 feet, my No. 2 noticed that the nose-wheel of my Meteor was jammed, and instead of coming down straight it was lying athwart the aircraft's centre line, so that unless it straightened up on touching the runway there might be a spectacular landing. After a low pass over the control tower I decided to land with it as it was, and not to try to retract it, as it might well cause further damage. I did a normal landing and held the nose-wheel off the ground as long as possible, and fortunately the shock of finally touching the runway turned the wheel fore and aft and a normal landing run ensued, but they were an anxious few moments. We did several more scrambles, some in Meteors and some in Vampires, but on the final day of the exercise as we sat waiting beside our aircraft reading novels in the sun we had the ignominy of being 'beaten up' by a squadron of Hornets that swooped down un-announced out of the blue and caught us on the ground. That took some living down, for were we not supposed to be the experts in air fighting?

It was now the rugby season again, and I was pleased to be selected to play for the West Raynham first team, who were good and contenders for the Fighter Command Cup. I had two games during the week, and in the second I broke my own rule and carried out a half-hearted tackle and received someone's boot in my face, subsequently requiring two stitches. Luckily this did not stop me flying, as two days later I was pleased to be asked to do an aerobatic display at the Royal Air Force College on the occasion of a Battle of Britain commemoration parade. I took the smart blue Meteor, the record breaker, which itself was much admired, and did a fifteen-minute aerobatic routine over Cranwell's parade ground before returning to West Raynham. The next day, a Sunday, I took the Anson up to York to pick up the commandant, Air Cdre Atcherley, after he had taken the salute at a Battle of Britain church parade at the cathedral, and we returned to West Raynham VFR on a beautiful afternoon. Returning to his office, Atcherley received a nice message from the commandant at Cranwell thanking those concerned for the aerobatic display of the previous day, which had been well acclaimed.

On the 25th two of my AFDS colleagues flew up to Manchester in the Anson and joined relatives and friends at a reception at the Manchester Midland Hotel, to mark the occasion of my marriage to Eve, my erstwhile air observer in Hong Kong. After a happy honeymoon in the Lake District we returned to duty in time for a dance in the West Raynham officers' mess. Back at work the next day, I again led a 'finger four' of Meteors up to 40,000 feet to carry out head-on attacks on B-29 bombers There was a conference at the Radar Establishment at Malvern a few days later, and I flew down with several colleagues to attend. This was followed by a visit to Manby to give a lecture to the senior course at the Flying College.

On 11 November after a Remembrance parade, we borrowed a service 30 cwt lorry and moved all our belongings into a married quarter on the now deserted airfield at Great Massingham. It was only a glorified brick hut, but it was our first home, and after cleaning it up and moving in our few belongings it seemed like a mansion.

In early December all the aircrew from the Central Fighter Establishment were required to take part in an escape and evasion exercise. We were driven out into the open Norfolk countryside, some fifteen miles in a covered lorry, and dropped off, one at a time, at intervals and told to find our way home without being caught by the opposition, in the shape of Army patrols or RAF police. I reckoned I walked or ran about twenty-five miles and waded through an icy stream up to my middle, but I still got home first, undetected, as the sun was setting, and I could see the welcoming lights outside the guardroom. But I was arrested by my own service police, as the rules stipulated that station security had to be breached and I had to reach the Intelligence office without being detected. A bit unfair, I thought, but it served me right and I should have given attention to the small print in the rules.

Early the next morning, I took off in a Meteor on a sortie to measure

G forces during low-level high-speed flights. But there was no indication of the impending catastrophe that was to follow. As I got airborne the undercarriage retracted normally and locked up with a reassuring 'clunk', and the warning lights went out. I flew out to the low-flying route and carried out two runs at 250 feet AGL, increasing speed up to 460 knots while recording the G meter readings on my kneepad. Turbulence was considerable and the ride very uncomfortable, but I steeled myself to do one more run. As I reached maximum speed the red warning light for the port wheel indicator flashed on, and almost simultaneously the port undercarriage leg came down with an almighty bang, and the aircraft pitched up and swung to port uncontrollably. As soon as I had managed to get the dive brakes out and slow the aircraft and get it under control, I realized that the undercarriage leg would be damaged and would never lock down. The Meteor had received a nasty 'tweak', but apart from the undercarriage it did not seem to have suffered other damage. But after Birdie-Wilson's similar experience at high speed and at low level, when the Meteor broke up and left him sitting in his ejector seat, I was very cautious and limped back to Raynham to do a low, slow pass over the tower. They confirmed that the port wheel was dangling down, but could not see any other damage, so I decided to make a two-wheel landing on the grass to the left of the runway. I approached as slowly as possible with safety and gently touched the starboard wheel on the grass and kept the port wing up for as long as possible with full aileron while closing down both engines. The nose-wheel touched at the same time as the wing dropped and the port engine nacelle ploughed through the grass, and the aircraft entered a gentle swing to port. By now the speed had dropped off, and the aircraft came to a halt, happily not requiring the aid of the approaching ambulance and fire tenders. It suffered surprisingly little damage and was flying again in a few weeks' time. That same afternoon I flew a speed trial in a Vampire at all heights between 20,000 feet and sea level, and happily these went off without incident. The rest of December was taken up with Vampire trials, except for one Meteor flight to ascertain fuel consumption during a powerless glide down from 40,000 feet to landing and switch-off at dispersal.

In the New Year performance trials on both types continued, but at the end of the month I carried out some Vampire flying for a film company making a Royal Air Force recruiting film. On the 27th I drove down through London to give a lecture to No. 500 Auxiliary Squadron at Maidstone. On my return to West Raynham there was an ominous atmosphere of gloom in the mess, and I was shocked to hear that Neville, one of our most experienced pilots, had been killed when his aircraft had crashed into high ground when descending through low cloud.

In February, representatives from *Flight* magazine visited with their photographer, and while I led a squadron formation of Meteors and Vampires the photographer took shots from various positions from a Martinet flying in company. The next day John Cunningham came over from de Havilland to discuss cannon- and rocket-firing trials from the Vampire. We agreed to fit these trials into the busy flying programme towards the end of March, when I did four Vampire flights over the Holbeach ranges, firing sixteen rockets, the last releases being filmed by de Havilland. During the month I was thrilled to get the opportunity of a flight in a Spitfire XVIII on air test. At the beginning of April I did two Vampire flights to work out an aerobatic routine before going to Ireland, where we had been asked to carry out demonstration flights over several Ulster cities. I was never told the purpose of these flights, but on the 6th I flew a Vampire to Aldergrove, and from there did demonstration flights over Belfast, Larne, Bangor and Newtownards. The following day I repeated the programme over Londonderry, Strabane and Belfast again, and from there returned to West Raynham, a 35-minute flight. On the 11th I took an Anson to Valley and Aldergrove with six passengers to a meeting to discuss the impact of the 'showing-the-flag' flights that we had done a few days before. While all mine were well received, unfortunately Bill, who had done similar demonstration flights over other towns, had flown into some electric cables when pulling away from one town, which was situated in a natural bowl surrounded by higher ground. Luckily the aircraft was not badly damaged and he returned safely to Aldergrove, but there were a number of very disgruntled local Irishmen knocking back their Guinness by candlelight that night.

The next day I went down to RAF Newton to play in the finals of the rugby Fighter Command Cup. Age was now beginning to tell, and I now played at full back. It was a very hard-fought game that we unfortunately lost to RAF Pembrey. I returned to West Raynham in the Oxford with the commandant and his deputy, who had watched the game. I recalled this game because the previous day the commandant had had me into his office and congratulated me on another 'Exceptional' assessment as a fighter pilot. In the closing moments of the game the opposing wing three-quarter, who had already scored three tries, was well on his way to a fourth, hurtling down the touchline, when I was able to make a super flying tackle and we both finished up in a tangle on the touchline among the spectators. As I struggled to my feet, I looked up to see the commandant gazing down at me in amazement and saying, 'Well tackled, old chap', then a pause and, 'Dashed if I knew you played rugby too!'

On the 27th I dined in with the C-in-C, Basil Embrey, and we had cocktails beforehand with the deputy commandant, Edwards-Jones.

They were both interested in the results of our head-on attacks on the B-29 bombers, and I explained that the trials were still at an early stage and would be continuing to the end of the month, and well into May.

As a change from the current trials that AFDS were engaged in, I was tasked by Bristol University to carry out cosmic ray investigation trials at maximum altitude. For this purpose I was provided with a large, sealed thermos flask, containing I knew not what, and took it in the Meteor up to 40,000 feet to let it soak there for a minimum of twenty minutes. After landing, an official of the university checked the seals on the flask and whisked it off, presumably to the laboratories at the university. This trial was repeated to the same ritual on 2 June, and a week or two later I received a letter of thanks from the University of Bristol, together with the same thermos and an invitation to keep it with their compliments. It was now unsealed, of course, but I never knew what it had contained and never had the courage to use it for our own drinks.

CHAPTER TWENTY

A Demonstration
for Royalty

June 1949 to January 1950

The month of June brought the annual CFE Convention again and the chance to meet old friends and see flying demonstrations of new fighter aircraft. Exercise Foil followed a week later, involving our participation in interception trials. In July testing of aircraft performance in both Meteors and Vampires continued, with Meteor night-flying and the evaluation of the new airfield approach and runway lighting at USAF Lakenheath. With memories of the old wartime glim lamps as runway markers, and no approach lighting at all, I was amazed at the modern lighting now available for night approaches and landings. Certainly a great deal of stress had been removed from the conclusion of each night flight, and in some ways the comprehensive lighting layout made night approaches and landings easier than in daytime. I also carried out trials on the new electric artificial horizon in the Vampire. This instrument had the advantage over the old design in that it would not 'topple' during aerobatics or violent manoeuvres, and added greatly to the safety of instrument flying in all conditions. In August I did a similar trial with this horizon fitted in the Meteor. On a very hot day in the same week I flew a Vampire in a cockpit cooling trial, for it had become very clear that the aircraft could never be operated in desert conditions without some form of air conditioning. This became very evident to me in later years when I commanded a Venom wing in Iraq, where we were most grateful for the cooling in our cockpits.

In the middle of September a party from de Havilland visited, and Mr Blithe allowed me to fly their de Havilland Dove on a familiarization flight. In the meantime the technicians in the party discussed the progress of the several trials currently in progress on the Vampire. At the end of the month trials were carried out with the Meteor towing a ten-foot sleeve on the end of a 600-yard tow line for use as a target for air firing. On the first attempt it broke free at 260 knots, but in subsequent flights it was successfully flown out to the ranges and brought back to the airfield, where it was safely dropped and recovered. On 27 October I flew several members of the squadron on a liaison visit in the Anson, when we went from Raynham to Bovingdon and thence to Defford, Old Sarum and back to Bovingdon, where we discussed new techniques and exchanged views on the current trials before returning to Raynham.

At this time two events occurred that upset my normal routine. Firstly an officer, who shall remain nameless, was put under close arrest for apparently misusing service funds. This meant that an officer of equal rank (squadron leader) must remain with him at all times in his room in the officers' mess. This duty seemed to come round all too frequently, and I found it intensely frustrating and a dreadful waste of my time when I had so much to do. The other irritant was the advent of promotion exams for squadron leaders, which meant a lot of swotting in preparation for them, a situation that I thought I had left behind when I left school. Somehow it seemed rather undignified to see a clutch of squadron leaders huddled together in a corner of the mess anteroom, struggling with problems of Air Force law and administration.

On the last day of August I received the tragic news of the sudden death of my mother in Cheltenham. I found it most upsetting, as for some time I had meant to make greater efforts to see more of her. Even though much of my time was taken up by my flying duties, I realized that it had been very remiss of me not to make a greater effort to get away to visit her. And now it was too late, and it made me sad and ashamed as well. For some time after her funeral my life seemed to be full of melancholy and regrets.

Early in September the clutch of squadron leaders descended on Bing Cross, who commanded Horsham St Faith airfield, and were secreted away for the promotion exams. With these over at last I could soon return to work, and after a few days back at West Raynham I collected a Meteor 7 from Farnborough and did a comprehensive acceptance air test before it was taken on strength at CFE. In the middle of December after landing from the last of a series of Vampire and Meteor high-speed, high-altitude, head-on attacks on the B-29s, I was told that I was to attend a Staff College course. While this was good news from a career point of view, it meant the end of my rewarding research job at the Air Fighting Development Squadron at the Central Fighter Establishment. I would certainly leave that with considerable regret.

However, I was not to go until the following June, and I would get a lot more jet flying before then. And indeed I did so, with more hours on high-level interception trials and bombing and rocket trials with the

Vampire. But what was shortly to follow must surely mark the brightest light of my flying career, and it occurred with little warning and quite unexpectedly.

The King and Queen with their family were in residence at Sandringham, a few miles down the road from West Raynham. They were clearly well aware of the jet flying going on from the airfield, and they suddenly decided that they would like to see the aircraft at close quarters and meet the pilots who flew them. Accordingly the commandant was asked (or perhaps commanded) to provide facilities for a private visit to the establishment. It is doubtful whether a royal visit could be called private, but as it turned out it was very informal.

On 23 January the King and Queen arrived with Princesses Elizabeth and Margaret and an ADC, and were escorted straight down to the hangar without any honour guard, where they were shown round the Meteor, Vampire and the other fighter aircraft, and met officers, airmen and airwomen of the Servicing Squadron. They were then escorted out onto the airfield, where the aircrews were introduced to them. There were only two pilots in flying overalls – George Baldwin, a Fleet Air Arm lieutenant-commander, who stood in front of a Vampire, and me standing in front of the Meteor. The two of us had the honour of being selected to carry out demonstration flights for the royal party.

As the spectators took their places on the top of the control tower, George took off in the Vampire and did his usual polished display of aerobatics, finishing with a very fast low pass over the tower. Even as the strident note of the Vampire still hung in the air, the watching crowd's attention was drawn to the Meteor as it roared down the runway with a very proud me at the controls. I held the aircraft down close to the runway as the wheels retracted, and when I had built up adequate speed I pulled the Meteor up into a vertical climb and completed a half loop and roll-out immediately overhead. Admittedly both George and I had had two days to polish up our display, but all agreed that we did a display fit for a King. After completing my display, and not to be outdone by George, I flew close alongside the control tower very fast and very low, finally disappearing behind the higher ground to the east of the airfield. I waited until the royal party were walking across to the mess for tea before I came in quietly to do a short landing and put the Meteor in the hangar.

At tea all the royal party were full of praise and enthusiasm, and chatted away with everyone there in a friendly and relaxed atmosphere. Princess Elizabeth, who had been wearing a becoming hat with a jaunty pheasant's feather, in the course of conversation with me said, 'I found your last flypast very thrilling. I thought you were going to knock off my feather.' Clearly they were all enjoying the occasion, and long over-stayed their schedule. The King finally turned to the commandant, expressing his thanks, and said, 'We must go home. Where are our girls?' Margaret was missing, and when I went out to see that the royal cars were ready, I found her in the entrance hall sitting on the sofa with the ADC, Peter Townsend! So ended a most remarkable and enjoyable day. A few days later, when I recalled Princess Elizabeth's remark about the feather, I could not help thinking the unthinkable, that not many people would find themselves in my situation, where they might have so easily knocked the head off a future Queen of England! Perish the thought!

The night following this thrilling royal visit, the commandant, David Atcherley, was dined out on his appointment to SASO at Fighter Command, but I was still not finished with the Development Squadron. After flying some trials with the Meteor towing a 16-foot glider and the Vampire fitted with the new Ferranti electric horizon instrument, I was dispatched to the Canal Zone to talk to the squadrons there about recent developments in jet fighter flying. With two colleagues we flew in a York to Fayid via Luqa. At Fayid, the next day, a khamsin, (a horrible hot gale) was blowing, lifting the sand in clouds and reducing visibility to almost nil. However, we managed to get to No. 205 Group Headquarters, where we gave a lecture and showed our film, followed by a welcome swim at the officers' club. The next day we drove up to No. 324 Wing at Deversoir, which flew Vampires. After a lecture and discussions with the squadron pilots, I borrowed a Vampire from Crowley Milling, who was commanding 6 Squadron, and enjoyed a very interesting reconnaissance of Suez and the canal area, with a few aerobatics thrown in before landing. The next day we took an Anson 19 from Deversoir to Fayid, and then across to Nicosia in Cyprus. Here we lectured to No. 32 Squadron and showed our film. That night we stayed at the officers' club and were taken out to see the cabaret at the Ambassadore's, where we made the acquaintance of 'Black Helen'. We flew back to Fayid and took the York back to Lyneham, refuelling at Luqa (Malta).

On my return to West Raynham to make my final clearance, I was very pleased to see that the commandant had given me another 'Exceptional' assessment in my logbook. A very satisfactory way to go; but I still had two more sorties to do before my departure. The first was another trial assessing the stability of the Vampire while dropping bombs, and the second was a gratuitous flight in a Meteor, when I was given freedom to do as I pleased. I took off and climbed on a north-westerly heading to 43,000 feet. Here I throttled back and in what seemed almost complete silence within my pressurized cockpit I surveyed the fantastic panorama below. Looking north beyond the Wash I could see the Humber with Spurn Head curling below it. Looking west over the murky conurbation of the Midlands I could just make out the glorious dales of Yorkshire. Beyond Liverpool and Manchester, both swathed in smoke, I could just make out the muddy waters of the river Mersey, down which I had sailed out to the Pacific War all those years ago. I was amazed how easily the memories came flooding back. North Wales, the Dee estuary and Snowdon with its last remaining fringe of snow stood out clearly in the spring sunshine. The scene unfolded below me as I cruised at that high altitude: the Welsh mountains, the Brecon Beacons and then the Severn with Gloucester at its head. My birthplace, and where I had first enjoyed the magic of flight. Down the Bristol Channel to Bristol and Filton, the airfield just to the west, where I had done my initial training. I could follow down the coast to Devon, the Valley of the Rocks, my mother's favourite spot, and then Cornwall, tapering off to the end of the land. And around to where I could just pick out the smudge of land that was France, becoming clearer as my gaze moved up the Pas de Calais. And more directly below, the English south coast, standing out as clear as could be all the way from Weymouth to Folkestone. Just behind stood Hawkinge, the airfield where my first squadron had been based, and where, as a sergeant pilot, I had flown the fantastic Fury, even now comparable with the magic Meteor from which I now surveyed the country below and relived the memories that came flooding back as the scenes unfolded. With great reluctance I put down the nose of the Meteor, extended the dive brakes and, as though in a dream, made my way back to West Raynham to land there for the last time. But even as I approached the runway, the warm feeling of elation that had accompanied my 'command performance' a few days ago came over me, and I revelled in the feel of the responsive aircraft under my hands. I slipped the Meteor in over the hedge, taxied up to the hangar and switched off the fuel cocks, and as the engines died sighed deeply as I slid back the hood to face reality again.

CHAPTER TWENTY-ONE

Air Ministry Staff London

April 1951 to May 1954

On 1 May 1950 I reported to RAF Andover to join the No. 8 Staff College Course. While Andover lacked the prestige of the Bracknell Staff College, it was much more fun and had the advantage of including among its students officers from several foreign air forces, thus giving a far more interesting cross-section of opinions on many relevant subjects, as well as interesting insights into the affairs in other countries. It had the other advantage that there was never any shortage of off-duty parties, as there was nearly always some special national day to celebrate from one or other of the nations represented. A very happy relationship built up among the students as a result, and many friendships were made. There were representatives from Greece, Argentina, America, Portugal, Sweden, India. Pakistan, Finland, Norway, Ireland and several others. We were particularly fortunate in having on the course two very agreeable American colonels with charming and friendly wives who loved being in England, and we were constant visitors to each others' homes.

As the course began, our son Charles was born on 3 May in Manchester, and the family were all together in a charming little cottage at Appleshaw near Andover by the 27th. As the course progressed it became clear that between lectures and doing exams there were often gaps when students were supposed to be studying, but the time could equally be used for keeping in flying practice. So I soon made contact with the OC Station Flight at RAF Andover, and I had already flown three sorties in their Tiger Moth and three in the twin-engined Dominie by the time the family arrived. Several senior officers and leaders from the aircraft industry came to lecture the course, and to add to the interest, external visits were made to places of relevance to our studies. A day was spent aboard HMS *Theseus*, when we had the experience of being submerged under the waters of the Channel for several hours, and on another occasion the course was taken on a tour of the Port of London. In the middle of June the Station Flight pulled an ancient Spitfire out of the back of the hangar and managed to get it serviceable for an air test, which I did with great pleasure. They also produced a Proctor in which I did several sorties, giving another of the students dual instruction. Jack was a navigator, but often hankered after a pilot's course. and while the Proctor had dual controls it was not a very good aircraft for instructional purposes, but Jack enjoyed the flying and made steady progress, although there was little prospect of him going solo. When 4 July came around, Joe and Bruce, our Americans, gave a splendid Independence Day party in the mess, and at the end in rollicking good humour we all did our best to render some ten different national anthems.

The rugby season had not yet got under way, but I was taking up tennis again. I hadn't played seriously since school days, when we were lucky enough to have our own court at my home. Weekend tennis parties there were very popular, and I remembered how my father led the way with a demon of a serve that somehow managed to curve well out of reach of his opponent, which everyone thought was most unfair. At Andover there were several keen players, and the courts were busy out of working hours. The commandant was also very keen, and was working up a team to play in the Inter-Command Cup competition. The finals took place at Amport House, and I was picked to play, rather as an afterthought, for I had to admit that I was not up to the standard of the rest of the team. As in several sports I had moments of brilliance but was seldom consistent. The competition, when it finally took place, dragged on a bit, and as the evening sun was throwing heavy shadows across the courts honours remained even right up to the final game When the commandant came onto the court and looked for his ace partner, he was told to his horror that he had already gone home. And guess what? I was the only player available to join the commandant on court. On this occasion, happily, my moment of brilliance came to the fore, and my senior partner and I walked off with the cup, to the delight of the commandant and my surprise. Thus, rather by accident, I qualified for my command sports badge, but I never had the face to wear it on my blazer.

The next away visit for the course was to Saunders Roe at Cowes, and a few days later to the Malgam Steelworks situated in the Rhondda Valley in South Wales. After the bank holiday that followed, the members of the course were sent off on a month's leave. Before going away, Eve and I had Captain Robertsen from Norway to dinner at the cottage, and the next day I flew him in the Dominie to Ouston to catch his ship to Norway from Newcastle for his leave.

After a few days' holiday on the Gower coast of South Wales with my brother, I returned to Andover in time to go with the course to the SBAC Show at Farnborough, which I enjoyed as usual and managed to get a lunch in one of the companies' entertainment tents. The middle of September saw the beginning of the rugby season, when we had our first practice match. The next day I was delighted to hear that the Station Flight had acquired a splendid Spitfire XXII. This was one of the top of the range, with a very powerful Griffon engine, and quite a handful to fly near the ground. In a few days it would be Battle of Britain Anniversary Day, and the airfield at Andover would be staging a flying display for the public. The Spitfire would clearly be on display, so I was asked to give it a thorough air test. I got away at the end of afternoon lectures and spent a glorious hour of uninhibited flying, getting all I could out of this magnificent flying machine. Finally returning to the airfield, my exuberance overcame my normal caution and I dived down and flew very low and fast over the officers' mess. Grinning to myself, I thought there would be quite a few upset teacups down there. But it turned out to be even more embarrassing, as my beat-up took me directly over the tennis court, where the commandant was poised to deliver one of his ace serves to clinch his game. Needless to say, he was not amused, and while still in his white flannels he telephoned the deputy commandant and told him to deal sternly with the 'show-off'' in the Spitfire!

I was duly summoned to the deputy commandant's office at nine o'clock the next morning, where Giles, who was a good friend, had me on the mat and administered a mild reprimand and said, 'Not again'. With a grin he then said, 'You can relax now because Sylvia and I would like you and Eve to join us for drinks this evening when a few friends are coming to celebrate the Battle of Britain.' At his home towards the end of that evening, Giles came across to me, and taking me on one side said with a grin, 'By the way, the commandant has agreed to my suggestion that you should fly the Spitfire on Saturday to do an aerobatic show. He has also agreed that you should fly the Spitfire in the handicap air race that I am organizing.' So all was forgiven, and Saturday was a most exciting day for me. The Spitfire show was to be aerobatics 'on request', when I was required to carry out the various rolls, loops, stall-turns, etc. sent up to me by radio by enthusiastic youngsters in the air traffic tower. Working out the handicapping for the air race was quite a problem, as the Spitfire was about three times as fast as the slowest competitor, the Tiger Moth. Between these two were the Dominie, the Proctor, the Oxford and a visiting Anson. On the day all these aircraft were lined up on the airfield with engines running, and were flagged off in turn. Long after the sound of all the other aircraft's engines had faded away, my Spitfire was still awaiting the flag. The large Griffon engine was not at all happy at being at tick-over for so long, and the temperature of the engine coolant started to rise alarmingly. Eventually I had to insist on being allowed to go, or I would have to shut down altogether. So I was flagged off early, regardless of handicap, and with great relief I roared off in pursuit of the others, but reluctantly limiting my speed a little to be fair. After screeching around the three turning points I straightened up on the final run into the airfield and could see the gaggle of aircraft ahead. The Tiger Moth seemed to be almost at the airfield, so I opened up the Griffon to full power and dived for the finishing line. It must have been a thrilling and beautiful sound for the spectators as I pulled up the Spitfire into a vertical climb over the finishing line, but the Tiger won by a short head.

On my birthday on 1 October we had a party in our cottage at Appleshaw for the Americans and their wives, and several of the other foreign officers with their partners. A few days later I played rugby against Basingstoke, and in the course of the game I was badly trampled in a ruck and came out of it with a very painful chest. I managed to struggle on for the rest of the game, and was relieved to get home, only to be told that we had been invited out to supper that night. The food was good and the company delightful, but just sitting still was agony. The next day I was driven to Tidworth for an X-ray at the Army hospital, and two cracked ribs were evident. Having been strapped up I was told to take things easily for a day or two. Not much sympathy was shown, and it was two weeks before I was really comfortable again. For two days running I had to sit through long lectures, one by Basil Embrey and the second by Pete Wickham-Barnes on his operations in Korea. They were very good talks and the discussions that followed were of great interest, but I still suffered and found it difficult to concentrate.

There followed a very interesting visit to Germany. The course assembled at the Hotel de France in Dover, and the next day took the ferry to Dunkirk, where we had a lecture on that momentous evacuation of the majority of the British forces from France in May 1940, when thousands were plucked off the beaches and ferried home by every available craft that could make the journey across the Channel, including privately owned little yachts and motor boats. This was an operation of great skill, courage and determination, but it was brought about, it should be remembered, by an ignominious defeat and retreat.

From Dunkirk we went on to Brussels, where, after visiting a night club, we booked into the Palace Hotel at 3 a.m. The next day we went to Cologne, where we were accommodated at Royal Air Force Butzweilerhof for the night. On the following day we were taken round Cologne in a coach to see the results of the Allied bombing during the war, and were later asked to make our own assessment of its effect on the course of the war. Our coach then took the autobahn to Essen. After lunch at the Black Diamond Club we toured the great factories of Krupps, where production recovery already seemed well under way, thanks to American dollars from the Marshall Plan. Thus is the idiocy of war revealed! When we talked to Germans on the spot, although they were surprisingly friendly, they considered it only just that as the Allies had knocked the factories down in their bombing campaign they should pay for their reconstruction! On 14 November 1950 the course visited the headquarters of BAAFO at Bad Eilsen, where we were given a talk by the Commander-in-Chief, and after lunch taken on a tour of Wünsdorf. A train from Hanover took us to Hamburg, where we were given a tour of the city by coach and launch. The bomb damage we saw was appalling, mainly caused by the fire storm that followed the incendiary attack, and it left us wondering whether the effects of such desecration on the national will could possibly justify such dreadful devastation and casualties. The argument is set about by so many imponderables that there is still no clear-cut answer today. That night in the Regina in Hamburg many opinions were offered and discussed, some with passionate intensity, well into the small hours of the morning. The next day we went on to Düsseldorf by rail, where we had dinner at the Yacht Club, and afterwards were the guests of both the sergeants' and officers' messes, and went late to bed. But the next day was an early start to tour Düsseldorf city and then to move on to Brussels for an early night and a chance to catch up on some sleep. Leaving Brussels early the next morning to catch the ferry to Dover, the course arrived safely and intact in London by early evening.

Back at Andover our course continued with a visit to London Airport, Heathrow, and I managed to get in another flight in the Dominie before the end of the month. With the approach of the Christmas holiday there was a noticeable increase in the number of parties and dinner nights. Joe and Lola, the Americans, invited several of the course instructors and students to dinner in Salisbury, and on the 22nd Eve and I threw a large party in our little cottage, with hot punch, and all the guests, including Portuguese, Greek, Indian, Americans, Scandinavians and other representatives from the course joining in carols round the Christmas tree. A really lovely party, long to be remembered. On the 31st the course instructors gave a New Year's party in the mess with all present, and once again this was a roaring success, starting the New Year with an attempt to render all the national anthems, one after the other in no particular order of precedence, for no one dared to rule on the matter.

In February the course was taken on an industrial tour in the north, starting with the steelworks at Corby. Next, we all put on hard hats and went down the coalmine at Donisthorpe, spending two very interesting hours underground. We barely had time to wash down and get rid of the coal dust on reaching the surface, before we were whisked off by coach to see the charming ballet *Coppelia* in the Leicester Theatre. Its charm was in stark contrast to the gloom and grime of the recently abandoned coalmine. It was only at the last moment that we remembered to remove the hard hats and leave them in the coach!

Back at Andover, on returning from a flight to St Athan in the Dominie, I was told the bad but not unexpected news that my next posting was to the Air Ministry, London.

CHAPTER TWENTY-TWO

Jet Refresher

May to June 1954

I anticipated that after Staff College I would almost certainly go to a staff appointment, but had hoped that it might be at a command or group headquarters. I dreaded the thought of three years commuting up to London to a boring job and far removed from any flying. However, having called at Gieves and bought my bowler hat, the accepted uniform for the Air Ministry, I reported to Whitehall and was introduced to the three other members of the 'office' of Air Staff Policy 3 situated down the corridor from the Planners, with whom we would work hand in glove. I was to cover the Far East Area of Interest, and the task of the 'office' was to prepare briefs for the Chief of Air Staff for his guidance at the Chiefs of Staff weekly meetings with the Air Minister.

I was thrown in at the deep end, and had barely settled into my chair when I was told that the Chiefs would be discussing the future of General MacArthur at their meeting the next day and the CAS would require a brief by 9 o'clock in the morning. Frantic scanning of the files and discussion with my colleague in Plans produced very sketchy material for a brief, particularly as it had to include a recommendation at the conclusion. By ten o'clock that evening I had managed to put together enough material to arrive at the conclusion that General MacArthur, by his deliberate involvement in the politics of the Philippines, had far exceeded his military brief and should therefore go. With some trepidation I sent the brief down to the CAS's office and went home. The next day, the day of the Chiefs' meeting went without incident, but that evening, on my way home, I grabbed an *Evening News* as I clambered onto my train, and braced in the corridor, as usual, I opened my paper and was shocked to see the headline in inch-high letters: 'MacArthur Sacked!' Good God, what have I done? I thought to myself.

There was very little interest in my job after that first excitement, and the days, months and years went by all too slowly. I quite enjoyed being in London for a time, and spent my lunch hours exploring and visiting the famous sites, museums and art galleries. Happily my American friends from Staff College were also in London, and we frequently lunched together at one of our clubs. Many other friends came up to London visiting the Air Ministry from time to time, and provided a welcome diversion from the daily boredom. The job became more frustrating, and if the truth be known I really did not have enough to keep me occupied. I must have got through fifty novels while sitting at my desk waiting for a briefing task, but the Far East was fairly quiet at this time. The famine of flying niggled me as much as anything, and when I hadn't flown for six weeks I decided I must get out of the office and into the air again. I discovered that there were aircraft at RAF Hendon that staff officers were permitted to fly to keep in flying practice, so it was not long before I was at the controls of an Anson after a quick check by an instructor. However, I was lucky if I could get in more than two or three trips a month, and the road out to Hendon was a nightmare. Even when I got airborne it was a tedious business to get clear of the air routes and controlled airspace round the capital's airports, before I was in clear air where I could carry out unrestricted flying practice. Before the end of the year the Air Ministry moved into part of the new Ministry of Agriculture and Fisheries Building, and our new office on the fifth floor gave a fine view of the Embankment, which relieved the tedium a little.

Two things occurred at the beginning of 1952 that were of note. Firstly, I was promoted to substantive wing commander, and secondly, my family moved from our small rented house in Radlett to the directly opposite side of London, where we took a very pleasant house on a common south of Dorking. Here we had a few acres where we became keen gardeners and raised chickens and children. The journey to London was equally tiresome, but at least we were out in lovely countryside. On 5 February I took the Americans to Twickenham to see the rugby between England and the Springboks, and they were amazed that the players didn't get killed without the armour customarily worn by American footballers. We returned from the match to hear that the first of the 'V' bombers, the Valiant, had crashed, apparently having broken up in mid-air. The aircraft subsequently had a very restricted service life compared with the other two, the Vulcan and the Victor, which played a significant part in the game of bluff of the Cold War.

In March, determined to improve the flying situation, my enquiries came up with the information that an Air Experience Squadron at Redhill were all too willing to have pilots help with flying Air Cadets in Tiger Moths to give them air experience. I could now easily get over from my home to Redhill on days off, and the airfield was situated in a more open area as regards controlled air space, so that my flying would be less restricted. However, although the Tiger Moth was fun to fly, there was a limited amount of flying practice that could be achieved, and it was not even fitted with radio. However, from time to time I continued to fly an Anson from Hendon when there was a useful task to be done, like collecting spares or taking staff officers on their periodic visits.

On the morning of 6 February the country woke up to the sad news that the King had died during the night. On the 16th we reported for work in our best uniforms and black armbands on our sleeves. From the window of our office in the Ministry of Ag. and Fish Building we watched the funeral cortège move slowly down Whitehall accompanied by the tolling of the great bell of the Abbey, one stroke for every year of the King's life. Later the muffled roar of the salute fired by the guns of a troop of the King's Own Fusiliers echoed up from Hyde Park, resounding from the walls of the tall buildings around as though issuing from every street. As the sound died away an uncanny silence followed, pregnant with the deep sorrow of the London people grieving for the king who was one of the most beloved sovereigns of modern times, remaining, as he did, among them to share the perils and horror of the German air bombardment.

In the middle of May I flew an Anson from Hendon to Aldergrove in Ireland, and returned as the beginning of a thunderstorm broke over London. I had an unpleasant drive back to Dorking, and the storm increased in intensity during the night. The next morning there were widespread floods all over the home counties, and in our garden the little stream that came down from Leith Hill was a roaring torrent and had swept away my recently built dam, but luckily the water had not come into the house.

On 16 July I left my office at lunchtime and took the train to Southampton and thence by ferry to Cowes. After a night and breakfast in the Gloster Hotel, Desmond and I joined the crew of Treve Holman's 40-foot yacht and sailed out of Cowes as a competitor in the Ocean Race to Dinard, France. After passing the Channel Islands and the Casquettes during the night, we crossed the line at Dinard, not among the first three, but not disgraced. After a drink and meal ashore, Desmond and I had to get back to the Air Ministry before we were missed, and so caught the night ferry, Falaise to Southampton, and arrived back in London at 9. 30 a.m., having achieved my object of qualifying for membership of the Royal Ocean Racing Club.

At the end of the month I was pleased to hear that the Air Experience Flight at Redhill had re-equipped with Chipmunks, and I lost no time in getting a trip in the new aircraft, which I found much more versatile than the Tiger, and more useful for keeping in flying practice. In August I did two flights in the Anson – one to St Athan near Cardiff, and the other to Shepherd's Grove to collect radio spares for Hendon.

In September my two colleagues and I visited the SBAC Show at Farnborough, and the next day went to a cocktail party with the Burmese Mission at Carlton Terrace, where we met Anthony Eden, who was trying to promote the sale of British aircraft and equipment to Burma. The Air Show at Farnborough that year was unfortunately marred by the crash of the de Havilland 110, which broke up in the air after a supersonic run and crashed on the airfield, killing John Derry, a friend of mine, and Tony Richards, his flight-test observer. The two Avon engines from the aircraft fell among the watching crowd, and several were killed and many injured. This accident raised fears in some quarters that supersonic flying might have some unknown dangers that had, so far, not been detected, as these were the early days of supersonic 'bangs' over Farnborough. Such fears were not substantiated, and the bogey was soon dispelled, although the design of high-speed aircraft was modified considerably to alleviate the onset of 'compressibilty'at the speed of sound, mostly by sweeping the wings. This accident was caused by rapid flutter due to the lack of torsional friction in the wing as Derry pulled the aircraft round in a very high G turn at high indicated airspeed, one wing breaking off, followed by the tail.

On Battle of Britain Sunday that year, Eve and I went to the commemorative service at Westminster Abbey, and this marked the beginning of a few days' leave. We set off by car to South Wales and booked in at the Rhosili Hotel on the Gower coast. We knew the village well, and had explored the surrounding sandy beaches and the splendid three-and-a-half-mile-long Rhosili Sands several times during previous holidays.

CHAPTER TWENTY-THREE

RAF Habbaniyah, Iraq

September 1954

On returning to London in mid-October, my job continued with little to relieve the tedium of not enough to keep me busy. I managed to get two Chipmunk flights at Redhill, and that evening we were asked by our American friends to a farewell party, as they had been posted to Frankfurt. We were invited to cocktails and dinner at Whitfield House, Barbara Hutton's mansion in Regent's Park. It was a very happy evening, tinged with regret that Bruce and Betty were leaving London. They, and Joe and Lola, had been such very good friends over quite a long period, and we had become very fond of them. It came as a great shock a few years later when we heard that both the colonels had been killed in two separate air crashes in the United States. Our deep sympathies went out to the two wives who had been so devoted to their men.

At the end of October I managed to get in two more Chipmunk sorties, but the weather to the end of the year was cold and unsettled, and the only Chipmunk flight in December was curtailed, as I was recalled because of a gale warning.

The New Year started off with snow and freezing weather. I was pleased to hear that my old squadron, No. 96, disbanded soon after the end of the war, had been re-formed at Ahlorn in Germany and reverted to its old role as a fighter squadron, now equipped with Meteors. I was relieved to get through my annual medical in the middle of the month, and although I remained quite fit I always had a fear, quite unreasonably, that the medicos would find something to ground me. So I felt free to try and organize some flying, but the weather continued bad. At the end of the month, in fact, snowstorms and gales returned with a vengeance, and there was widespread flooding down the east coast and many people were drowned in Holland and some in East Anglia. The Irish Ferry foundered on its crossing from Stranraer to

Larne, and many small boats were lost or damaged around the coasts.

After the early storms February turned out to be a more settled month, and I managed to get in four more flights in the Chipmunks at Redhill, and four more in March, to keep my hand in. After Easter I got the opportunity to renew my love of sailing when my brother-in-law and I chartered a small sailing yacht from Bosham and enjoyed a week's cruising in the Channel, calling at Lymington, Yarmouth (Isle of Wight), Beaulieu, Cowes and the Hamble. On our last day, as we felt our way back up the Solent in thick fog, to our embarrassment we found ourselves in the middle of the Canadian fleet that was just arriving to take its place in the Royal Naval Review in the following week. In early June I managed to get two seats in the Mall to view the Queen's Coronation Parade, and I shared the great spectacle with Eve's cousin. It poured with rain, but this did not spoil the magnificence of the parade made all the more remarkable by the sight of no fewer than four air marshals valiantly struggling to keep their seats on four excited horses towards the end of the parade. The thrill of the day's events was greatly enhanced by the hot-from-the-press news that Edmund Hillary and his companion Tensing had reached the summit of Everest, the first ever to do so. What a memorable day for the British! A few days later another happy event occurred when our daughter Emma was born.

Shortly afterwards I was lucky enough to be given a berth in SS *Braybury* to witness the Naval Review, which consisted of many ships from the Commonwealth and friendly nations as well as those of the Royal Navy. The whole of the Solent and Spithead were so full of ships that there did not seem to be room for a single one more. This was a most stirring sight and one to stir even the most cynical landlubber! The last few days had given a wonderful lift to my national pride.

In the middle of July 1953 I realized that I was well into my tour at the Air Ministry, and it was time for me to start thinking about my next posting. By all the rules I should soon be in line for another flying job, and although I had kept in flying practice it was only in light and slow aircraft. I thought I would have a better prospect if I were to be up-to-date on more modern types of aircraft, so to this end I borrowed a Chipmunk from Redhill and flew down to West Malling to see my old friend Peter Walker, with whom I had trained, and who was now commanding this fighter station. Peter kindly arranged for one of his instructors to give me a check ride and then authorize me to fly a Meteor 7 to do one and a half hours' solo handling. I thoroughly enjoyed the experience, and soon found the Meteor cockpit becoming quite familiar again. The trip back to Redhill in the Chipmunk was very dull in comparison. This visit was shortly followed by another to West Malling, and this time Peter had an instructor check me out in a Vampire T.11, followed by one hour ten minutes of solo handling flight to familiarize myself with this delightful little single-engined jet fighter.

At the beginning of September I spent a day at the SBAC Air Show at Farnborough, and was detailed to escort a party of German aviation industrialists round the stands and aircraft. I found this very interesting, particularly as I had been away from aircraft for so long, but luckily I had swotted up the details of the new aircraft, so I could provide reasonably intelligent answers to the Germans' questions, and there were plenty of those.

After another visit to West Malling, when I was able to fly another two hours ten minutes in the Vampire, I then felt confident enough to go and see Bob Hodges at Air Ministry Postings and enquire about my next posting. As is the habit of officers in the Postings job, he was very cagey, but said he would arrange an Instrument Flying refresher course for me in the meantime. Accordingly, before the end of the month, I was attached to No. 10 Advanced Flying Training School at Pershore for a concentrated Instrument Flying course on Oxfords. Here I did eighteen hours 'under the hood', using the method of 'two-stage amber', whereby the aircraft's windows were covered in amber screens through which the instructor could see as though through tinted glasses, but the pupil wore amber goggles, which turned the windows black but still allowed him to see his instruments. The flying involved take-offs, approaches, landings and recovery from unusual flight positions thought up by the instructor, all on instruments only, a stressful exercise needing great and unrelenting concentration. However, after a while, confidence returned and I drove away from Pershore with my 'green card' again tucked away in my logbook.

After a period of leave I returned to my 'mahogany bomber' in the Air Ministry, and life continued in its previous boring manner, with only an occasional Chipmunk sortie to relieve the tedium. The new year of 1954 brought snow and very cold weather, and at one point we all joined in skating on the St James's Park lake. Another visit to the Personnel Postings staff came up with the offer of a job as Air Attaché in Lisbon. This sounded very attractive, but I was advised that it would probably be a bit of a dead end, and not favourable for my future career. However, in a few days I was given the very welcome news that I was to take over a Venom fighter wing at Habbaniyah, in Iraq, a posting that suited me in every respect, and I started my preparations in high spirits. I would have to do several refresher courses in different places and spread over several weeks, so I decided to buy a caravan to accommodate the family and myself. On 3 April, I completed my allotted term of three years at the Air Ministry almost to the day, and my relief arrived to take over. With my bowler hat clutched in my hand I marched down to Westminster Bridge and tried to lob it down the funnel of a passing tug. This was a traditional act by RAF officers on completion of their staff tour in London. A few days later the caravan arrived, and after piling in all our belongings and the family we set off for a couple of months like a family of gypsies.

With a few days to spare before my first course began, I accepted an offer from the station commander at Thorney Island to park our caravan on a remote dispersal on the far side of his airfield. From here we could enjoy a few days visiting some of the delightful places on the south coast, like Dell Quay, Bosham, Birdham, and Hayling Island. I also took the opportunity to go sailing with the station commander in his sailing dinghy.

At the end of this little holiday we packed up everything into the Vanguard and caravan, and set off from Thorney Island with the intention of travelling by night to avoid the worst of the traffic. Just before midnight disaster struck when a wheel on the caravan collapsed and the tyre burst. Luckily this occurred almost outside a country hostelry where the family could be accommodated for the night while I went off in search of a garage. Again we were lucky when I found a treasure of a young mechanic who turned out with surprising enthusiasm at midnight, and within a couple of hours he had welded the wheel and found a tyre to fit at very reasonable cost. After a welcome breakfast with the family in the pub, we were able to set off again for Weston Zoyland, the Royal Air Force station situated on the Somerset Levels to the east of the Polden hills, with Sedgemoor close by. After settling the family in the rather scruffy caravan site, I reported to No. 209 Advance Flying School. On my first day of duty the weather was poor, with drizzle and low cloud adding little to this rather dreary part of Britain. However, I was able to start my refresher flying on the Meteor, and was soon feeling familiar with the aircraft again, and thoroughly enjoying the thrill of 'real' flying once more. I was doing one or two sorties a day on aerobatics, instrument flying, simulated single-engine approaches and landings, as well as navigation exercises. Towards the end of the course I met up with several old friends and got to know a few new ones during a get-together at the local pub and restaurant. My old boss from Singapore, Richard, and his wife Imogen were there, and we spent several enjoyable occasions over drinks and dinner, talking about old times at Changi. I was also pleased to meet Peter Ellis, who was to be one of my squadron commanders in Iraq. Here began a very firm friendship that was to last many years.

I successfully completed my Meteor refresher course on 20th June, and set off from Weston Zoyland having renewed my instrument-rating green card again. I had a few days at Old Sarum on a Weapons

Demonstration and Army Liaison course, and there were enough of my old cronies also on the course to make up a very enjoyable get-together at the Rose and Crown in Salisbury. Back at Weston Zoyland I now planned to take the family in the caravan to my brother's home at Minchinhampton for a day or two, as this would be on the way to my next duty in South Wales. But again disaster struck, when, in the Avon Gorge, a violent gust of wind took the skylight off the roof of the caravan and it was lost for ever in the muddy brown waters of the river; and then, a few miles further on, when the same caravan wheel fractured, appropriately enough, at a place called Old Sodbury. Here we were very lucky, as we were just getting up a good speed to tackle a steep hill that we could see ahead, when Eve noticed that we were pretty low on fuel and suggested that we call at the garage at the foot of the hill for petrol. As I reluctantly pulled in to the forecourt we were surprised to see the proprietor staring at the back wheel of the caravan with a look of horror on his face And no wonder, for the wheel had split and the tyre's inner tube had come out like a huge red balloon as big as a football. A few more yards up the hill and we could have been in real trouble. As we were not very far from my brother's house, the family were able to move in there while I spent the remainder of the day searching for a wheel and tyre that would fit the caravan.

Before moving on we had a few days' leave to spend with my brother, and the opportunity to revisit my old haunts in the Cotswolds, which brought back so many happy memories of my school days. Games of cricket against Wycliffe College in their lovely grounds at Stonehouse, riding an old hack with Suzette through the splendid woods at Cranham or the family race to the top of May Hill to count the Scotch pines on the summit again, to confirm that there were still a hundred there. I discovered that Gp Capt Gilson was now commanding Royal Air Force South Cerney just down the road, so we arranged to meet him and Sylvia at the Highwayman Pub on the Fosse Way for a pub lunch, and for them to meet my brother and sister and her husband, who lived just up the road in the lovely village of Brimscombe. It was soon time to move on, and having lost confidence in our poor overloaded caravan we decided to give the job of towing it down to South Wales to an expert hire company. Consequently I set off with our dog Ben, temporarily leaving the family at Minchinhampton, and drove on down to Wales over the Brecon Beacons and through Llandovery to Pembrey, situated just inland from Pendine Sands, where in the old days attempts were made to beat the land speed record. As far as I could recall, it was Sir Malcolm Campbell in his car Bluebird that finally achieved this aim.

Pembrey was primarily a Gunnery School, and on arrival I was billeted out in a small hotel in Llanelly, as there was no room in the officers' mess. As soon as I had reported to the headquarters of No. 233 Operational Conversion Unit, I was airborne in a Vampire again and, as always, enjoying the experience. On the third sortie I managed to fly over Minchinhampton on a navigation exercise, and was able to check that the caravan was no longer in my brother's front garden but presumably on its way to Wales. Two days later I was able to pick up my family at Llanelly railway station, and we were able to move into our caravan. The station commander had been good enough to let us park it on one of the remote dispersal hardstandings, which we thought would be a nice quiet spot where the children could play in peace. However, we soon discovered that it was not always so peaceful. At weekends the Air Cadets would be flying their gliders with their winches only a hundred yards or so from our caravan, or if the wind was from the other direction, the gliders would approach to land very low over our camp. Not only that, however, as during the weekdays our dispersal would be used to arm up the Vampires with live rockets, much to our young daughter's interest and her mother's alarm. However, we were very content to be there, although, being on the other side of the airfield, we had to wait for a green light from the air traffic tower before we could cross the runway on our way to the NAAFI, as there were Vampires taking off and landing regularly throughout the day.

There followed a period of rain, as was not unusual in those parts, although the flying continued, but it was only when the sun came out at last that the family discovered the wonderful sandy beach a few minutes' walk from the caravan. On sunny days this was a delight for the family, and at weekends some of the pilots, led by Peter, would drag a long net through the surf to catch the odd flounder or flat fish. It was also a favourite place for Peter to practise his golf drives.

Vampire training continued with battle formation tactics, practice rocket attacks, high and low interception practices and instrument approaches and landings, including one to Weston Zoyland and return. Our pending departure overseas was foreshadowed when Pete and I were summoned to the Medical Centre to have our innoculations. Before our departure we had Peter and the station commander over to our caravan for farewell drinks, and we were lucky in managing to re-rent our caravan to a squadron leader at Pembrey. Our other worry had been what we were going to do with Benny, our well-loved spaniel, when we went abroad, but this problem was solved in a most satisfactory way. Even though we had been situated on the far side of the airfield, the postman came over every day with our mail, and Benny took a great liking to him and greeted him every time he came with much fuss. Clearly this liking was reciprocated, and it was agreed that on our departure Benny would go to the postman. Both parties were delighted that they would be together, and after we left we received several postcards from the postman to say how delighted he was with Benny and assuring us that our dear dog was completely content.

At the completion of the course I had done twenty-three hours on the Vampire and was looking forward to getting my hands on the Venom, which I would be flying in Iraq. To this end Peter and I borrowed an Oxford and set off for Benson, where Digger McGill was trying to arrange for us to ferry out two Venoms to Iraq. The weather was awful, with very low cloud, but Pete and I elected to fly visual flight rules to Benson, as it was only a short distance and we hoped to wriggle in under the overcast. But our endeavours were very nearly cut short when a Viking civil airliner descending into Cardiff over Porthcawl passed very close to our Oxford, so close, in fact, that we experienced severe turbulence as we flew through its propeller wash. We reported the air miss to our control radar and continued on our way, landing safely at Benson with a radar-controlled approach. After lunch, when the weather had lifted a bit, we boarded our Oxford and flew on to Hatfield, the home of de Havilland, where we were given a lecture on the Venom systems and engine handling, and we discussed with their test pilots the handling and performance details of the aircraft. I was able to meet John Cunningham again, and asked him about his very busy life as de Havilland's chief test pilot. He was currently occupied with delivering Vampires to Switzerland and lecturing their pilots and engineers about the aircraft He was also very busy with development flights on the Comet, which he had first flown in 1949 on his birthday, 27 July. He reported that up to a few weeks previously the Comet had been hailed as a great achievement as the first jet-propelled civil airliner, and it was already flying with several airlines. But then a BOAC Comet taking off from Rome Ciampino had to abort the take-off and was damaged beyond repair, luckily without casualties. But some months later a Canadian Pacific Airline's Comet on its delivery flight to Australia suffered an exact repetition of the Rome accident at Karachi, but with fatal results when the aircraft was destroyed. After the Rome accident John told me that he carried out exhaustive trials on Comet take-offs, during which he discovered that if the nose-wheel was lifted off the runway too early in the take-off the aircraft was reluctant to accelerate, and in extreme cases the aircraft would not lift off before the end of the runway. John immediately issued a warning to all Comet pilots, and introduced the first concept of the critical 'rotation' speed now adopted worldwide. The captain of the Karachi Comet had done a full conversion course at Hatfield, and the importance of 'rotation' speed had been drummed into him, as well as being demonstrated. He had considerable experience as an airline captain, but little experience of jet-powered aircraft, and on this occasion was doing a night take-off, with ground haze obscuring the horizon and a fully fuelled aircraft for a non-stop flight to Rangoon. From tyre scuff marks and tail bumper marks investigators were able to prove that the captain had raised the nose of the Comet too high and too soon, and the aircraft had ceased to accelerate and had struck a wall at the end of the runway and burst into flames. After these two accidents the Comet was modified with drooped leading edges, and with John's specific briefing there were no further accidents of this nature. At this time John had just returned from beating his own speed record between Hatfield and Cairo, this time flying the Comet 2. He had so many interesting tales to tell me, and I was reluctant to leave Hatfield. But we had another visit to make, and flew on to the Central Fighter Establishment at West Raynham, where my old squadron was able to lend me a Venom for a short handling and evaluation flight. After landing and refuelling, Peter was able to do a similar flight in the same aircraft. Feeling that we had achieved a very satisfactory day, we had a few drinks in the mess and retired early to bed in a room in the mess kindly provided by the PMC. The next day Peter and I flew back to Pembrey in the Oxford, and spent an evening celebrating the successful conclusion of our course with the CO and instructors.

CHAPTER TWENTY-FOUR

Three Squadrons of Venoms

September to November 1954

Having satisfactorily disposed of the caravan, we piled into the Vanguard and set off for Manchester, where we would be staying in Pat and Miles's new house to spend our embarkation leave. We had a lovely drive through the Welsh mountains, and arrived with the prospect of an exciting time planning our trip out to Iraq together. But what followed was the first and only time that I had what was a rather bitter row with the service authorities. Right from the start of the announcement of my posting to Habbaniyah, it had been made quite clear that an ex-officio married quarter would be available for me and my family to move into on arrival. I had no reason to doubt this, as it was normal practice for unit commanders to be accommodated on the camp in a married quarter. However, on going to London to buy my tropical uniform, I went in to see the Personnel staff to confirm our travel arrangements, only to be told bluntly that the policy had been changed and no married quarter would be available, and I would have to go out to Iraq unaccompanied. To say I was angry would be putting it mildly. How, I asked, at that late stage, was I expected to arrange accommodation for my family in the UK and also to find schools for our children. No answer was forthcoming and no help of any sort offered. The attitude of authority on this occasion came as quite a shock, for I had never experienced anything like it during the whole of my service up to then. No protests had any effect on the decision, so I had to go ahead and make the necessary arrangements to meet the new circumstances. Happily Pat and Miles could take care of the family, and were glad to do so until I could get them out to join me. So with my sincere thanks and gratitude to the Bentons I settled the family down, kissed them goodbye and on 23 September I set off for the Middle East on my own. I took a taxi to Manchester station and then a train to RAF Lyneham, where I was accommodated at Cliffe Pipard for the night. The next day

152

I took off in a Hastings bound for Iraq, staging through Idris in Libya overnight. Thus it was that I arrived at Habbaniyah on 25 September on my own, and on our wedding anniversary, to add a final twist to my resentment. As I disembarked from the Hastings on the satellite plateau airstrip that overlooked the main airfield, I was reminded of the desperate situation that had faced the station in April 1941. Raschid Ali, who had seized power in Iraq at that time with the understanding that he would receive German support, had laid siege to the airbase by moving a strong force of artillery to this very place where I now stood on the plateau. Under constant bombardment for two weeks, the airmen at Habbaniyah put up a spirited defence with their training aircraft, which they had adapted to carry bombs, and carried out constant air strikes on the Iraqi guns. Looking down now from the plateau at the sitting targets of hangars, buildings and aircraft that must have been presented to the Iraqi gunners, I was amazed that they had not been more effective and that the RAF had been able to hold out for so long. The base was relieved by a brigade-sized flying column (Hab-Force) that had crossed into Iraq from Palestine and arrived at Habbaniyah on 18 May. It was only just in time, as German aircraft had already arrived at Mosul in North Iraq and were poised to lend their weight to the attack on Habbaniyah. In the south an Indian division had secured Basra and the other British airbase at Shaibah, and advanced northwards to join Hab-Force to threaten Bagdhad itself. With air reinforcements now arriving in the shape of a flight of Gladiators, the Iraqi leader, Raschid Ali, withdrew his artillery force and fled into Persia. and Iraq support for the Axis collapsed.

Habbaniyah was built in 1934 under the Anglo-Iraqi treaty that allowed Britain to establish a military base in the country. It now stood as a bastion and an important stabilizing influence for Middle East peace, and it became clear that the building up of my Venom fighter wing to operational status would be a task of some importance. However, before settling down to the job, my exploration of the huge station filled me with wonder. Its primary purpose was as an airbase, of course, but its remote position way out in the desert forty miles from Baghdad made it clear that the provision of recreation and sporting facilities was of primary importance to maintain the morale of its personnel. These were provided in abundance, and there was just nothing that could not be done on the base. There were at least seven different units accommodated here, and each had its own mess where regular social activities were held. So at times like Christmas and other holidays, dances and mess balls would be taking place nearly every night for a week, and invitations would come pouring in. Each mess would vie with the rest to produce the finest decorations and transformations, and in truth it was sometimes impossible to believe that you were not in a Chinese heroin den, the cave of Aladdin or a main-line railway station.

For the energetic there was a riding school, a polo club and even what is now termed 'blood sports' in the shape of the Exodus Hunt, which met regularly and went out into the desert to chase the jackals that were out there in abundance. There were regular meetings of horse-racing at the station racecourse, presided over by the group captain commanding the RAF Regiment. Most sports were provided for, and the tennis courts and swimming pool were always popular. Lake Habbaniyah, which was only a mile or two from the station and used to be a staging post for BOAC flying-boats on their way to India, provided safe swimming, and there was a yacht club with several dinghies providing good racing for sailing enthusiasts. The 'Jewel in the Crown' was perhaps the command gardens, where exotic tropical trees, plants and flowers were attended by a whole army of Arab gardeners, whose system of irrigation was a marvel of ingenuity and consisted of a series of channels criss-crossing the gardens and dug out from the Euphrates river, which ran alongside the station. There was never any shortage of water, and the gardens were flooded once a week to keep the whole station green and verdant, and resplendent with bougainvillea and oleander blossom everywhere. The flooding also included the married-quarter gardens, which was all very nice but could be a little embarrassing, as we often took our beds into the garden to sleep in the hot-weather season and could wake up to find a foot of Euphrates water swirling round our beds.

Having played an energetic game of tennis, cooled off in the swimming pool and fallen off one of the polo ponies, I thought it time I got down to serious work. On 1 October I took over command of the fighter wing, which consisted of Nos 6 and 73 Squadrons. On my first flight I took a Venom and carried out a low-level reconnaissance of the surrounding desert, making note of the few useful pinpoints in the locality. In the afternoon I flew another sortie, going wider afield, and this time experiencing the unforgettable thrill of low flying over the desert. Contrary to expectations, this was never monotonous, and the ever-changing colours and contours were a joy to behold. I soon had my first experience of a desert exercise when we set up camp on the far side of Lake Habbaniyah and slept out under the myriad of bright stars before returning by launch the next day – a magical experience. I was now flying regular Venom sorties, alternating my flights with each of my two squadrons in turn. I would sometimes act as target for their interception exercises, or, flying high, would sweep down on a low-flying flight and try and 'bounce' them before they could reach their target. It was not long before the squadrons reached operational standard, but there was a marked difference in their performance, and one squadron was notably more efficient, with the benefit of a squadron commander who could get the best out of his pilots, my old friend Peter. However, at this point I reluctantly feel I ought to tell of a most unfortunate episode that did little towards that squadron's reputation. The junior flight commander on a night training exercise, his aircraft having gone unserviceable, asked me if he could borrow my own personal Venom RCH. I rather reluctantly agreed but was not unduly worried as I knew Mike was a dependable and reliable pilot. Alas, my confidence was unjustified, and within an hour my favourite aeroplane lay a pathetic twisted wreck on the runway where Mike Hobson had placed it with its wheels still tucked up inside its belly. There was no way that I could excuse Mike's lapse, and I had to report it to my station commander as a serious but untypical error of judgement by an otherwise reliable pilot. Poor Mike, it was a most unfortunate setback, coming just after he had returned to duty from attending his father's funeral in the UK.

CHAPTER TWENTY-FIVE

Six Venoms Down in the Desert

November 1954 to January 1955

As well as being the commander of the Venom wing I was also Wing Commander Flying at Habbaniyah, and had responsibility for all the flying at the base.

Habbaniyah was one of three bases built in Iraq under an Anglo-Iraq treaty in 1930. By the treaty Britain fully recognized the independence and sovereignty of Iraq, which in turn agreed that British troops should be based in the country in a peacekeeping role. Iraq at this time was suffering under uprisings of different factions and tribes, and we were able to contain these with the help of RAF aircraft. Thus Habbaniyah became a vital base to meet the uprisings of the Mullahs, particularly from over the North-West Frontier with Afghanistan. The base was made especially for the Royal Air Force, and was built on a desert site on a bend in the Euphrates, forty miles west of Baghdad. To the south was Lake Habbaniyah, a considerable size of freshwater lake, where Imperial Airways flying-boats used to land and refuel on their route to India in the 1930s. When I arrived at the base I discovered that there were no fewer than seven different units based there. Apart from the Flying Wing of three fighter squadrons and a Communication Squadron, there was a hospital, a ground-defence unit consisting of the RAF Regiment and Iraqi Levies. There was, of course, the usual ground support wings of Aircraft and Radio Servicing.

As well as flying the Venoms, I quite often made a point of flying the aircraft of the Communications Squadron into Baghdad and back, so whenever there was a flight required in either an Anson or the new Pembroke I took the opportunity to vary my flying in a useful way, as well as gaining flying experience on all aircraft types on the base.

Flying regularly over the desert and the considerable extent of the waters of Lake Habbaniyah, more than six square miles, I soon realized that the Desert Rescue Unit that was already in existence should be given regular training against the eventuality of an aircraft going down in the desert or in the lake. There was no chance of obtaining a proper air-sea rescue launch, so I had an existing launch fitted out with the necessary rescue gear, and an Iraqi boatman was trained to operate the craft from the yacht club where it was kept at readiness. A reference grid covering Lake Habbaniyah was devised so that any aircraft force-landing on the lake could be plotted accurately and thus the time for a rescue could be reduced as far possible. Overland the unit operated with special one-ton trucks fitted out with the necessary navigation and communication equipment. I was aware that my adjutant, Clive (Flt Lt Clive Leech), was already a very enthusiastic member of the team, and on the posting of the current leader I agreed to release him to take command of the unit. He was given the responsibility for bringing it up to a high level of readiness, and he undertook the task with his usual energy and enthusiasm, being perhaps a little over-eager to take his Austin one-ton trucks out into the desert for radio checks or other exercises when he might have been better employed as my adjutant. However, the usefulness of the unit and its efficiency was proved in a most dramatic way in the months ahead. To gain experience of their role I spent a day or two out with Clive, and we went north from Ramadi to Samara, a desert town with a glorious golden dome over its holy tomb, which provided an excellent landmark from the air visible for miles around. From here we crossed over the Euphrates by the ferry at Haditha, and returned to Habbaniyah via Hit, a very hot and dusty trip but full of interest.

On 20 October Pete Ellis arrived with Gp Capt Corkery, the new station commander, and there followed several welcoming parties at the various messes. Arthur Ryall, who commanded a considerable force of Iraq Levies (local Assyrian soldiers) on the station, was the first to welcome the group captain and his wife at the Levy mess at a guest night. The next day there were cocktails at Air House, followed by a ladies' guest night at the Station HQ mess. On the 23rd I took several officers into Bagdhad in the Pembroke to the trade fair, and on my return I was flying a Venom when, while I was doing simulated rocket attacks, the hood of the aircraft suddenly flew open. Although no damage was done, it was a noisy and uncomfortable depressurizing experience, not to be recommended. Exercise Consist the following day required me to move out onto the airfield and control the operation from my caravan. This was only a one-day-and-night exercise, and after moving back inside the perimeter fence, when all was packed away, I went to lunch with the station commander and his wife; that evening the pilots gathered in the Flying Wing mess for a Pimms party that went on until the small hours, but the next day being a Sunday, thankfully there was no flying.

In early November Ivor Broom brought six Canberras through on a reinforcement exercise, and while they were being refuelled I had a chat with Ivor about the aviation news from the UK. I was anxious to hear about the Comet disasters, and as Ivor had recently spoken to John Cunningham he was able to provide details of what had happened. For almost a year BOAC had operated its Comet fleet with outstanding success in the first-ever jet airliner operations in the history of aviation. The aircraft proved safe and reliable and had operated at a profit. But following the Comet take-off crashes, just two hours before the end of that first year, BOAC and de Havilland were dealt a succession of devastatingly cruel blows. On 2 May 1953, Comet G-ALYV broke up in very severe turbulence at cruising altitude when climbing through a cumulo-nimbus cloud after taking off from Calcutta, and six crew and thirty-seven passengers were killed. Eight months later, after another Comet had taken off from Rome en route for London, and had reached cruising altitude, a catastrophic explosion occurred and the wreckage fell into the sea a few miles south of Elba. Only a few months later another Comet 1, after taking off from Rome en route for Johannesburg, met with a very similar disaster, and at cruising altitude in clear air an explosion occurred, the aircraft disintegrated and crashed into the sea south of Naples. After the most painstaking investigation, during which three-quarters of the wreckage of the Comet was recovered from the sea-bed off Naples and reassembled at the RAE Farnborough, the cause of the disaster was narrowed down to a hairline crack in the corner of one of the square windows, caused by metal fatigue. All Comets were returned to Hatfield and their fuselages modified in accordance with the findings of the investigations regarding fatigue resistance of pressure cabins. From then on the Comet 1s had no further failures, and all the succeeding marks were most successful and would surely have led the way to worldwide jet airliner operations had it not been for these unfortunate tragedies. All modern airliners now have circular windows.

On 11 November, after Ivor had taken his Canberras on their way eastwards, the whole station was assembled for a Remembrance Parade on the padang behind Station Headquarters, and after the parade we enjoyed a holiday, but the next day Black Robbie (Sqn Ldr Roberts) and I took two Venoms down to Shaibah and then on to Bahrein. After landing we were taken out in a seaplane tender to visit the Royal Navy in HMS *Newfoundland*, where we were to discuss a forthcoming exercise. On our flight back to Habbaniyah we had to turn back due to low cloud at base, but after a couple of hours' delay we were able to proceed, though we had a long and rough descent through thunder clouds before emerging into the clear over the lake at a few hundred feet. Two days later I was again down the Gulf, landing at Shaibah and going on by road to Basra to visit HMS *Newfoundland*, then lying in the harbour. I had further discussions about the pending exercise, and after a small pink gin I flew the Venom back to Habbaniyah.

At this time I was persuaded to take over as president of the Country Club, and after organizing a few entertainments there I realized how much I was missing my family, and the married quarter business began to wrangle once more. I made up my mind to pursue the matter as soon as I had time. But at the moment I had to lead a formation of six Venoms down to Bahrein for Exercise Shop Window. We had a dawn take-off from Bahrein, and landed at the sand and oil airstrip at Sharjah, where the pilots were picked up by a coach and rushed to Dubai to catch a boat by the skin of our teeth that was taking the local Sheik and his guests out to HMS *Newfoundland*. Once we were all safely aboard, the Navy organized an exercise afloat, and after she had returned to her anchorage the Arab guests and the Royal Air Force were given lunch, the latter being plied with liberal pink gins beforehand. After further discussions in the afternoon we were invited to dine with the Admiral, and a very pleasant evening was enjoyed on board this powerful ship. The next day was spent in Dubai, and some of us went back aboard *Newfoundland* for further Navy hospitality. It was then time for the squadron to return, and the six Venoms left Sharjah early the next morning, landing back at Habbaniyah around teatime, having staged through Bahrein and Shaibah.

Before the approach of Christmas 1954 I did several low-level Venom exercises against desert targets such as Samara and Fort Ukedir, and again revelled in the thrill of low flying over long stretches of desert. Night-flying, too, was a wonderful experience, the air delightfully smooth, the myriad of bright stars above contrasting with the unbroken velvet blackness of the desert below. On this December night I remembered night-flying over the airfield and looking eastwards, seeing not a single light until the loom of Baghdad came into view some forty miles away. After that experience the events of the following days were even more unbelievable. I was working in my office, aware that both squadrons had several aircraft airborne, when the air traffic controller rang to say that they had received reports of a bank of fog approaching the airfield. I could hardly believe this information, as fog was almost unknown, and certainly not without any warning, but I ordered an immediate recall of all aircraft and rushed up to the control tower. Mike was leading four Venoms of 6 Squadron about ten minutes' flying time away, and was able to lead them in on a direct approach to the runway. Even so, he could see the fog already engulfing the far end of the runway as he touched down with his three aircraft behind him. Then two

Venoms of 73 Squadron managed to scrape in behind them, but now the fog had effectively closed the airfield. Two more of 73 Squadron's pilots managed to find a gap in the fog where they could see open desert, and managed to land their aircraft with minimum damage. But there still remained a section of four aircraft airborne above the now impenetrable fog without fuel enough to reach Baghdad or another diversion airfield. I was now faced with a very difficult decision, but there was now no alternative but for me to instruct the pilots to abandon their aircraft and save themselves. Air traffic vectored them to a clear area north of the airfield, where they carried out a most commendable and admirable operation and ejected together, still in formation. All landed safely in open desert not far north of the airfield, and Clive and his Desert Rescue Team came into their own. We had already scrambled the team, who lost no time in making for the area where they had been briefed to search. Four of the pilots were soon located all together, and the remaining two after another hour's search. Sufficient to say that Clive and his team did a marvellous job and fully justified the time we had spent training the team and for him to be absent from his office in Flying Wing from time to time. All the pilots were back at base by early morning of Christmas Eve, and the Yuletide festivities that followed were all the more joyful in the knowledge that the potentially dangerous situation had been handled so well and no one was hurt. The Christmas festivities started with cocktails in the medical officers' mess, and the next evening cocktails with the station commander's wife, followed by a Flying Wing mess party. There was a seven-a-side rugby match the next day with a Pimm's party at SHQ mess, and this was just the build-up to Christmas. From Christmas Eve onwards there was not a day without some celebration, and not a mess not offering some sort of party, from cocktails to a full-sized ball. At one party Simmo (Wg Cdr Simms), an engineer officer also separated from his family, and I sat in a corner and turned to discussing the vexed question of married quarters. Finally Simmo came up with the brilliant suggestion of investing in a caravan each. This seemed a pretty ambitious scheme, but as he was shortly going back to the UK for a few days we agreed that he should look at a few caravans and get an estimate of the cost and also what the shipping charges would be. We decided that we would go into the whole scheme on his return after Christmas. Which we did; and much to our surprise the costs turned out to be remarkably reasonable, and all we had to do was to get permission from the station commander to bring two caravans onto the camp. But therein lay the biggest problem. He was rather reluctant at first to even consider the question, but we were under the impression that he rather admired our enterprise and audacity in trying to beat the system, and as he was that sort of chap we went about trying to persuade him of the benefits, and promising that we would be prepared to let the station have the use of the caravans when we were eventually posted home. We thought that we had almost persuaded the station commander when the medical staff heard of the idea and came down most firmly against it on the grounds that in that climate caravans would be quite unsuitable accommodation in which to house families. However, Simmo and I were so determined to get our families out without further delay that we agreed to go ahead in the face of all the opposition, and started the New Year by ordering two caravans to be shipped out to Iraq as soon as possible.

On 1 January the Under-Secretary of State for Air visited, and the senior officers were invited to Air House for cocktails. The next day there was a race meeting at the Turf Club on the racecourse, where I acted as a steward, although I was not at all clear what my duties were. Luckily all the jockeys behaved, there were no enquiries and the races went off well with great excitement and enthusiasm.

A rumour had been rife for some time that Habbaniyah was to be handed over to the Iraqis. This had now been confirmed, and it seemed that there would now be little delay in achieving the transfer. A squadron from the Iraqi Air Force was now moved in and the RAF undertook to help the Iraqis with their operational training. They arrived initially equipped with Sea Furies, a large and quite difficult fighter to fly, but they quickly re-equipped with Vampires, and this made the cross training with my squadrons that much easier. The Iraqi pilots flew quite well individually but showed little aptitude for aggressive fighting operations, and their weak leadership seriously undermined their effectiveness. Even after many years their air force never seems to have overcome this deficiency, as was seen by its pathetic performance in the Gulf War following the invasion of Kuwait in later years, when their aircraft never appeared. In the weeks following the Iraq squadron's arrival, several senior officers of the Iraqi armed forces visited Habbaniyah, and flying demonstrations and lectures on air fighting and tactics were given for their benefit. On 13 January, Col Abadi, a senior officer of their air force, visited, and Venom formations were flown and a supply-dropping demonstration was carried out on the plateau airfield. In early February a special demonstration was laid on for the Iraqi Crown Prince, who was a member of our mess and a regular visitor, and he took a particular interest in the Iraqi fighter squadron and its training. It should be noted that all the Iraqi pilots were fully integrated in our fighter wing, and we all got on extremely well; and all their senior officers who visited from time to time were friendly and appreciative of our efforts. A few days later I had to fly down to Sharjah in a Venom to act as president of a district court martial.

This lasted for three days, and on my return Peter Ellis and I took two Venoms to Amman and Mafraq to look at the possibility of carrying out a squadron exercise from that airfield. It would be a real 'field' exercise as there were few facilities at Mafraq, and it was all sand with no runways. This was the biggest problem, as jet aircraft taking off threw up an impenetrable dust storm, making it impossible to make further take-offs or landings for several mimutes. However, this would represent realistically the problems of operating a tactical squadron in the desert. At the beginning of March I flew over to Amman and on to Mafraq, where a control caravan with the necessary radio communications, a mobile air traffic caravan and supporting technical facilities were being moved in. That evening the Venoms of No. 6 Squadron flew in from Habbaniyah, and for three days they flew on tactical and interception exercises from the desert airstrip with no outside support. The aircraft were untroubled by the dense clouds of sand and performed well, and while the conditions were difficult all the pilots coped well in meeting the demands of intensive operations from a desert strip, which is what the exercise was designed to prove. On the return flight to Habbaniyah, some of our Venoms were diverted to search for a missing Iraqi Air Force Vampire, of which, unfortunately, there was no sign.

CHAPTER TWENTY-SIX

Handing Over to Iraq

April to November 1955

On 2 April the whole station was on parade to celebrate the Royal Air Force Birthday Anniversary, with appropriate festivities taking place for the rest of the day. Coming shortly after this happy day, the week was sadly blighted by the death of one of No. 6 Squadron's young pilots who lost control of his Venom at high altitude, got into a spin and for some unexplained reason was still in his aircraft when it crashed out in the desert. He was newly married and his young wife was at Habbaniyah with him. Mike and I had the heartbreaking duty of trying to comfort her on breaking the sad news that he had been killed. Good Friday turned out to be a very happy day, when Eve and the family arrived on the plateau airfield in a Hastings of Transport Command after a pretty rough flight through thunderstorms and turbulence en route. She and the two children were initially accommodated in the transit mess, but it was wonderful to have them near at last and be able to share all the fun and games that the splendid station had to offer. On the 16th we were invited to Air House to meet the AOC and his wife, and as No. 73 Squadron was about to depart to Cyprus, several farewell parties were in train, culminating with Flying Wing's Spring Ball. On 2 May Royal Air Force Habbaniyah was handed over to the Iraqis with a formal parade and flypast by the departing squadron. Little did I think at the time what repercussions might be sparked off by this retreat of British forces from the midst of Arabia. It was hardly credible that within a few months of our going King Feisal and all his family, and our friend the Crown Prince, would have been murdered and the perfidious family of Saddam Hussein would later on be able to seize power in Iraq? And not more than a few weeks hence, Egypt's Col Nasser felt secure enough to seize control of the international waterway of the Suez Canal.

It was perhaps of little value to speculate on such possibilities, but in

163

the eternally volatile situation in the Middle East such eventualities were not inconceivable. It was the height of irony that after so many months of training with my Venom wing that one of my squadrons would be in action carrying out rocket and bomb attacks on Egyptian targets at Suez when I had only just relinquished command and was on my way back to the United Kingdom. It was particularly so as the family were travelling home by sea and we were almost trapped in the Canal. But that was in the future, and for the moment things carried on much the same, and relations with the Iraqis on the camp remained amicable.

On 5 May I was relieved to pass my annual medical, and on the same day was excited to hear that the caravans had arrived at the southern port of Basra and would be put on open trucks of the Iraqi railway for Baghdad. A day or two later, while doing a low-level reconnaissance down the Euphrates, I was able to intercept the Basra–Baghdad train, and there, low and behold, were two caravans on a low-loader truck ahead of the guard's van. I was tempted to escort them right into Baghdad freight yard, but resisted the temptation and hurried back to land at Habbaniyah and find Simmo to tell him the good news. Our excitement was far more than if we had been allocated an ordinary married quarter, and we couldn't wait to set our caravans up on the camp. The station commander had finally relented and agreed for a site to be provided for the caravans behind the officers' married quarters, and electricity and water supplies would be laid on for them. Once we had received notification that the caravans were available for collection, I flew into Baghdad, and Spud Spurdens (Sqn Ldr Spurdens, my operations officer) followed by desert road in a Jeep fitted with a suitable hook. The caravans had travelled well and were undamaged, apart from a broken window apparently caused by a stone thrown by urchins outside the yard. After a seven-hour tow our van reached its future home, and amid great excitement was positioned and connected up to its power supplies. We had erected a structure of reed mats overhead, and the caravans settled nicely in the shade under them. In no time the families moved in and were very comfortable and content. Before I could do much towards the move in, an urgent call was made to collect a patient from the K.3 Oil Station. I took off in the Pembroke with Earnie (Sqn Ldr Earnshaw), my air traffic controller, and a medico called Stewart, and set course for K.3, following the pipeline that was clearly visible from the air. The flight was uneventful and the patient was safely delivered to the Habbaniyah Hospital within two and a half hours of the call-out. The next day I took off in a Venom to watch the No. 6 Squadron flying team rehearsing an aerobatic programme that they would be demonstrating at various stages during a forthcoming flag-waving flight down to the Cape. I told Mike that I was very impressed with their formation aerobatics, but made sure that he didn't get too big-headed by reminding him that his show wasn't quite up to the stuff that in my day used to be done, when nine Furies were looped and rolled in formation and tied together from take-off to landing! Nevertheless, on 24 May, with justifiable pride, Mike took off with four Venoms for Amman, the first leg of Exercise Quick Return Six that would take them down to the Cape. With a supporting Valletta, they staged through Khartoum, Entebbe, Tanganyika, Pretoria and finally to Ysterplaat outside Cape Town. The squadron carried out a demonstration of formation aerobatics at most stops, both on the way down and on the return flight, and these were very well received and applauded on all occasions.

On 12 June, which was a Sunday, we were all gathered around the swimming pool when we were thrilled as Mike led his three Venoms in to land back at Habbaniyah after a most successful flag-waving exercise, which did a good deal towards enhancing the reputation of the Royal Air Force down the South African route.

On 5 October I collected a Pembroke from the maintenance hangar, and with Flt Lt Green and a rigger airman took off to give the aircraft an air test after its servicing. Up to then I had never had any problems with the Pembroke, and was taken by surprise when, directly after take-off, the aircraft began a severe pitching motion, which as the speed increased became quite violent. I guessed that I was exaggerating the pitching by over-controlling, so I reduced speed as much as I dared and made a conscious effort to anticipate the direction of pitch and use very small control movements. I called the tower and received permission for a priority landing, and at the same time told my passengers to look out and see if they could detect anything unusual that might affect the control surfaces. They could not, of course, see the tailplane, where I thought the trouble probably was, from the cabin, and I did not want to risk a low pass over the tower to find out if they could see anything from the ground. I decided to try and get the aircraft back on the runway as soon as possible, as I had managed to reduce the rate and extent of the pitching, and had established better control. I approached the runway with plenty of power on to give the maximum airflow over the tailplane, and with wheels and flaps down I did my best to judge the hold-off as the aircraft pitched up and, with a fair amount of luck, made a tolerable landing. After relaxing with relief at the end of the landing run, I taxied in, switched off the engines and stepped out and walked round to look at the tailplane, but as far as I could see all was normal. Then my rigger said, 'Come and look at this, sir.' The hinged leading edge of the port wing, below which the wiring and controls for the outer wing ran, had not been secured after inspection, and it had sprung open and was acting as an effective air brake, to cause considerable turbulence over the elevators and thus the instability and pitching and a few nasty moments in the air. Clearly some unfortunate rigger had to be severely dealt with.

A few days later there was a station parade, and Black Mac (Gp Capt MacDonald, the new station commander) insisted on taking the salute while on horseback. If he had only known how ridiculous he looked he would never have undertaken the bravado. He was no horseman, anyway, but at least he did not fall off until after the march-past. Perhaps it was in an attempt to redeem himself that he flew the senior officers and their wives into Baghdad to attend a Reception at the British Embassy. After the party, Mac and I and twenty-five passengers assembled at Baghdad airport and scrambled into the Valetta, each somehow having acquired a ripe melon or two. The flight back to Habbaniyah was a little erratic, with Black Mac flying the aircraft and myself as second pilot in the right-hand seat. Despite a rather apologetic warning from me that Mac's approach to the runway at Habbaniyah seemed both too high and too fast, he was oblivious, and the aircraft touched down well down the runway, so that it was only with a good deal of heavy braking that we managed to stop before its end. The near-hysteria inside the cabin was partly caused by the avalanche of ripe melons that were cascading down the central aisle, impelled by the deceleration, and bowling into the cockpit, where I was trying to field them and stop them from obstructing Mac's efforts to retain control of the aircraft. It wasn't his day or night!

The next day I took the Pembroke with seven passengers to Amman and on to Nicosia, and returned on the same day with Ben Boult and several others, ending with a night landing at Habbaniyah. A day or two later Clive persuaded me to take the Pembroke and try and rendezvous with him and his Desert Rescue Team out in the desert for an affiliation exercise. I did find him some miles south of Sulaymaniyah, and exchanged messages, and I dropped some urgent spares for one of his one-tonners.

The next day a call came in to air traffic that a Venom had forced-landed some forty miles out in the desert, so Spud and an engineer officer accompanied me in a Pembroke to try and locate the downed aircraft. We were soon able to spot it, and after a low flypast or two to examine the adjoining terrain we landed on the sand alongside the Venom. After assessing the help that would be required to get the aircraft airborne again, we took off for a return to Habbaniyah. I did two more flights out to the grounded Venom, landing on the desert strip alongside and off-loading some engine fitters. On the second trip I took Peter with me, and he then flew out the restored Venom and I took the remaining personnel off in the Pembroke and returned them to Habbaniyah. The next day I flew Arthur Ryall to Mosul via Baghdad and returned in time for a guest night in Flying Wing's mess. On 4 July I flew Eve and family in a Valetta to Amman for a few days' leave. We stayed in Mike and Barbara's flat there, which was fine except that water was only available in the middle of the night, when one had to rush to the tank and collect it. One day we took a taxi out to Jerash, a Roman town whose remains still held the magic of their ancient civilization. We spent half the day among its crumbling buildings and aged stones. On our return to Habbaniyah we were sorry to have to say goodbye to our good friends, Ben and Peggy (Boult), who were off to Akrotiri in Cyprus.

On the flying side our original Venom 4s were now being replaced by the new, more powerful Venom FB20, which had power controls and was consequently far more manoeuvrable and pleasant to fly. On 20 July I had my first flight in the FB20, and was duly impressed. The next day Mike flew me in the Meteor 7 for my instrument rating test, and I coerced him into awarding me a Master Green, a rating that I managed to retain until the end of my flying days. We both celebrated in the Flying Wing mess that evening. And I went well content to bed. The next day great interest was shown when the first of the 'V' bombers, the Valiant, came in. Regrettably this type ran into early structural problems and was never a success as were the Vulcan and Victor bombers. In August I took the opportunity to have an instructor check me out on the Valetta so that I could carry out some flights to Amman and Baghdad in a bigger aircraft that could carry more passengers. At the end of August I took a two-week break to take the family for a holiday in Cyprus. We went aboard a civil Viking, 'Lord Rodney', flown by Capt Benson, and landed at Nicosia, where we hired a taxi out to Karenia and booked into the Dome Hotel. Our arrival in Cyprus coincided with the start of four years of guerrilla warfare against the British Administration. Since 1925 Cyprus had been a British Crown Colony, but now the Greek Cypriots were demanding union with Greece (Enosis), spurred on by the tyrant priest Makarios and the leader of the terrorists, Grivas. We were in Cyprus again in 1959, when I would be involved in the future political shaping of the island, but for now the situation was comparatively quiet and we were able to enjoy walking through the beautiful mountains of Karenia and swimming from its superb beaches. We returned to Habbaniyah in a Pembroke on 9 September 1955. The following week it was Battle of Britain Day, and the wing flew a large formation of Venoms and Vampires over Baghdad before returning to fly the whole formation over the airfield to salute the ground crews who had worked so hard to get the maximum number of aircraft serviceable for the occasion. After landing there was a cocktail party in the Flying Wing mess with a toast to 'The Few'.

October saw several more Venom flights, including a reconnaissance of the Golden Dome at Samarkand, which was to be the location to make contact with Clive and the Desert Rescue Team. The next day I took the Pembroke out to rendezvous with them and drop some urgent vehicle spares. After a Meteor sortie a few days later to practice aerobatics and a bad-weather approach, Earnie and I set off in the Pembroke to search for a lost hunting party, who eventually turned up having found themselves trapped on the wrong side of the Euphrates. A wide error of navigation! They were Army!

There was a long-weekend holiday at the beginning of the month, when a gymkhana was held on the padang with jumping and tent-pegging competitions, and a parade of some fifty horses of various shapes, colours and sizes, but all Arabs. The star was the all-black Arab stallion Midnight, a truly splendid animal, very fast, a great jumper and yet of the gentlest disposition. At the beginning of November I took Earnie up in the Meteor to do a series of trials of the air traffic equipment and training for the controllers. On 3 November, in the middle of a rugby game versus Kuwait, Sir Claude Pelly arrived with Digger Aitkin (an old wartime colleague), and they were duly entertained in the Club. After several very happy and comfortable months in the caravan, the family were allocated a married quarter in Palm Grove. Happily we were able to sell our caravan to another family, who were very grateful, and it continued to rest in its shady corner among the palm trees, with the doves cooing over it and surrounded as always by the sounds of the cicadas and bullfrogs. But it was a joy to be settled in our tropical-bungalow-like quarter, particularly as we were expecting the birth of our third child within a few weeks.

CHAPTER TWENTY-SEVEN

A Visit from King Faisal

December 1955

In early December No. 6 Squadron returned from its annual armament practice camp in Cyprus, and Venom training flights continued. Pre-Christmas jollifications got into their stride with cocktails with the AOC and drinks at the Air Headquarters mess, followed by a party at the Club with the habitual game of roulette. Apart from all the happy Christmas celebrations our break was taken up with settling into the married quarter and exchanging visits with other friends on the 'patch'.

On the second day of the New Year the aircrews went out to the Army exercise ranges, and were taken for a ride in Centurion tanks to experience a battle tank in action. After that experience there was not one of us who would have swapped our Venom for a Centurion in which to go to war. Later I flew a Pembroke into Baghdad with four large, well-muscled passengers who were required, after landing at the airfield, to lift and manoeuvre an upright piano into the Pembroke. It was a tight fit, and I seem to remember that we had to fly back with the rear door slightly open. The next night the piano came into use at a Vamps and Tramps Ball in the Club. Three days later a crowd of our aircrews were invited by Brigadier Ismail to an excellent 'koosie' at his home in the nearby village of Ramadie. Our parties with the Iraqis were always interesting and enjoyable, but inhibited a little, as, being Muslim, very few of our hosts would drink alcohol, and their visitors felt a little embarrassed in accepting the gins and whiskies which were invariably offered. On the last day of January the CAS Dermot-Boyle visited and had lunch with the AOC, and we all met him at cocktails in the evening The next day I flew the CAS and AOC to Baghdad in the Pembroke.

In February I did two Venom low-level strike exercises, one on Sharaban and another on Ukidir, and a low-level reconnaissance of Ba Quaba and Jaiuala. A flight to Baghdad and Kirkuk ended back at

Habbaniyah in a dust storm, and as always, Earnie helped me in to land in very poor visibility with an immaculate QGH, which was as good as any radar talk-down. We were still awaiting our talk-down radar equipment. Early in March I had to take a Pembroke down to H.3 with a doctor to pick up an airman patient who had been accidentally shot and see him safely delivered to the Habbaniyah hospital, where he was soon comfortably settled. In the same month I took off in a Venom to do a low-level navigation exercise over the desert at night. This flight brought all the magical experiences of the desert, together with the thrill of high-speed flight at low level, with the desert lit only by the canopy of stars. A memorable flight ending only when almost empty fuel tanks bought me back to a reluctant landing at my base. On the 13th, Brig Hayes asked to be taken on a reconnaissance up the river to search for a launch party that had set off up the Euphrates earlier in the day. We went off in the Anson, but despite covering some fifty miles saw nothing of them. They were found later, embarrassed but safe.

On 10 March I was very pleased to meet Percy Gick again (Admiral Sir Percy Gick), who called in with Sir William Dixon, and we spent a happy hour at the bar talking over old days together in Hong Kong, when we used to take a couple of naval Corsairs from Kai Tak and go chasing Chinese pirate junks over the China Seas. Later I took him in the Pembroke to Baghdad, where we picked up the Air Marshal and flew him to Nicosia. I returned with my navigator to Habbaniyah later that night. On 12 March Lord and Lady Mountbatten staged through Habbaniyah, and in the absence of the station commander Eve and I had the interesting experience of dining with them in the Club, just the four of us. We had very interesting talks with our guests, but they ate very little of the steaks we offered, and were clearly tired and grateful for an early night. They flew on the next day, and later I received a very nice personal letter of thanks from Earl Mountbatten. During the following week the Iraqis held Exercise Nisir at El Rashid, and I flew the AOC and SASO in the Anson to view the flying programme.

The next day I flew AVM Boyce to El Rashid for the same purpose, and at the end of the exercise I flew them all back in the Iraqi Air Force Dove to Habbaniyah. Afterwards a series of farewell parties culminated on the last day of the month, when many friends of Mike and Barbara assembled to say farewell to this popular couple on their return to UK on Mike's promotion. They took off in a Dan Air York and arrived back home on their fifth wedding anniversary.

On 2 April, Easter Monday, we had organized a regatta on the lake, and also a gymkhana on the padang, followed by a dinner dance in the evening at the Club. A few days later, on 5 April, King Faisal, accompanied by the British Ambassador, flew into Habbaniyah to perform the opening of the Ramadi Barrage. This was a project to build a waterway with controlling sluices to divert some of the flow of the Euphrates waters into Lake Habbaniyah when the flood waters came down from the melting snows up in the mountains of its source, in Turkey. Many guests were invited to the ceremony, and were accommodated in a huge and magnificent royal Arab tent, resplendent with gold hangings and liberally carpeted with Turkish rugs underfoot. After the ceremony everyone moved to the lawns of Air House, where a sumptuous 'koosie' was laid out for all to enjoy, but the special delicacy of the feast, the sheep's eyes, naturally enough, and thankfully, were kept for our Arab guests.

The next day I took the Anson into Baghdad and returned to Habbaniyah with Sir David Wright, the Ambassador, and Brig Shaw. The occasion was the ceremonial departure of No. 6 Squadron, Royal Air Force. The squadron's Venoms were lined up on the tarmac with a pilot in front of each. Peter Ellis took the Ambassador with several senior Iraqi officers down the line, introducing each pilot in turn, and then they returned and took up their respective positions on or behind the saluting dais. On a signal from Peter the pilots climbed aboard their aircraft, and at another signal twelve Coffman starters belched out their black smoke and twelve Ghost jet engines screamed into life, scorching with their jet flames the asbestos mats draped over the tailplanes of each aircraft, placed there to prevent the tailplanes themselves being scorched. Peter led his snake of Venoms out to the runway and they took off in fours. As they flew by, the reviewing officers saluted their final passing, the Iraqis politely, but inwardly, no doubt, with the sentiment of 'good riddance!'

On 12 April Black MacDonald threw a cocktail party on his imminent posting home, and the next day I took over command of Royal Air Force Habbaniyah. On the last day of the month the station moved into summer working routine, khaki dress was donned and Hughie Edwards (Gp Capt Hugh Edwards VC, the new station commander) arrived, in blue uniform.

It was unfortunate timing that the AOC's Inspection was due on the day after Hughie arrived, as I had rehearsed the parade and he had not been involved in any of it, but for some reason the AOC sent a message from Cyprus that Edwards was to take the parade. It turned out to be quite impracticable, so that on the arrival of the AOC I was on the parade ground in charge of the parade and Gp Capt Edwards met him as he descended from his aircraft. He gave Hughie one look and said, 'I expected you to take the parade', and without another word turned round, re-entered the aircraft and told his pilot to take him back to Cyprus. Needless to say, the two of us were dumbfounded, and furious that the AOC had left some 500 airmen expectantly lined up on the parade ground. We were both even more astounded the next day when a signal from Air Headquarters was received ordering us both to report to the AOC in Cyprus at once. We both agreed that the situation was ridiculous, and Hughie said that he was not going but it was up to me whether I went or not. I, of course, supported Hughie, so neither of us went to answer the summons to Command Headquarters, and nothing further was ever heard of the extraordinary event. I had the greatest admiration for Hughie Edwards, who was the kindest and most considerate of men with none of the prejudices of the average Aussie. His courage was of lion proportions, evidenced by the award of the Victoria Cross for his Blenheim operations in the war. I did not meet Clayton Boyce, the AOC, again until years later, when he turned out to be my boss in the Ministry of Aviation, and then he could not have been a more pleasant officer with whom to serve, and he never mentioned the Habbaniyah affair. Perhaps he did not even remember it!

CHAPTER TWENTY-EIGHT

The End of my Tour in Iraq

June 1956

With the departure of No. 6 Squadron, Habbaniyah had no operational role, and became a staging post on the Far East Reinforcement route. However, I still retained my Venom and there were Meteors in the Communications Squadron, as well as the passenger aircraft, so I was never short of something interesting to fly to keep in flying practice. On 11 May I took a Meteor down to Karbala to meet the Desert Rescue Team, and on the 13th I took several officers, including Hughie, in the Iraqi Dove to El Rashid for Iraqi Air Day. On the 24th I did a night reconnaissance exercise in the Vampire T.11, and shared again the wonder and thrill of night-flying over the desert, this time with Flt Lt Pemberton in the right-hand seat. June was a memorable month because our second son was born on the 8th, in the Habbaniyah Royal Air Force Hospital.

As he grew up, Robert had no great aspirations to fly like his dad, and I certainly did not encourage him in that direction. After qualifying as a quantity surveyor he practised for a short time in Sydney, and on returning to England he joined the British Steel Round the World Yacht Race, which he completed despite their yacht being dismasted in the Southern Ocean. Before departing on the last leg of the race from Cape Town, by the greatest good fortune Robert met the lovely Andrea, step-daughter of Pat Quinn, another member of the yacht's crew, and they were later married in London, where they have now settled with their three delightful daughters.

On 15 June I was left once more in charge at Habbaniyah when Hughie left for the UK for the VC Commemoration Ceremony. On the 20th there was a great gathering around the swimming pool when a swimming gala was organized, which caused great excitement for the youngsters, as this was the first time that they had been encouraged to take part in the races and diving competitions. In the meantime, out on the airfield, feverish work was going on to complete the fitting out of the ground radar equipment in the air traffic tower. Once completed and the ground radar at last in place, I was kept busy flying Meteor sorties to calibrate the equipment.

During the first week of July I did several trips into Baghdad, and on returning from the last, while practising a single-engine landing, the failed engine's propeller would not unfeather, so I was committed to landing with only one engine working. This presented no problem as the Pembroke had a very good single-engine performance, which I regularly practised. The next day after the ground engineers had worked on the propeller I air-tested the aircraft and had no further trouble, and I took it into Baghdad that night to collect Lady Slim (wife of General Slim who led the revitalized Fourteenth Army to defeat the Japanese in Burma). She came to dinner with us that evening and was accommodated in the VIP quarters for the night before flying on to Britain the next day.

On the 19th I took a Pembroke into Baghdad and picked up AVM Stephenson and flew him to Amman. The last time that we had met was when the AVM was commandant of the Staff College and I received a reproof from him for beating up the mess in a Spitfire at Andover. Happily the subject was not raised on this occasion. The following week I went off in the Pembroke with Wg Cdr Beer, the senior engineer at Habb, and a keen ornithologist, and flew down to Lake Kerbala to photograph the birds. The lake is the favourite breeding ground for the Arabian Flamingos, and that day we saw and filmed thousands of the birds, both in the shallows of the lake and also in the air, where they formed a huge pink cloud against the blue of the sky. On our return flight, following the Euphrates northwards, we flew over the amazing remains of Ctesiphon, an ancient palace no great distance from the ruins of Babylon. It still contains a remarkable arch some 130 feet high, built of brick with no supporting pillars. It must surely be one of the highest arches of its kind anywhere, and it makes a most wonderful landmark soaring into the sky from the desert floor. It deservedly took up all our remaining film before we returned to land back at Habbaniyah. On the last day of the month I had to act as president of a district court martial on the RAF Base at Mafraq, so I took a Meteor to Amman and got a staff car to take me to Mafraq.

In the middle of August I was due for some leave and arranged for the family to have a few days up at Sersing in a hotel in the foothills of Northern Iraq not far from the King's Summer Palace. I flew them up in a Pembroke to Mosul, and while Hughie flew the Pembroke back to Habbaniyah the family took a taxi to Sersing, where the British Vice-Consul, John Burgess, kindly took us to our hotel in his official car.

The hotel was rather basic but quite pleasant, with a refreshing, babbling stream running through the gardens, but the cool weather that we had been promised did not materialize and the weather continued stiflingly hot. However, the environment was relaxing and the change helped us enjoy the break At the end of our stay, when we came to leave, John Burgess kindly drove us to Mosul to catch a train back to Baghdad, and I had the opportunity to repay his kindness a few days later.

At the beginning of September Peter Casement came through flying a Shackleton, and stayed to supper. I had last seen Peter when we were on the Planning staff together at the Air Ministry, and our families used to get together for Sunday lunch from time to time. Peter was a well-decorated officer who had sunk more than one German U-boat during his wartime tour in Coastal Command.

When I wrote to the Vice-Consul in Mosul to thank him for his help on our holiday, he asked me if I could help in getting his shot-gun and his new puppy-dog up to Mosul. I was mystified how they had turned up at Habbaniyah, but there they were, through the Diplomatic Bag perhaps? But I was only too pleased to repay his kindness up at Sersing, and flew the gun and 'Peter the Pointer' up to Mosul on a reconnaissance flight, and handed them over to John Burgess at the airport, where his thanks were almost entirely stifled by his little dog's delighted welcome.

The King of Iraq was a keen sailor and sometimes used to come to Habbaniyah to sail on the lake. His Dragon-class yacht and a Chris-Craft high-speed launch were kept at our yacht club and were maintained by Chris Rothshjaers, the skipper of the royal yacht, which was berthed at Basra and rarely left port. On one occasion Chris invited several of the officers and their families to a moonlight picnic on the launch. It turned out to be a most beautiful night and a memorable occasion under a sky full of stars reflected in the lake, calm and still under a breathless tropical night. Again I felt the appeal of this compelling country, but my pleasant reverie was soon cut short by the news of the arrival of Jock Cassels, who was to take over from me in a few days' time, at the end of my tour in Iraq.

The day Peter Casement came back through with his Shackleton, we heard the news of the Vulcan crash at London Heathrow. This was a tragic accident that should never have happened, and was brought about by over-confidence and bad judgement. Sir Harry Broadhurst and Sqn Ldr Howard, who had demonstrated the Vulcan 'V' bomber very successfully on a world tour, had arrived back in the UK planning a grand touch-down at Heathrow, no doubt to impress the waiting reception. The weather was bad and below safety limits for the Vulcan, and although several diversion airfields were open with better weather conditions, the decision was made to try a landing at Heathrow. One attempt was made, but the landing was aborted, and on the second attempt the aircraft hit the ground hard, causing severe damage to the machine, but an attempt was made to take off again After gaining a little height, the air marshal and Howard ejected, but the three crew members who had no ejector seats or time to get out were killed. All the favourable impressions that had been created on the tour round the world were erased in a flash by the impact of this tragedy.

Before my final departure from Habbaniyah, I was determined to experience again the fascination and appeal of the desert, so while poor Eve got on with the packing I set off with the Desert Rescue Team on a protracted exercise. I drove one of the one-ton trucks, and we set off north to Samara, Tikrit and Kirkuk, and thence to the most northern Iraqi town of Sulaymaniyah, where we were found by the Habbaniyah Pembroke and were glad to receive the supplies dropped from the aircraft. The next day we soldiered on to Jahula Ba Quaba and various small villages for another night stop out in the desert. As we sat around the camp fire relishing the calm beauty of the night, one of our party came dancing back into the light of the fire in his bare feet and advised us all that if we ventured out we should be sure to wear boots, as all the ground around the whole camp was swarming with scorpions, no doubt attracted by the firelight. The one-tonners of the team finally drew in at Fallujah Bridge, very hot and dusty, to finish up our rations, and my most vivid memory of that desert sortie was the sheer pleasure of finishing off a large tin of whole peaches, to ease my parched throat. Nectar of the Gods!

CHAPTER TWENTY-NINE

Home by Sea

November 1956

On my return to Habbaniyah I was able to find time to do another flight in a Meteor 8 on an air test after inspection ready for its allocation away to Cyprus. I also had time to sail in the regatta on the lake, and won the Battle of Britain Cup in the sailing race for dinghies in the Firefly that I had rebuilt. The racing was followed by a Regatta Dance in the Yacht Club, with the presentation of the winning cups.

On 17 October we gave our own farewell party of cocktails and small eats, and afterwards Hughie kindly invited us for dinner. He had been a splendid CO and always shown the greatest kindness to us, and I was glad and honoured that he had asked me if I would teach him to sail. We subsequently spent several hilarious hours on the lake gibing and changing tacks, invariably ending up with Hughie diving overboard and swimming ashore. After I left the service we were delighted to hear that he had been appointed as High Commissioner to Western Australia. He could be nothing less than a wonderful influence on his fellow Aussies out there.

The night following Hughie's most enjoyable dinner we were dined out in the NCOs' mess. The following day I flew the family and all our luggage to Baghdad in the Pembroke, and while Hughie flew it back to Habbaniyah the family boarded the night train to Basra Margil. Thus ended a most happy, interesting and rewarding posting, and we began an epic journey home.

As the train began to slow down on its approach to Basra we were woken up in our comfortable sleeper to see the sun rise over the Eastern Desert in a huge ball of red fire: an unforgettable symbol of our desert experience, although perhaps a sunset might have been more appropriate to our leaving. It had always been a happy perk if one could travel by troopship to or from overseas postings, and as we had not achieved this before I made strenuous efforts to get permission for us to return to UK by sea. Little did I know what I was letting us in for! After some efforts I was told that troopships were no longer sailing, but it was reluctantly agreed that we could go by a merchantman. So it was that we found ourselves at Basra preparing to catch a German heavy-lift ship bound for Rotterdam. At Basra our good friends Chris and Sheila Rothshjaers met us and were kind enough to have us in their house on the edge of town for the two days that we were waiting for the ship. We went shopping down town, and Chris took us to look round the Port Marine Dockyard. In a surprise visit he took us aboard the royal yacht, *Queen Aliya*. We were allowed to peep into the King's sleeping cabin and see the royal bed with his crest over the bedhead. On 24 October, the day of our planned departure, Sheila woke us with the news that there was a smallpox epidemic in the town, and we had to be smuggled out to the port through the back streets, so that we could catch a launch to take us down the Gulf to our ship lying in the Shat El Arab, where she was taking on her load of dates. The ship was the MV *Birkenfels*, a German vessel registered in Hamburg, with huge derricks, which were clearly not required for the dates, but we understood that she had lifted a locomotive aboard on her previous trip. We started down towards the Gulf past the flaming refineries of Abadan and entered the Persian Gulf on 25 October. The whole family were now very excited at the prospect of a leisurely cruise home and of going through the Suez Canal in a few days.

The coast that we were passing down our starboard side was familiar to me as I had flown over it many times, but it was all very exciting for the family. It was not long before we had turned west and were sailing along the southern coast of Arabia, and then with Aden on our starboard side we entered the Red Sea. As we basked in the sun lying on the after-deck contemplating the prospect of that leisurely cruise through the Mediterranean, we were astonished when the ship's First Officer rushed up to us shouting, 'It is war, it is war!' with typical Germanic enthusiasm. Having been deprived of English papers for a week we had not the faintest idea what he was on about. He gradually got us to understand that Egypt's Nasser had seized control of the Suez Canal, and that France, and Britain apparently, had moved against Egypt in support of Israel, whose forces were already advancing on the canal itself. Targets had been attacked in the Canal Zone, and supporting troops were following up. We could not believe that this crisis had developed so swiftly, and it took some time for the news to sink in, but when, after a day of dead-slow steaming up the Red Sea, a French frigate ordered our ship to turn back, we realized that there was a strong risk that we might be caught in the débâcle ourselves. Our ship turned about and later that morning entered the port at Aden on 8 November, presumably for the captain to seek guidance from the ship's owners as to what action he should take.

The Egyptians in a fit of spite had now sunk several ships in the narrows of the canal, effectively blocking it, and so it was soon decided that our ship would continue to Holland (its original destination), but would be routed round the African Cape. Rather than two weeks at sea the prospect now loomed of something more like eight weeks on board. Had it only been the two of us we would not have been too concerned, but with three young children, the baby only five months old, the prospects were truly worrying. The decision having been made, and the ship committed to the long haul round the Cape, we could at least take some action to ease our journey. I rushed ashore and found the Services NAAFI in Aden and filled a sack with all the tins of baby food I could lay my hands on. I found another sack and filled that with many other baby needs, small toys for the others, and books and papers for us. I had only been back aboard for a few minutes when the ship sailed again, having planned to take on oil and rations at Cape Town.

The ship was quite comfortable, with four reasonable cabins, and the food was adequate, but the all-German crew did not include a doctor or, as far as we knew, anyone with medical training. We hoped and prayed that the children would remain healthy over the following weeks. I had brought copies of the national newspapers aboard at Aden, and we eagerly scanned the latest news of the 'war' in Egypt. According to the papers Egypt had been secretly rearming, and in league with Jordan and Syria was planning to surround Israel. When news of this plan leaked out, Israel, in retaliation, carried out a pre-emptive strike at Egypt from Sinai and was quickly only a few miles from the Canal. Britain and France called on the warring sides to withdraw, and volunteered a temporary occupation of the Canal Zone. Egypt refused, and much against the American and USSR's approval, Britain and France set in train an invasion of Egypt. The Egyptians responded at once by seizing the Canal, and they later closed it altogether by sinking ships in the narrows. Diplomatic action from USA and USSR and the Arab states was so strong that the British and French had to withdraw from Egypt, but the Canal was blocked and was not opened to shipping again for several years, and condemnation of the impulsive British action was widespread. There were even allegations of collusion, and the whole incident was considered a disgrace. What was particularly ironic for me at the time was that, after all the training with my Venom wing in Iraq, Peter Ellis and his boys were now engaged in live attacks on Egyptian targets from Cyprus only a few weeks after Peter and I had been planning tactics for the squadron together. The squadron was now on active service only a few nautical miles away from where our ship had been turned back south of Suez.

But now we had to make the best of our predicament and keep the children happy, healthy and content. In an effort to maintain their interest – and mine, come to that – I had brought an atlas from Aden, and with the help of this I had produced a large-scale chart of the whole of our projected route, Basra to Rotterdam. Every day I would make a plot of our position so that we could all see the rate of our progress. It must be admitted that it was painfully slow, and I began to worry that I might not arrive back in the UK to take up my next appointment. We crossed the Equator going south on 12 November, and on a chilly, misty morning, we arrived at Cape Town, and with great excitement looked forward to seeing the town and Table Mountain when the mist cleared. But, alas, we were not allowed ashore, and after taking on fuel and stores *Birkenfels* made her way through the several troopships, including *Staffordshire* and *Stirling Castle*, which were entering or leaving harbour, and turned north for the long tedious haul up the length of the South Atlantic. We recrossed the Equator going north on 1 December, and in fine, sunny weather passed the most westerly point of Africa. When the Canary Isles fell astern we were glad to realize that we would soon regain our original intended route which would have taken us through the Mediterranean and be in home waters. The weather remained good except for a brief spell of rougher seas through the Bay of Biscay, and we passed Dover at dawn on a beautiful clear morning, but arrived off the Hook of Holland in a quite violent storm, and the final leg up to Rotterdam was tricky, accompanied by thunder, lightning, torrential rain and a blustery wind. We were soon ashore, and with our luggage were taxied through Rotterdam, gay with Christmas decorations, and down to the Hook of Holland, where we boarded the ferry *Arnhem*, which would take us finally to Harwich.

The last leg of the journey was very rough and noisy, but we arrived thankfully at Harwich soon after dawn, and the Customs officials there took pity on this exhausted-looking family, so that we were soon on the train to Liverpool Street. And suddenly the realization that we were home at last came over us and we were overcome with thankfulness and joy, made all the more so by the sight of a full English breakfast served in the restaurant car: eggs, bacon, sausage, fried bread, the lot. We claimed it as the best meal that we had had since leaving home all those months ago.

The date of our arrival at London was 14 December, the very day that I had estimated for our arrival when starting my plotting at Aden in that school atlas. I lost no time in reporting to the Air Ministry to hear about my next posting, and by an extraordinary chance I met Peter Ellis on the Ministry steps, also looking for a job. We had a quick coffee together in the canteen, but I could not wait to hear confirmation of my appointment. I felt myself most fortunate when 'P' Staff told me that I should lose no time in travelling up to Edinburgh to take over command of Royal Air Force Turnhouse, near Edinburgh. So on 19 December 1956 I took the *Flying Scotsman* to Scotland, where I was met at Caledonia Station by a staff car and found myself at Turnhouse, usefully employed in counting money from the Christmas draw in the officers' mess the night I arrived. After all the rush and anxiety I had suffered in getting there on time, I was a bit put out when Archie Winskill said he was surprised to see me before Christmas, and seemed in no hurry to hand over command. However, I was delighted to find Mike Hobson was at Turnhouse commanding No. 603 Auxiliary Squadron, and I lost no time in renewing old friendships when I was invited to dine with Mike and Barbara in their married quarter the following night.

Once again Pat and Miles had hastened to help us, and had taken the family into their home in Nottingham before my family could come north to join me in Scotland. As I was not apparently expected to take over my command at once I was able to travel south again and spend Christmas with the family. After the débâcle of our married quarter in Habbaniyah it was a pleasant contrast this time for us to be able to move without delay into the station commander's residence at Turnhouse. Almond House on the little Almond Beck was a huge Type One married quarter, and on 1 January 1957 Eve drove up north with the children in our new Morris Traveller, and we moved in and were soon unpacking and rattling around in the unaccustomed space. As soon as I had taken over command from Archie I settled into my office and gloried in the feeling of having my first station and, looking out of the window, realizing that all I could see was mine to command.

Firstly there was Mike with his 603 Squadron with Vampires, the Auxiliary Squadron of the City of Edinburgh. Across the country there was No. 602 City of Glasgow Squadron, which together with 603 formed a Vampire fighter wing over which I was nominally in command. There was a University Air Squadron with Chipmunks, an Air Experience Flight and a Communications Squadron – all my responsibility and providing a source of flying machines to keep me in flying practice. Turnhouse was also the civil airport for Edinburgh, and BEA operated two Viscount flights each day to London and return, and also civil flights within Scotland and to and from Ireland. Air Traffic Control and Safety Services were mostly manned by RAF personnel, and the civil air terminal and restaurant were civil controlled under a civilian manager.

To familiarize myself with the local area and the approaches to the airfield I borrowed a Vampire and did an hour's local flight, ending with two radar approaches to the main runway. The secondary runway was short, with bad approaches and invariably across the prevailing wind. My next duty was to go across on the Firth of Forth ferry and pay my respects to the Flag Officer, Scotland, the General Officer Commanding the troops in Scotland and the Senior Royal Air Force Officer in Scotland, all of whom had their headquarters on the north side of the Firth of Forth. As a result, and remembering that there was no bridge across the Firth at this time, Eve and I were often asked to stand in for the senior officers at high-level functions in Edinburgh, a duty that we invariably enjoyed, especially the rugby at Murrayfield where I was given a box seat for every international game! My next duty was to visit the Edinburgh City Chambers, where the Lord Provost kindly invited me to luncheon.

On 9 January I flew a Vampire across to Abbotsinch to visit the CO of No. 602 Squadron, Don Bartman, and the next day flew a Meteor 8 down to Ouston to call on my AOC. I was delighted to meet Spud Spurdens, who had been my operations officer in Iraq and was now on the group staff there.

On the 10th a station parade was held at which I had to announce that all auxiliary squadrons were to be disbanded in two months' time. This news was greeted with utter dismay, and my thoughts went back to No. 600 Auxiliary Squadron with whom I served in the Battle of Britain, and I remembered the great debt that we, as a nation, owed to those few 'weekend' pilots who fought and many died in the desperate air battles at that time. How short the memory, how deplorable the reward!

I soon discovered that Turnhouse was the gateway into Scotland, and I spent a great deal of time meeting and greeting important visitors flying in on visits. Within a week I had shaken hands with General Murray, Mr Kuppinger, the United States Consul, Chief Superintendent Fleming of the Scottish Police and the Duke of Edinburgh, flying his own de Havilland Dove. On another flight in a Vampire I landed at Acklington to call on Ben Boult, who was posted in to command the station from Cyprus. On the 27th I acted as ADC to Air Commodore the Duke of Hamilton, who took the salute at the farewell parade of No. 602 Squadron in Glasgow on its disbandment. After this melancholy and stirring march-past with the bagpipes wailing the lament, I picked up Eve and we drove back to Edinburgh and arrived in time to watch the international rugby match at Murrayfield.

On the 18th the Queen's Colour of No. 603 Squadron was laid up in St Giles's Cathedral with due reverence and solemnity, marking the end of this very distinguished squadron's history.

After some investigations I was pleased to discover that there was a

Hunter established for the use of the sector commander, who very seldom visited the station. The aircraft was kept at Leuchars, so I asked if it could be established at Turnhouse, where I would take on responsibility for its servicing and, incidentally, keep it in flying trim. The sector commander agreed provided I went across to the Hunter squadron at Leuchars for a full course of flying training on the type. So on almost every day for a week I flew over to Leuchars in the Chipmunk and flew the Hunter, Exercises 1 to 10, as a pilot of the squadron under the eye of the squadron commander. Finally I took control of a personal Hunter 4, fully competent in aerobatics, instrument flying, bad-weather approaches and landings. It was a special thrill when I looked out of my office window to see the Hunter lined up outside the hangar with my other steeds, and I often flew it from Turnhouse.

On 11 March the Spitfire that stood in the garden outside the gate of RAF Turnhouse was officially dedicated to those members of No. 603 Squadron who had been killed in the war; and there it still stands, a proud testimony to the brave, to be seen by all who drive by and hopefully remember in gratitude. Two days beforehand there was a farewell dinner held in the officers' mess at Turnhouse to mark the end of the auxiliary squadrons. As might have been expected, the occasion was marked by a fairly wild party, ending at two in the morning with a hut of the mess being set on fire and the early-morning Viscount arriving at Heathrow plastered with the squadron's crest on its shining fuselage, announcing 'Gin Ye Daur'! It was not with a whimper that the squadron did its final landing!

In addition to my duties at Turnhouse itself, I also had administrative responsibilities for several outstations in the Hebrides, and it was often necessary for me to pay them a visit from time to time. I occasionally took the civilian manager with me, as he also had some responsibilities on the islands. Thus, on the 28th, Jock Halley and I set off in the Anson to Machrihanish Port Ellen, Port Leverl, Tiree and Benbecula, and after a long day returned to land at Turnhouse in the dark. Early in April Jock and I went in the Anson to Sumburgh and Kirkwall to pay visits to our staffs, and returned to Turnhouse late in the evening. I was becoming very conscious of the fact that the control of civilian airliners, and the safety of passengers, was in the hands of my air traffic people on the approach to, and departure from, Turnhouse, so I spent a good deal of my flying keeping my controllers in a high state of training. To this end I also took the controllers flying on approach and landing exercises to help them appreciate the pilots' viewpoint. On 26 July I flew the sector commander, Air Cdre Robinson, on a staff visit to Ouston and Valley in Anglesey, making a point of thanking him for letting me fly his Hunter.

At the beginning of August I was fortunate enough to be able to borrow a civilian Dove from the local airline and fly the family, including Robert's nanny, Ruth, for a sightseeing flight across the Firth of Forth and around Edinburgh. I had promised that I might fly them under the Forth Bridge, but perhaps just as well it was shrouded in mist on that day. At the end of the month I managed to get in two night flights to keep in night-training in the Meteor. However, even though I landed after midnight, being August in Scotland it never really got dark, so although I called it night-flying in my logbook I would have to wait until later in the year to get real night-training. In August a guard of honour was assembled for the arrival of General Montgomery, who was visiting the GOC, Scotland. Monty took the trouble to inspect the whole of my guard of honour, but he made no comment to the guard commander or me. A few days later, I, the sector commander and other officers were flown in a Ferranti Dove to Ringway, and then on to Blackbushe, from where we were taken in a coach to Farnborough for the SBAC Show. On my return to Turnhouse I was kept busy making plans for the Battle of Britain Open Day when our air display was to be the only one in Scotland. I remembered the air race that was organized at Andover, which I almost won in a Spitfire, and which turned out to be a most popular event, and I thought I would organize a similar handicap race at Turnhouse. I did several sorties in the Hunter to plan a suitable route, and had my navigation officer work out a handicap for each of the several types that would be competing. This was no easy matter, as the competitors varied between a Chipmunk, an Anson, a Meteor, a Vampire, a Javelin and the Hunter, and the aim was to have them taking off at staggered times to keep the interest alive at the airfield, and hopefully for them to arrive over the finishing line in a bunch, after a twenty-five-mile circuit. The Battle of Britain Show took place on 16 September, which dawned bright and sunny, with only a smattering of cloud that served to emphasize the beauty of the Pentland Hills as a background to the flying programme. There were several interesting visiting aircraft, including a Vulcan and a Valiant, resplendent in their 'anti-flash' white paint, the first time that the 'V' bombers had been on public view in Scotland. A wartime Mosquito flew in with a woman pilot, Mrs Veronica Volkersz, a wartime member of the Air Transport Auxiliary who had flown many aircraft types. The air show went ahead with aircraft demonstrations, formation aerobatics by Hunters of No. 43 Squadron from Leuchars, and some brilliant individual aerobatics by a pilot from No. 92 Squadron. The air race, which was the first of its kind in a Battle of Britain air show in Scotland, was clearly the most popular event, and the thrill was evident when six different types of aircraft suddenly appeared approaching the finishing line on the airfield, the Hunter and Javelin sweeping ahead of the rest just over the boundary, and I just got the Hunter a millisecond ahead of the Javelin, both doing over 600 mph in a deafening thunder of noise. No prize was offered, but it was decided to make the race an annual event to compete for a silver cup. The local press were full of praise for the air show, so I later approached the editor of *The Scotsman*, asking if he would agree to present the cup at future shows. He promised to put the suggestion to the management.

In October 1957 No. 151 Squadron was re-equipping with Javelin aircraft, but as the runway at Leuchars was being resurfaced the aircraft were delivered to Turnhouse. They were ferried in ones and twos and had to be parked on the far-side dispersal. This gave me the opportunity to familiarize myself with the drill for starting up the engines and the cockpit layout of the Javelin when I took the opportunity to taxi each one of them to their dispersal. By the time the squadron CO arrived with his pilots there was a full complement of Javelins awaiting them. The CO was the only one who had any Javelin experience, and before the conversion programme could start all the aircraft had to be air-tested, so I offered to do some of the testing.

So on 15 October, already familiar with starting-up procedures and the cockpit layout, I took off in Javelin 5 XH 689 for a familiarization and handling flight. Compared with the Meteor the Javelin was considerably larger and heavier, but I was surprised to find it was light on the controls, highly manoeuvrable and with an enhanced rate of climb and top speed. After an hour in the air I felt thoroughly confident, and after two approaches and touch-and-go landings I taxied the big machine in with a feeling of satisfied achievement. I did another flight in the Javelin in October, landing in heavy rain, and the following month flew a Javelin on an air-to-air gunnery trial. Later in the month I took a Javelin 5 up to 45,000 feet and did a supersonic run over the sea, followed by a QGH/GCA at Leuchars on its delivery there.

At the beginning of March 1958 I was attached to the Flying College at Manby for a Guided Weapons course, and while there I flew four Meteor sorties, one at night, from Strubby. I also managed to borrow a horse from the riding school and did a recce of the local countryside on horseback. On my return to Turnhouse I did several Meteor flights in cooperation with the local Army light ack-ack regiment at Dunblane, and these continued into April with flights for another Army light ack-ack company at Linlithgow. In May I took the Anson to Benbecula and Tiree via Acklington with a load of staff officers, and flew several Meteor sorties, including an aerobatic demonstration for the University Air Squadron's 'At Home' day. A Meteor 7, that belonged to the Royal Navy and had force-landed at Turnhouse with a failed engine, came out of the hangar after the engine had been replaced, and I did a comprehensive air test before the Navy collected it. On 26 June I flew with Major Bounds in an Army Whirlwind to get some dual handling experience on helicopters, as up to then I had not qualified on rotary-winged aircraft but was very keen to do so. It was not until I was at the Test Pilots' School at Farnborough that I was able to do this.

In July I took some leave and went caravanning up in the Highlands with the family. On our return from the north, August was mostly taken up with training controllers and calibrating the mobile homer. However, I did take a Chipmunk across to Leuchars and borrowed a Vampire T.11, and used that for more training of my controllers. The comparatively few air movements at Turnhouse meant that I had to supplement these whenever I could get an aircraft to keep my controllers up to date in their training. At the beginning of September 1958 I went with Capt Allen in a Heron to Ringway, Blackbushe, and I captained it on the return flight. On the 18th I flew the Hunter on an aerobatic sortie, and the next day in contrast I flew in a Troop Transport Beverley with Flt Lt Kirk and eighty soldiers of the Royal Scots Regiment on an air exercise. I flew with Mr Blair in a Twin Pioneer the next day on an aircraft evaluation exercise. But I was then disappointed to hear that the sector commander's Hunter was now to be returned to Leuchars to be taken on the strength of No. 43 Squadron. So for the last few days of September I made sure of getting in four more flights in the aircraft before I had to take it to Leuchars on 1 October.

The month was mostly taken up with flights in the Anson to the Islands, where our annual inspections were due. Jock Halley, the civil airport manager, and several staff officers came along and we visited Port Ellen, Tiree, Benbecula and Stornaway, and returned to Turnhouse via Kinloss, concluding with a night landing. On the 18th, Exercise Sunbeam took place at Leuchars, and I flew across in the Chipmunk to act as observer. I was back at Turnhouse by teatime but had to return to Leuchars after dark for the night phase of the exercise. However, the weather clamped right down and the exercise was cancelled as it was below limits for the jets. But I took off in the Chipmunk and immediately went into cloud, and only emerged at 250 feet over the end of Turnhouse runway after a radar talk-down. I was pleased to get one up on the fighter boys. In November my instrument rating was due for renewal, so I flew across the Firth to Leuchars in the Chipmunk and took my test in a Meteor 7 with Flt Lt Richards, and managed to hold on to my Master Green Instrument Rating. Now that the resurfacing of the runway at Leuchars was completed, the Javelin squadron had moved back and none of their aircraft remained at Turnhouse. Not to be deprived of the odd flight in a Javelin, I flew over to Leuchars in a Chipmunk. In a borrowed Javelin, I did a climb to 45,000 feet with

Flg Off Hamilton in the morning and a low-level navigation exercise with Flg Off Woods in the afternoon, followed by several QGH/GCA practices at Turnhouse, before handing the aircraft back to the squadron at Leuchars and flying the Chipmunk back to Turnhouse. at night. On 11 December I joined forty-nine other passengers on a demonstration flight in a Fokker Friendship of Air Lingus, and after landing, at a champagne buffet in the civil terminal. This aircraft was an early version of the Fokker 50, the type that Charles, our eldest son, flew when he was with Air UK several years later. He had transferred from his engineering profession to become a professional commercial pilot, and we were full of admiration, for it took a great deal of hard work for him to obtain his commercial licence. He undertook the task with commendable zeal and effort, and with the greatest support of his wife Sandra, who is also an accomplished pilot. Charles is now flying Boeings on long-haul flights for British Airways. And Sandra is a flying instructor at a civil flying club near High Wycombe.

CHAPTER THIRTY

Officer Commanding RAF Turnhouse

December 1956

Unfortunately all the jet aircraft had now been withdrawn to Leuchars from Turnhouse or allotted elsewhere, so as I was anxious to keep my jet rating I had to take the Chipmunk across to Leuchars to fly a Meteor, Vampire, Hunter or Javelin. But during the month I took to the air in a Sedburgh Mk 3 glider, and after three winch launches with an instructor I had a solo launch and flight, but my total time in the air amounted to only eighteen minutes! Winter weather had now moved in on us and on several occasions during the month there was snow and ice on the runway at Turnhouse. I had to do regular flights to assess the suitability of the runway for the civil aircraft to land, and runway snow clearance was an urgent and painstaking job for the Turnhouse ground staff. An air test was a necessity before aircraft could be accepted for landing, and for this I only had the Chipmunk, but in fact it turned out to be quite adequate for the purpose.

As a matter of interest no flight was ever diverted for runway surface unsuitability while I was there, but this did not, unfortunately, extend to cross-wind conditions: because of the orientation of the only long runway and the prevailing winds, the cross-wind component for landing was sometimes outside the limits for the civil aircraft, and they had to be diverted to Glasgow. It was not until the end of the month that I was able to get over to Leuchars and get a flight in a Meteor 7 for instrument flying and aerobatics, and later in the day a Hunter for a climb to 45,000 feet. On my approach to the airfield I steeled myself to do a practice manual controls landing, which meant switching off the power controls and using a great deal of strength and judgement to overcome the very heavy stiffness and lack of feel in the elevator and ailerons to effect a safe landing. I never experienced a failure of power controls in earnest, although I did have the failure of flaps to extend on one occasion when landing a Hunter at Turnhouse, but this was no great problem.

But manual reversion was such a marked contrast to the usual sweet controls of the Hunter that it was a much more difficult problem.

Flying in February was confined to a handful of Chipmunk sorties, including one at night, but in March I had to take the Anson to Benbecula with several 'Bloodhound' technicians who wanted to carry out inspections of the missiles before a test firing against a glider target from Llanberis. On the 17th I got a few days' leave, and Eve and I were flown in a Pionair (Dakota) to Dyce (Aberdeen). The next day, with a new captain of the Pionair, we flew on to Dice, Wick, Kirkwall and Sumbrough in the Shetlands, where we had booked in to a hotel for two days. After enjoying a welcome break of walking and exploring in the Shetlands we returned to Turnhouse in the Pionair.

Before the end of the month I did my last flight at Turnhouse in a Chipmunk. and notification of my next posting marked the end of my most enjoyable stay in Scotland. I flew down to Ouston in the Anson to say my farewells to the AOC and his staff, and returned to give the good news to my family that we would all be going to Cyprus for our next tour.

After several cocktail parties to say farewell to the many friends that we had been fortunate enough to make, including several notable people in Edinburgh, such as the Chief Constable and the commander of the American forces north of the border, we were finally dined out at Turnhouse and were able to get down to packing our bags. Before I was due to take up my new appointment as Wing Commander Administration at Akrotiri Cyprus, there were several spare weeks in hand when I could take some leave, so I applied and was given leave to travel out to Cyprus by sea. After a week or two showing our young family the exciting sites of York and London, we travelled down south by the night *Scotsman* from Edinburgh, and early the next morning boarded the troopship *Dunera* lying alongside the dock in Southampton. After a delightful and relaxing few days at sea we arrived off Limassol in a full gale, and as the *Dunera* was moored offshore, we had a very wet and exciting trip ashore in a small motor boat. It was very rough and spray was coming into the boat, and it seemed an unduly perilous situation for the Mediterranean that we had been looking forward to. However, once ashore we were soon enjoying the warmth and sunshine that we had promised ourselves.

My predecessor was reluctant to give up his married quarter on the base, so the family and I were temporarily housed in a hotel in Limassol. This meant travelling into my work every morning by car, but I soon got into my administration job, and it did not take me long to realize that I was going to be very busy. My good fortune continued, however, in that I found my new commanding officer was one of the nicest men of my experience. The true charm and kindness of both Andrew and Agnes Humphrey were a delight, and as a commander Andrew could not have been more helpful and understanding. I was made to understand at once where I stood, as Andrew told me bluntly that he expected me to get on with my administrative job without worrying him with non-essentials, and if I was not able to cope I would have to go.

From that moment on we worked together with perfect under-standing. Andrew was a very wise and brilliant officer with a fine war record, having shot down a number of enemy aircraft after the Battle of Britain, and I was not surprised that he went on to become the Chief of Defence Staff in the years ahead. Sadly he was to die prematurely while in the post.

There were three Canberra squadrons and a communication squadron at Akrotiri, and despite the heavy load of my office work I managed to find time to keep in flying practice. I quickly got the commanding officer of the comm. squadron to check me out on the Pembroke and to do a solo flight to familiarize myself with the local area as far as Nicosia. I remembered that the family had spent a holiday in Cyprus in 1954 at the beginning of the guerilla war against the British Administration, and I was interested to find that talks were now taking place at the end of four years of this unrest. Happily, Grivas no longer lurked in the mountains, and Makarios had been released from his incarceration. He now joined with the Turkish representative, Denktash, in talks with the British in an attempt to agree a formula for granting independence to the colony. But Cyprus held a key strategic position in the Middle East, and although in 1960 sovereignty was finally granted under their joint presidency, it was essential for Britain to retain a military foothold on the island. As a result two Sovereign Base Areas were set up, one at Dhekelia for the Army to the east, and Akrotiri for the Royal Air Force four miles to the west of Limassol, with Episcopi, the headquarters of Middle East Air Command, close by. Sporadic fighting between Greek and Turk continued for several years, culminating with the Turkish invasion from the mainland in 1974, when the Turks seized and occupied a third of the island in the north, despite worldwide protests.

Attempts to stabilize the situation were made, but the Turkish community in 1983 declared itself independent as the Turkish Republic of Northern Cyprus, and all that the Western Allies could do was to put in United Nations troops to patrol the border to keep the two sides apart.

The future situation at Akrotiri was to be influenced a good deal by the events that followed. There was endless traffic of civilian and military people through the station involved in the political negotiations. In addition an urgent and substantial build-up of military equipment and stores, together with the associated building, had to be put in hand in the base areas, and their security was of first priority, for some of the natives were by no means friendly. In a short time Akrotiri became by far the largest overseas base, and I had my hands full as its senior administrator. I was prepared to work late hours and took files home to keep pace with the relentless pressure, but I was not prepared to forego my flying. I had on my staff a Flt Lt Andrews, a navigator who shared my enthusiasm to get airborne, and Andy had the time to keep his eyes and ears open for a chance to do some useful flying. In June we took five passengers into Nicosia in the Pembroke, and after landing back at Akrotiri I managed to get my hands on a Meteor 7 from one of the Canberra squadrons. As it was clear that I was going to be busy during the day I arranged for a night check on the Pembroke so that I could do the Nicosia run when needed at night. Happily, Andy was glad to come along. On one day in July Andy and I were scrambled in the Pembroke to carry out a search for a shark reported off one of the bathing beaches that surrounded the peninsula on which the base stood. On this occasion it was 'everybody out', but normally the families could spend many happy hours swimmimg and snorkelling from the several surrounding beaches. I, unfortunately, could not normally get away from my office except to join the family for a brief swim before the sun went down.

It never ceased to amaze me how various types of flying machine seemed to appear from the depths of the maintenance hangars and became available to fly. On one occasion, quite unexpectedly, the main-tenance crews produced my old friend a Chipmunk, and I was asked to fly over to Episcopi to assess the suitability of the mini landing strip that was part of the sports field at the headquarters. I found it too short for regular use, but subject to wind direction and strength it could certainly be used in an emergency. That evening I flew the Air Marshal and his SASO into Nicosia in the Pembroke, and returned at night and took the opportunity of making myself thoroughly familiar with the runway approach and landing lights at both Nicosia and Akrotiri.

I was also asked by the Air Staff to fly over and assess the suitability of the small landing strip at Limassol for use in an emergency. There was always a possibility at this time that terrorists might set up road blocks to cut off communications between the base areas, and these little strips might prove of valuable use. My recce of the Limassol strip and the touch-and-go landings in the Chipmunk were fun in themselves, but the pleasure was greatly enhanced as I flew over by the sudden eruption of a cloud of pink wings, providing a wonderful sight of hundreds of flamingos as they took off from the nearby salt lakes that were their breeding ground. On 26 September Andy and I flew Sir William

MacDonald to Nicosia and took him back to Akrotiri on the night of the 28th with the Permanent Under-Secretary Sir William Dean. It will be appreciated that there was a great deal of air movement into Nicosia associated with the current negotiations for Cyprus independence at this time, so I was given a day and night check by the senior flying instructor so that I could be officially appointed a VIP aircraft captain.

My regular flying provided a welcome relaxation from my intense administrative tasks, which seemed to grow each day. The one bright spot was my friendly relationship with Andrew Humphrey, based on mutual trust and confidence. We were both under severe pressure in our own fields, and yet Andrew always found time to pop into my office and have a friendly chat. He was a fairly heavy smoker and was always running out of cigarettes, so I made a point of keeping a packet or two in my desk drawer, which I knew Andrew appreciated. Our weekly tour of inspection together around the huge station took up a great deal of time, but it was the only period when we spent more than a few moments together. Notes were made of all the many things that needed to be done, and Andrew soon came to appreciate that he never had to ask twice for appropriate action to be taken.

In addition to the routine administration there were several royal visits to the station, including one by the Queen, which involved a lot of tidying up and the provision of special facilities for her comfort. The greatest efforts, however, were required for the visit by the Duke of Gloucester when he came to present a new Queen's Colour to the Middle East Air Force. The whole station was to be paraded, including a Colour Escort Squadron and the MEAF Band. A special stand had to be built for the visiting guests to view the parade, and the Presentation, the March-Past of the Colours and the Royal Salute, which had to coincide exactly with the Fly-Past by the Canberra Squadrons. Happily all went well, except that, because of a mistake by the Palace, the Duke arrived in blue uniform when the station was all in summer rig and the day was very hot. The Commander-in-Chief, too, decided that he should also wear his blue uniform, as a gesture to help ease the unfortunate situation. Happily the parade went off very well, and the roar of the Canberra formation led by Guy Hogan coincided exactly with the Royal Salute as they flew over the glittering line of bayonets at the present arms. Hardly had the last bars of the National Anthem faded away, together with the diminishing roar of the Canberras, when the Duke and the C-in-C were whisked off to the mess to cool off with the help of an iced drink. A formal luncheon rounded off a very satisfying day for all concerned, albeit a trifle hot and uncomfortable for the principal participants.

As a change from my regular flights in the Pembroke to Nicosia and an aerobatic sortie in the Meteor, on 14 November I flew in a Shackleton piloted by Flt Lt Waddington on a maritime special operation off the coast of Israel. Although Israeli aircraft did not participate, several small, high-speed torpedo-type craft were busy along the coast. The following week I went into Nicosia in the Pembroke to collect Air Marshal Earl. On the return flight Tubby came up to the cockpit and settled down in the right-hand seat and took over the controls. It was a beautiful, clear morning, and we thoroughly enjoyed flying only a few feet above the summit of Troodos Mountain to have a good look at the radar unit perched on the top and glistening under several feet of snow. After a gradual descent and a landing on the runway at Akrotiri, we got out of the aircraft to find, in sharp contrast, a very hot noon day. The beautiful Mediterranean weather continued, and the family took every advantage of the superb swimming and snorkelling on the surrounding beaches while I was beavering away at the heavy administration burden and only occasionally joining them when work would allow. But there were occasions when I could get away briefly for some leave, and on 7 June we boarded a Comet at Nicosia that was to take us to Athens. I was rather surprised to see as we mounted the steps to board the aircraft that it had recently been resprayed, and I could see under the new paint the letters RAE Farnborough. This turned out to be the same aircraft that we had at the Test Pilots' School at Farnborough for the test pilots to fling around to work out G forces in steep turns, etc. I didn't let on to Eve before we took off.

We enjoyed a memorable two weeks during which we took passage in a small motor yacht and visited the ancient Greek cities of Epidaurus, Mycene, Corinth, and Delphi. We were entranced by the all-pervading feeling of mystery and ancient Greek legend, and descending into the catacombs of Delphi we were persuaded that the Oracle decreed that we must leave Greece and return to Cyprus, which we reluctantly did during the night of the new moon in the same BEA Comet.

Two days after my return I took off in a Beverley captained by Flt Lt Lang, with his crew and eighteen paratroops and two heavy platforms of military equipment. This was part of Operation Swiftsure, when I witnessed the stores and parachutists being dropped at Morphu.

A few days later I flew in a Canberra with Flg Off Blewitt to Thorney Island in the UK, staging through Luqa in Malta. The purpose of my return to the United Kingdom was to visit the Air Secretary's Branch to discuss my next appointment. To my surprise I was summoned to an interview with the Air Secretary himself and told that the Promotion Board had agreed my promotion to Acting Group Captain for my next job, yet to be announced. I was convinced that this happy event was entirely due to Andrew's recommendation on my last Confidential Report at Akrotiri, and it was with happy anticipation that I returned to Cyprus on 9 January, when I boarded an RAF Comet at Lyneham, flown by Flt Lt Hartman and also having Sir Dudley Ward on board. We landed back at Akrotiri early that evening.

February and March were very busy months, and I only managed to get airborne twice to Nicosia and to grab a quick flight in the Meteor. But in May I got away for another leave break, and on the 15th, Eve and I boarded 'Bald Eagle', a Boeing 707 flown by Capt Randle, to fly from Beirut to Istanbul. After a wonderful week exploring the fabulous mosques and ancient buildings of modern Constantinople, we took a ship through the Dardanelles to Izmir, which still showed the scars of the calamitous earthquake. We visited several of the famous ancient Greek temples and toured the town over the next few days, before returning to Istanbul in a Dakota of an internal Turkish airline. It was a reasonable flight, but we were amused to find that the in-flight refreshments that were advertised turned out to be boiled sweets, served with a flourish after take-off. We returned to our hotel in Istanbul only to find that, through a misunderstanding, the management had relet our room, and while full of apologies, they regretted that no other rooms were available. After remonstrating to the manager and arguing that for the sake of one night our romantic holiday would be spoiled by the incompetence of his staff, he relented and we were moved into the bridal suite, complete with a king-sized bed and 'his and her' dressing gowns hanging behind the door, not to mention the most superb view of the Golden Horn from our balcony. Back down to earth the next day, we boarded a BEA Comet and were flown to Ankara and then on to Nicosia, where I took over a waiting Pembroke and flew us back to Akrotiri that night.

A few days later, for the first time in my flying career, I landed from a flight without my aircraft. Command HQ had decreed that senior officers should experience a parachute descent, and so the RAF Regiment's CO, Tony Sullivan, who was an enthusiastic parachutist, called for volunteers for the first drop. Andrew was always recognizing his responsibilities as station commander, and to set a good example immediately put his name forward. He, as always, assumed that I would be supporting him, so I added my name as a matter of course. So it was after a short period of instruction in the hangar that we and a handful of staff officers led by Tony took off in a Hastings that climbed to 1,200 feet over the sea off Lady's Mile beach and disgorged us from the side door in a string. After the noise and slipstream that buffeted me as I left the aircraft, the gentle and peaceful descent, gently swinging beneath the canopy of my parachute, was a delight, but all too soon the waves seemed to rush up towards me, and wriggling out of my harness I was quickly plucked from the water by the rescue boat. After a quick shower and a change back into uniform, the parachute party gathered in the bar for a celebratory gin amid the plaudits of the rest of the flyers who had yet to jump. But were their congratulations tinged with jealousy and resentment that they were not the first? There was no time to dwell on the follow-up to our achievement, as during the following week the family and I had packed up. I had handed over my duties to two newly arrived wing commanders, and after several farewell parties and a dining-out in the mess we left in a Britannia of Transport Command with another one hundred passengers to land at London, Stanstead, on the afternoon of 6 October, at the completion of a very busy tour, but one of great interest and achievement, which earned me the award of an OBE.

CHAPTER THIRTY-ONE

Flying the Phantom

November 1962

After a few days to settle down back in England we spent the first three weeks of November in house hunting. I had learnt with great interest and excitement that my next appointment was to be Staff Officer Flying at the Ministry of Aviation in London, so our search was for a house in the home counties with reasonable access to the city. We were fortunate in finding a nice property near Woking coming on the market in the near future, with a very good train service to Waterloo, but it would be some time before all the negotiations with agents and solicitors could be finalized, and for a while I would not be able to move the family down from Ratcliffe-on-Trent, where they were staying with the Bentons. I was not due to take up my new job for some days, so I joined my brother in a week's holiday in the Mediterranean. We left Heathrow in a Viscount and flew to Gibraltar. The flight was pleasant enough en route, but we ran into a thunderstorm just before reaching the Rock. The tropical downpour left inches of water on the runway, making landing very difficult, and the captain obviously found the brakes were having little effect, as the tyres were aquaplaning over the surface water and we were lucky not to run out of runway. We stayed in a pleasant hotel in Algeciras, and happily it did not rain during the rest of our holiday, and we took a hired car up into Spain on a widespread visit to places of interest and charm, which we thoroughly enjoyed.

On landing back at Heathrow I lost no time in reporting to the Ministry to find out the details of my new post, Staff Officer Flying at the Ministry of Aviation. Although it was essentially a desk job I was delighted to hear that I was to have responsibility for supervision of all test flying of military aircraft by civil manufacturers throughout the United Kingdom under the Director-General of Flying. I was alarmed to discover that the Director was my erstwhile AOC in Cyprus with whom Hughie Edwards and I had fallen out. But happily all was forgiven and I could not have had a more considerate boss. We got on well, particularly as he just let me get on with my daily task without interfering, and it must be said, without showing a great deal of interest. I was also to have responsibility for the testing, research and development flying at Boscombe Down and the conduct of flying training at the Empire Test Pilots' School (ETPS) at Farnborough. Thus I would be expected to travel all over the country in pursuance of my duties, to meet all the civilian test pilots, and have close contact with the development of new service aircraft. How else could I cover all this ground in the time available than by air? Plenty of flying was in prospect and my cup of happiness was filled to the brim. I considered myself fortunate indeed, particularly as I was now a group captain!

Even without my dropping a hint it was recommended that I should get my jet rating up to date before taking up my job, and on my own recommendation I was attached to the Empire Test Pilots' School for a flying refresher course on the Meteor. I completed the course on 7 December, when I did my instrument rating test with the senior instructor and went away with my Master Green Card safely tucked in my log book once more. After a short break after Christmas and the New Year, I travelled up to London and found my office in the Ministry of Civil Aviation Building at the top of Tottenham Court Road. Awaiting me was a staff of eight civil servants, including a secretary who turned out to be absolute perfection, knowing everything and everybody that mattered in the job. She made my task through the coming months very much easier, enjoyable and rewarding. On my first day I brought Peggy an African Violet for her desk, not knowing then that she was an ardent gardener. By the time that I left the Ministry the office looked like a flower festival with wall-to-wall African Violets! Among her many talents she certainly had green fingers. She was a perfect secretary and never once was there ever a cross word or misunderstanding between us. My staff were mostly experts in some field of flight safety, such as air traffic, fire and rescue and the professionalism of personnel employed by contractors doing Ministry of Aviation aircraft flight testing. My office laid down the criteria that the Ministry required for the flight-testing of military aircraft at civil contractors' airfields. Thus, regular inspection was a necessity, and I was also responsible to the Director-General of Flying for ensuring that civil test pilots were fully qualified and competent and in up-to-date flying practice for the highly skilled and responsible job of flight-testing very valuable and high-performance aircraft belonging to the Ministry of Defence. The question of flying practice requirement became a matter of some significance, as will be seen later. It was always a matter dear to my heart, as will be appreciated.

I started in the new job at the beginning of January, and was glad to find out that I could call on the Test Pilots' School at Farnborough for an aircraft whenever I needed one for my staff visits. It was very seldom that they ever failed to produce something flyable, and to prepare for my visiting I went down to Farnborough to be checked out on their aircraft. After being cleared on the Devon, I took it to Warton with two of my staff to visit English Electric and discuss their set-up for flight development of the Lightning and flight-testing of production aircraft. I returned late in the day for a night landing at Farnborough. I only got to Farnborough twice in February, getting checked out on the piston-engined Provost and doing dusk landings on the first occasion, and on the 19th taking the Devon to Lyneham and return for VOR/ILS practice approaches. At the beginning of March I flew down to Dunsfold in the Meteor 7 to talk to Bill Bedford about the early trials on the P.1127, later to become the Harrier. This vertical-take-off fighter was the first of its kind and already showing great promise, but as so often seemed to happen in the United Kingdom, support for it was so half hearted that it took years to get it recognized as the invaluable tactical fighter that it eventually became. Even the Americans bought it! The Test Pilots' School was fortunate enough to have a Vickers Viscount 810 on their establishment for multi-engine flight-testing training, and I persuaded Wg Cdr Laidler, the chief flying instructor, to give me some dual on the aircraft. We did an hour's flight, including landings with one engine stopped, and lastly with two engines stopped on the same side. I found the aircraft beautiful to handle, even under those conditions, although admittedly it was very lightly loaded at the time. I would have another chance to fly the aircraft when we took it to the States on a visit to Edwards Air Force Base and also on shorter trips to the continent. At the end of the month, after two flights in the Meteor I was fortunate to join the test pilots in flying the American F4H Phantom, a very advanced and sophisticated aircraft that became the standard fighter/strike aircraft of many air forces throughout the world. It was a comparably large and heavy aircraft, but the power-assisted flying controls made it exceptionally manoeuvrable and straightforward to land.

On 5 April I took my signals expert to the Radar Establishment at Pershore and return, and on the 11th I visited Rolls-Royce at Hucknall. Here their chief test pilot, Capt Rogers, took me on a demonstration flight in the Ambassador G-37-3 fitted with two Rolls-Royce Dart engines and with reverse thrust. We accomplished some remarkably short landings. The following week I took the Meteor 7 to visit Marshals of Cambridge, where Mr Worsdell let me fly the company's Aztec, which was waiting outside his office like a taxi – a very gentlemanly way of checking their air traffic control facilities at Cambridge. On the 18th,

using the Devon, Eric and I did a similar exercise at Chalgrove and
Luton, carrying out ILS and GCA approaches at both airfields. Before
the end of the month we had visited Tarrant Rushton, Turnhouse and
Prestwick. In June I was busy catching up with paperwork in the office,
where Peggy kept me going on copious cups of coffee – the real blend,
for she did not hold with 'instant'. When I managed to get out of the
office again I flew over to Hatfield to see my old night-fighter friend
John Cunningham. Over a good lunch at the Comet, John told me about
the Trident programme, which had run into problems and suffered two
aircraft crashed. Investigations had shown that the aircraft had been
allowed to enter a deep stall from which recovery had been impossible.
John explained that with aircraft with tailplane and elevators positioned
high up on the tailfin it was possible to raise the aircraft nose so high at
low speed that the airflow over the wing blanketed the flow over the
elevators and made them ineffective for recovery. John had emphasized
this danger in his briefing for operating the Trident, and droop flaps on
the wing leading edge had been modified and warning systems fitted.
John was now engaged in proving the remedial action taken by de
Havilland, and after lunch he invited me to go with him on one of these
test flights. So we boarded Trident G-ARPA, together with Peter
Buggee, and did an hour carrying out trials on the stalling characteristics of the Trident under various conditions with a clean aircraft, with
various stages of flaps and slots and full landing rig with wheels and
flaps down. Quite alarming at times, with a horn screeching, the
stick shaker going madly and the aircraft doing all sorts of antics, not
like a well-behaved passenger airliner. But it was a convincing
demonstration, nevertheless, clearly showing that it would be very difficult for an airline pilot to reach a stalling situation inadvertently, and
that even if he did the Trident would recover easily if handled right.
After landing I complimented John on the calm way he handled the
aircraft, but he said he had no worries as he made sure the aircraft was
fitted with an anti-spin tail parachute before the trial. The Trident went
on to be quite a successful feeder airliner with BEA, and it was the first
to be fitted for fully automatic blind landings, which I observed in flying
trials at Bedford. On 20 July Eric Mather and I went across to Yeovil in
the Chipmunk to visit Westland Aircraft Company, the principal helicopter firm in the UK. After lunch we flew to Weston-super-Mare to see
the flight-test division of the firm, and then back to Farnborough
that evening. There was something very captivating in flying a light
aircraft on a still summer evening, apparently with the sky to ourselves
and the air as smooth as silk. I remembered us both saying what a shame
it was that we had to come down to the chaos of traffic round
Farnborough and back to London. The next day in my office I realized

that my knowledge of helicopter operations was very limited. I there-fore thought it was a good reason to go to my Director-General and suggest that I might gain experience by doing a helicopter flying course. To my surprise he agreed and sent me off to Farnborough for a short helicopter conversion course, and ETPS was as usual only too pleased to agree. Before the end of the month I had already done an hour and a half of hovering, cyclic handling and use of the collective control in the Dragonfly helicopter.

On 1 August I was at Rearsby to evaluate the little Beagle Terrier G-ARLF and to look at the firm's air traffic and safety facilities. The following week I took Mather and a lieutenant-commander in the Devon to Sydenham (Bedford), where we landed in heavy drizzle with 400 feet cloud base, using Decca for our let-down and approach. Our return to Farnborough the next day was by contrast in the clear. I was busy at the beginning of the month with the commandant of ETPS and the instructors considering the flying demonstration programmes of the company test pilots at the SBAC Show at Farnborough. We considered two things were paramount: firstly, the safety of the public spectators, so the flight paths of the demonstrated aircraft had to be over a safe route and well away from the crowd enclosures; secondly, of course, the safety of the valuable development aircraft themselves and their test pilots. There was clearly a temptation to fly to the limit of their per-formance to impress the onlookers and potential customers, particularly foreign buyers, but some curbs were essential to ensure, as far as possible, that no catastrophe happened to spoil the show. While flying programmes were clearly up to the test pilots themselves, their routines had to be cleared by the show committee, of which I was a member This was a very responsible job, and the details took us some time to work out and agree. Happily the show went off without a hitch and I was lucky enough to fly in the new VC.10 G-ARTA with Jock Bryce and Bryan Trubshaw on its demonstration flight: a most impressive display in a really beautiful aircraft.

Visits to various company airfields continued into November, including a flight to Luton where I managed to get a flight in a Jet Provost, an aircraft I had not flown before. I returned to Farnborough in my piston-engined Provost and landed in a snow storm with a cloud base of 400 feet. At the beginning of December I took the Devon to Shoreham, where Mr Mitchell briefed me on the handling of the twin-engined Beagle 206 G-ARRM, which I flew solo for an hour, enjoying the comfort and light handling of this delightful aircraft while checking the air traffic controllers in the tower. After lunch I flew the little Airdale, G-ARNP, for half an hour before flying home in the Devon. There was no flying at Farnborough during January as the airfield was closed on and off with snow, and it was not until the middle of February that I managed to get down to Farnborough again. On the 19th I took Sir Charles Gardener in a Devon to Northolt, where Mr Pike from de Havilland took him and other ministers on a demonstration flight of the new Dove 8. I went as second pilot to make up the numbers.

At the end of April a visit was arranged to some French test-flying establishments, and on the 23rd I joined Ray Watts and several test pilots from ETPS flying in the Viscount to Istres. Here was the French Helicopter-Testing Establishment, where we had a session comparing notes on test procedures and training. The next day Ray and I were flown in a French Alouette for a demonstration flight by their Commandant Hablo. After some interesting handling performance the commandant said, 'Now I will show you something really interesting', and much to our surprise descended to tree-top height and made for the coast. After a few minutes we circled a sandy bay so low that the sand began to swirl around, and out of the murk appeared a bevy of naked girls waving with great enthusiasm. No doubt the commandant and his lads were regular visitors to this nude bathing beach. We did find it most interesting, but it hardly added to our understanding of the French flight-testing procedures.

Two days later we took the Viscount from Istres to Bretigny, where we spent the day with French test pilots and were generously entertained in the evening with choice French wines and cuisine. The next day we returned to Farnborough, having called at Manston to clear customs. The excisemen always seemed much stricter at Air Force stations than at civil airports. For some weeks the Dragonfly helicopter had been on trials, but it now become available again, and in July I had been able to continue my flying training on the helicopter. After more dual with Sqn Ldr Stevens, including hovering, auto-rotation in the event of engine failure, approaches and rolling landings, I did my first helicopter solo flight on the 18th, and thereafter six more solo flights before the end of the month. In no time I was revelling in this new challenge and thoroughly enjoying the helicopter experience. Admittedly it was noisy, with uncomfortable vibration, but what a thrill to be able to land the chopper with ease on its hard standing between the hangars.

In August and September I continued to build up some helicopter hours, interspersed with visits to the Bristol Engine Company at Filton and to Colerne. Similarly, in October, I finalized my helicopter course with practice solo auto-rotation forced landings and side and backward manoeuvres. In November I had the opportunity of more second-pilot hours on the Viscount when ETPS test pilots flew to Italy on a liaison visit to the Italian Flight Test Centre. We took the Viscount to Luqa, and then a night landing at Nicosia, and the next day to Ciampino airport, Rome. Two days later we flew back to Farnborough via Lyneham to clear customs. I did a little Meteor and Devon flying during December, but was looking forward to an exciting visit to the United States that had been planned for the New Year.

CHAPTER THIRTY-TWO

Helicopters and Edwards US Air Force Base

January 1963

With the backing of the Ministry of Aviation, the Empire Test Pilots' School and the American opposite number at Edwards Air Force Base paid regular liaison visits to each other's establishments. This January it was the turn of the British to go to the States, and I managed to join the party as the Ministry Representative. On 3 January seven test pilots, led by the ETPS commandant, Ray Watts, and I set off in the Viscount from Farnbrough to Lossiemouth in Scotland, where we refuelled and took off again for Keflavick in Iceland. No sun appeared while we were there to brighten the dreary, sad countryside, and we were glad to be on our way again, although the local people did all they could to be hospitable during our stop-over. Our next landing was at Sondrestrom in Greenland, where the weather was even more depressing and the whole place seemed to be immersed in low cloud and ice and snow. After a quick refuelling stop the Viscount was on its way to Goose Bay in Newfoundland, a place familiar with visiting British military aircraft, as we had an agreement with the Canadian government to keep a detachment there, and Vulcans, Victors and fighters flew in constantly to carry out exercises and gain experience of operating in sub-zero temperatures. When we landed it was certainly sub-zero, and we were advised not to leave the aircraft until it was in the hangar and the doors closed. Everyone there moved around in cars with their heaters going full blast, and one had to keep well covered up even in the short journey from car to the heated mess buildings. Fur-lined jackets with hoods were issued to all, and we never ventured out without them.

The buildings and the hospitality were equally warm, and we were sorry that we could not stay for a day or two, but we had a tight schedule to keep across the States, so the next morning we were bundled into the Viscount to avoid the freezing wind that was whipping up the powdery snow off the banks alongside the runway. The aircraft had only just come out of the hangar when Eddy Rigg (Yes, Diana's brother) got into the captain's seat for the next leg of the flights and prepared to start up the engines. After his cockpit checks he pressed the starter button of number one engine, and to his astonishment all four engines began to turn. Clearly something was amiss, and so back into the hangar went the Viscount. It was discovered that the starting solenoids had frozen up, even in the short time that they had been exposed to the outside freezing air. After the application of a heater-blower all worked normally, and in a very short time we were able to take off and climb out of Goose and leave behind the distinguishing white plumes of smoke coming from every chimney, where the moisture turned into ice crystals the moment they hit the sub-zero air.

Eddie took us to the American Air Force Base at Westover in three and a half hours, where we refuelled, and then Hubbard took over for the flight to the US Naval Air Station at Patuxent River. Here we had a stop-over of four days. This was a very interesting visit where we had lectures and demonstrations of the way the US Navy conducted its flight-testing operations, and some of the British test pilots flew a selection of their latest naval fighters. During the visit I was accommodated with the family of the senior instructor, who were most kind and generous. As well as being wined and dined at their attractive ranch-like house, I was taken out for a ride on a very presentable hunter. I enjoyed every moment of it, and discovered the New England countryside was quite breathtaking: the trees shone golden in the evening light of the setting sun as we cantered back and then slowed to a walk to let the horses cool off before putting them in the stables with a bucket full of corn on the cob for each of them.

On 10 January we flew to Scott Air Force Base in Illinois, and then on again with Robbie Robinson in charge of the Viscount, landing at Kirtland Air Force Base in Albuquerque. After refuelling we took off on the third flight that day, Eddie and Ray Watts sharing the flying, and landing at our final destination, the Edwards Air Force Base, in the late evening. After a long and tiring day we were all looking forward to a few drinks and an early night, but it soon became apparent that the welcoming party was all laid on for that night. What was even more tiresome was that the party was in the City of Los Angeles itself, and we had hardly alighted from the Viscount when we were hustled aboard a C54 Transport aircraft of the USAF, which took off at once, and we were soon circling the myriad of lights of the Los Angeles International Airport. Needless to say the airport was very busy and we were stacked overhead for what seemed like hours to us, the exhausted English guys. At last the C54 received landing clearance, and again our genial hosts hustled us out of the aircraft and into a series of 'limos' that shot off into the seething traffic of the city. At last we reached our destination and were ushered into a great hall containing many small tables and one larger top table at the far end. There must have been some one hundred men and women seated at the tables, but as the British team entered they all leapt to their feet clapping and cheering wildly. It soon became clear that we had arrived very late; the reception party had begun sometime before we were ushered in and the drinks had been flowing liberally. When I said that they all leapt to their feet this was an exaggeration, for many were already prone beneath the tables. Nevertheless the reception was overwhelming, and we were soon seated at the top table catching up with the drinks, our fatigue and sobriety forgotten. I was thrilled to find that Chuck Yeager was seated between Ray Watts and myself, so we enjoyed a feast of stories from this great American pilot who was the first to fly supersonically anywhere in the world. This was in the Bell X-1 research aircraft, which he flew at Mach 1.06 over Muroc Field – the future Edwards Airforce Base in California's Mojave Desert. He told us a lot of scary stories about incidents in his flying achievement, most recently in the pioneering research aircraft with turbojet and rocket propulsion. These were exploring supersonic flight and flight into the stratosphere, leading to the final goal – entry into space. Even that evening as he spoke, Chuck was gesturing with hands heavily bandaged, a result of a horrendous experience when he had to take to his parachute when his F.104 fighter went out of control while on a climb beyond the atmosphere. The burns were suffered when the rocket of his ejector seat set fire to the shrouds of his parachute and he had to extinguish the flames with his bare hands as he floated down a hundred miles out in the desert. Luckily he told us that he was soon picked up by a rescue helicopter.

As the evening wore on speeches were made by both teams, almost unintelligible for the most part, but there was no concealing the friendliness and mutual admiration between them. Even in my inebriated state I was very conscious of the fact that seated around the top table that night was a bunch of the most experienced test pilots in the world, some of them to gain fame as the future astronauts. Neil Armstrong was among them, and he told us about his experiences in flying the X-15 up to 125,000 feet and at twice the speed of sound, which he did before his space flight. The British team certainly learned a lot that drunken evening, probably more than their hosts intended. The next morning several of the American test pilots who had been at the party were on the flight-line at Edwards at eight o'clock sharp to continue their aircraft high-speed and high-altitude research programme The next few days were spent in very interesting demonstrations of future projects, including a brief sight of the Space Program's re-entry vehicle then in mock-up form (the Shuttle). We were all impressed with the Americans' confident attitude to bringing this vehicle back from space, re-entering the earth's atmosphere and generating incredible heat as they did so, and then approaching from great altitude and landing a powerless aircraft with a stalling speed around 200 knots. The skill and judgment required was prodigious, even though the whole operation would be monitored from the ground with a computer program.

The next two days were taken up with flying American fighters, when I was given the opportunity to fly the Northrop T.38, taking it up to altitude and doing a stall (very mild) and then a fast run to Mach 1.6 before returning to the huge runway for several touch-and-go landings. After lunch (strictly no alcohol) I flew the notorious F.104, the so-called widow maker, with Capt Switz as safety pilot. On this flight I was subjected to one of the most fascinating experiences of my flying career. After a long take-off run we climbed vertically, reaching 40,000 feet while still over the airfield. After some general handling and a level fast run to Mach 2 Switz said, 'OK, I've got her', and took over the controls. He again stood the 104 on its tail and engaged reheat on the special upgraded General Electric turbojet. As we climbed, the altimeter wound round so fast that I lost count of our true height. The sky gradually darkened and soon was a deep purple, and there did not seem to be any horizon. Although we were still vertical I had no feeling of that attitude, and then, to my consternation, Switz cut the engine and the aircraft just hung there, no noise, only a slight rumble from the engine ticking over, a feeling of weightlessness and sublime relaxation. Then the aircraft gently tumbled over and began falling, still with no noise of any slipstream, and an uncanny feeling of what I could only describe as wonder as the whole of California and probably bits of adjoining states was spread out below us in a fantastic panorama of shades and colours. At this point Switz chose to say, 'OK, you've got her.' To say I had control would have been misleading, for the 104 showed no inclination to respond to any of its controls. However, as we descended into less rarified air the control surfaces began to bite, and soon we were back on even keel and heading for the airfield. The 104 was quite straightforward to land provided one had plenty of space, but sharp turns near the ground could be hazardous. Coming over the hedge fast, the actual landing was no problem, but the aircraft is quite long, and the nosewheel and main wheels are both well behind the cockpit and situated close together, so if the nosewheel is not placed firmly on the runway there is a tendency to induce a rocking motion about the main wheels, and it is easy to touch the tail if care is not taken. Capt Switz warned me about this as we landed, and I taxied onto the apron well satisfied and thrilled with my first flight in the 'widow maker', but I was glad to have had Switz with me!

When I was not flying or at lectures or demonstrations, the American public relations officer took me in hand and proved anxious to show me as much of California as possible. He was a charming man and spared no effort to please. On one occasion we drove around Hollywood and I was shown all the homes of the stars and several of the studios and all the interesting places along the Boulevard. We stopped at the famous candy shop favoured by the stars, and he bought a box of delicious chocolates, which we gradually consumed as we drove around. I remarked on how delicious they were and how much my wife would have liked them. He drove straight back to the shop and bought another box for me to take home for Eve. Not satisfied with this kindness, he used to send Eve a box of the same chocolates every year for some time afterwards. The next day we went down to the Mexican quarter of LA, and browsed round the fascinating market and sat out in the sun sipping tequila out of large wine glasses topped with sugar. Back at Edwards the British test pilots were flying several of the American advanced fighters, and the air was full of sonic bangs until they had all landed and returned, well satisfied, to the Officers' Club.

It was soon time to leave this fascinating place, and the wide interests that were awakened by all we saw at Edwards and all the kind and hospitable people who had given us such a wonderful time. Their hospitality was not spent, however, and on our last evening the American team took us all to Las Vegas to an unforgettable experience of gambling, an obsession of wanton and unashamed pleasure seeking.

The next day we were scarcely airborne in the Viscount before two of Edwards's fighters took up station on each wingtip and escorted us well on our way to Moffet, where NASA had its headquarters at Ames. After half a day with NASA, with whom the Edwards test pilots were hardly on speaking terms, we flew on to Nellis (Nevada), where the USAF had its Weapons School. The team spent two days here, with demonstrations and lectures laid on for us, and before leaving the Americans took us across to San Francisco. We had cocktails at the highest bar in town (Top of the Mark), and then we were taken down to Fisherman's Creek for a splendid fish meal of lobster, crayfish and crab. After a tour of the picturesque city we were finally on our way home, when Eddy Rigg took over command of the Viscount as we took off from Nellis bound for Offot AFB (Nebraska). After a quick turnround we set course for Westover (Massachusetts), and en route we were able to fly very low over the Colorado River: the Canyon was a wonderful sight to see from the air. From Westover we picked up the same route across the States as the one we had flown on the way out some eighteen days before. We night-stopped at Goose Bay and Keflavick, and finally landed back at Lossiemouth on 21 January.

After a day or two catching up at the Ministry, Ray Watts and I sat down at Farnborough to write up our report of a very successful liaison visit to the States. While I had been away Peggy had amassed quite a lot of queries from the outstations, and it was necessary for me to embark on several flying visits. Peggy also drew my attention to the latest progress report on accident investigation. This reminded me of the very first day in my office when, after I took over from Pat, he came into the office and dropped onto my desk a large box. Throwing open the lid revealed a mass of electrical leads and wire spools. 'You had better take this over, it's a magic box that the Royal Aircraft Establishment are working on which records on wire details of an aircraft's flight conditions. The finished box will be crash-proof and will provide vital clues for the investigation team of an air crash in the future.' This was the birth of the 'Black Box'!

Now I had to catch up with all my visits. The first was to Boscombe Down in the Devon with Eric Mather for a conference with the com-mandant, and to take the opportunity for a check on their air traffic controllers. We landed back at Farnborough with an ILS and radar approach. In February I visited Rochester and Chivenor, and at the beginning of March paid two visits to Warton. On the second I flew with Jimmy Dell in a Lightning Tr.592 on a general handling exercise, during which we did a Mach 1 run over St George's Channel. After landing, Jimmy brought up the problem of continuation flying for his test pilots. While the Lightning was still doing development trials only a few aircraft were available and only a few development test pilots were able to fly them. Until the aircraft started coming off the production line he had several test pilots starved of flying hours who would not be in full flying practice when required. This was a problem shared by several other aircraft contractors, and I was able to solve the problem in the end, after a long battle with the Ministry civil servants who held the money bags, by getting them to authorize the attachment of civil test pilots to RAF fighter squadrons in order to maintain their flying hours – a solution that turned out to be satisfactory to all parties.

On 24 March Mather and I flew up in the Devon to Rolls-Royce in response to a request to go over and sort out a problem concerning the manning level of air traffic controllers. Our landing forecast for Hucknall was not good, but we decided to go and have a look. Arriving overhead we were offered a radar let-down, and on our final approach we broke cloud at 300 feet and a visibility of less than 900 yards:

very good practice for the controller and the pilot. We did land safely!

On my return to the Ministry the next day there was a note on my desk from my director saying that he was being pressed by the finance department to take urgent action to recover an outstanding account for the hangarage of a civil aircraft at White Waltham. Peggy looked up the file and found this was a long-standing matter with Douglas Bader, who owned the aircraft, having been given it by the Shell Company on his retirement. I knew Douglas well from Battle of Britain days, so I rang him at home to warn him what was afoot. When he heard that the Ministry's finance department was still chasing him for what was really a paltry sum, Douglas reacted as I guessed he would. His actual words were not repeatable, but he implied that while he and many others like him had been fighting to save their country those so-and-so penny-pinchers had been sitting on their fat arses in the underground shelters beneath Whitehall. 'It's not the money,' he said, 'but the principle of the thing that I object to.' I, like my predecessor, tucked the relevant file away in a remote cabinet, and my successor made sure that the file was finally mislaid and Douglas was never called on to settle this trifling debt.

In April I managed to get some more continuation flying in the Dragonfly, and did my first helicopter cross-country to Boscombe Down, where I began to feel that I could discuss helicopter operations with the experts with better understanding.

Later in the month I became involved with the BBC over a controversy regarding the erection of a new television mast near East Haptree. I flew into Heathrow with Capt Marlow in a Dove to pick up representatives of the BBC and Sir Julian Amery, and we flew over the Bristol area to make a detailed reconnaissance of the proposed site for the TV mast. It was clear that it would infringe the safety criteria of both the civil aircraft using Bristol Whitchurch and, what was of more concern to me, the military aircraft on test flights from Filton and also helicopters from Weston. After several days of acrimonious discussions with the BBC, which foolishly had already started the construction of the mast, it was made to abandon the project on the grounds of aircraft safety.

On 12 May I went down to Cowes and joined Mr Phillips for trials of the SRN 3 Hovercraft in the Solent. We finally ran the Hovercraft ashore on the beach in front of Osborne House, where Cdr Lambe landed his little Widgeon and picked me up and flew me back to Cowes, On 20 May Mather and I took the Chipmunk down to Cowes again and on to Sandown to look at the Decca AR 1 Radar. On the 27th I took the Meteor 8 down to Boscombe Down and on to Filton, where I joined Mr Williams, a test pilot of the Bristol Aircraft Company, in the cockpit of

Britannia XM 491, which he was flying for acceptance trials, including stalls and recovery and high-G turns. Finally Williams let me take over the controls and land this lovely aeroplane and taxi it back to the dispersal, where anxious ground crew were awaiting the 'thumbs up'! For a very large aeroplane, the biggest I had ever flown, it handled beautifully, but I was soon to have more experience on large multi-engined aircraft.

In June I managed to get down to Farnborough for another helicopter flight in the Dragonfly, and now that I was getting more experience I took the opportunity of asking if I could now move on to a more advanced helicopter. The Test Pilots' School was flying a Scout helicopter as part of its course, and it was fully engaged most of the time, but I was promised that I could have a flight when and if it became available. Unfortunately I left the Ministry before the promise could be fulfilled, but I always considered myself very lucky to have had the flying facilities at Farnborough that the commandant had generously offered. Later in the month I was given two dual flights in a Varsity, and then a solo flight on circuits and landings with a Master Engineer. On the 25th I took the Devon to Radlett, and after lunch and a briefing I joined Mr Allen in Victor 11, XH 672, and we flew down to Boscombe Down to flight-test the auto-land equipment fitted in the aircraft. The auto-land was also tied in to the ILS at Boscombe, and in the period of an hour we did seven 'hands off' landings. Allen brought the Victor into the ILS beam and selected auto-land, and both he and I folded our arms while the aircraft flew around the ILS pattern, turned itself onto the approach, flew down the glide slope and throttled back over the hedge, held off a few feet above the runway and settled down to a near-perfect landing. It was quite uncanny to sit back and watch the controls moving on their own to correct every deviation, and the throttles moving unassisted to maintain the correct airspeed. I couldn't remember whether we selected wheels and flaps down before the landings, but I was quite sure the auto-land would not have landed without them This was a very convincing demonstration of how modern equipment could now allow passenger aircraft to land in safety in blind conditions. It was a little ironic that quite often a small van with an illuminated sign saying 'Follow me' had to come out to lead the electronic marvel to its terminal.

CHAPTER THIRTY-THREE

TSR 2 and Hastings Conversion

February 1963

I started off July with two more helicopter flights, and did an ILS trial in the Varsity with Eric Mather. Later I took the Varsity to Woodford to discuss flight safety measures with Hawker Siddeley management. While there I joined Mr Harrison on handling trials of an HS 748 Andover, including stalls, single-engine flying and a demonstration of the aircraft's STOL capabilities. After lunch I took off with Mr Blackman in Vulcan 2 XL 384 on a minimum-speed handling trial, after which we did some coupled-ILS approaches at Manchester before landing back at Woodford, where I picked up the Varsity and flew back to Farnborough with Eric. On the 17th I joined the crew of Hastings 480 on a navigation trial from Farnborough, in which we carried out several homings, let-downs and approaches at airfields spread all around the country. At the end of the month I had an enjoyable trip to Nice, flying with Sqn Ldr Harper in Comet 2E XN 453 with six crew on a VLF radio trial lasting three hours twenty minutes and giving me some time in the second pilot's seat. Excitement was growing at the approaching first flight of the TSR2, and I was doing several flights to Warton to talk to 'B' Beamont, the chief test pilot, to work out the safety routes to be flown and special air safety matters required for the first flight. It took a little time, but finally 'B' took me into the secure hangar to see this remarkable aircraft and to show me its very advanced electronic fit and overall design. There was no doubt in my view that this was an aircraft well ahead of its time, a technical triumph that was more advanced than other possible rivals outside Britain. Designed as a tactical strike/recce aircraft by Freddie Page, it was initially to be built by English Electric at Warton, but the government intervened and ruled that construction should be shared with Vickers at Weybridge. This was to result in further delays to what was already a programme running late and beyond budget. This problem,

211

which was endemic in the design and production of all modern, sophisticated aircraft, was to become a vital factor in the future of this splendid aeroplane. The unbelievable, misguided opinions of government ministers at this time was epitomized by Duncan Sandys' declaration in 1957 that in his view there was no longer a need for manned aircraft as the country's defence needs could now be met by automated missiles! The newly elected Labour government, always conscious of votes, could not stomach the idea of spending millions of pounds of public money on the further development of the TSR2. In the meantime the aircraft had been taken down to Boscombe Down and made its first flight. Several more flights followed, with enthusiastic reports from 'B' Beamont that it had performed better than expected and continued to do so on subsequent flights.

The government's view at this time seemed to be blinkered by the short-term costs, and it lacked the vision to appreciate the value of having an outstanding strike aircraft that was badly needed in our own Air Force and would certainly sell to many other nations worldwide (the Australians had already shown a lively interest in the aircraft). Its production would provide great prospects for increased employment in the aircraft industry as well as useful foreign currency. But the company was not only up against the government in its efforts to convince opinions that the aircraft would become a world beater. Surprisingly, Admiral Lord Mountbatten, always jealous that the Royal Air Force would be given preference over the Naval Air Arm, made a special trip to Australia and actually persuaded their Defence Department to drop its preliminary intentions to buy the TSR2, and instead to buy the American F-111, which would be available sooner and cost less. In due course of time the Australians did buy the F-111, which was not a successful aeroplane, but it meant the end of the argument in favour of the TSR2, and the British government withdrew its support for the project.

Then followed two of the worst and infamous actions by any government in modern times. Instead of telling the company confidentially that the aircraft was to be cancelled, so that the management could break the news to its works staff in the kindest way possible, the Under-Secretary announced it first in Parliament. But the next act was even worse, and no one from the Prime Minister down has ever admitted to giving the order to this shameful and blatant act of vandalism. The company was told to destroy all the remaining airframes of the TSR2, so that, presumably, there was no chance of the aircraft ever being put into production. One can only imagine the chagrin and bitterness of all those skilled and dedicated men who had worked tirelessly to get this splendid aircraft into the air where it belonged, not to mention the Royal

Air Force squadrons which had eagerly awaited such an outstanding replacement strike aircraft.

On this sad note I left the Ministry of Aviation at the end of my tour. I had enjoyed the best possible support from all my staff, and Peggy had been wonderful in making all the arrangements for my many visits around the aircraft construction companies and running the office in my absence. I was pleased to receive a letter from each of the senior test pilots saying how much they appreciated the efforts of my office in looking after their interests while I had been in the hot seat, and wishing me the best of luck in my new job.

I realized how very fortunate I had been to get my acting group captain rank and step into such an interesting job at the Ministry of Aviation. I felt that my luck could not hold, but nevertheless I hoped that I might be considered to command a flying station. The chances of a fighter station were certainly very remote, for I had been away from fighter operations for a long time, but I did hope that I might be considered for a bomber base, as I had recently had a little experience of operating 'V' bombers. But this experience was minimal and I was not surprised when my hopes were not realized. But the Postings staff came up with a most satisfactory compromise. I was posted to command Royal Air Force Lindholme, which was a flying station with the Bomber Command Bombing School, training radar navigators for the 'V' Bomber Force. The fact that this training was undertaken in Hastings aircraft was rather a disappointment, but at least I would be getting some flying, even though of a different order from that to which I had been accustomed. Before taking up my appointment I was attached to No. 242 Operational Conversion Unit at Thorney Island to obtain my Hastings rating. On 17 August I joined Flt Lt Jackson in Hastings 587 as second pilot in a liaison flight to St Mawgan and return as a first introduction to this large, heavy aeroplane. Three days later I flew with Jackson again on a dual conversion exercise in the Hastings, and as he pointed out, this was a very different sort of flying from the fighters on which I had been brought up. The minimum crew required was a second pilot as a back-up and to assist with selection of flaps and landing gear, and an engineer to handle the four Pegasus sleeve-valve engines and their fuel system. A navigator was also carried. When the auto-pilot was disengaged I found that one needed both hands on the controls to manage the aircraft, particularly in rough weather, and therefore on the approach to land the control of the engine throttles was handed over to the engineer, who had duplicate throttles and engine instruments, and whose duty was to follow the instructions on power settings passed by the captain. On my first approach, as I wrestled with the control column with both hands, I couldn't help smiling to myself as I recalled my old instructor's remarks on my very first dual flight: 'Just use finger and thumb on the stick, it will give you a better feel for the aircraft.' This one had no feelings, and only brute force had results, but after a few hours I began to enjoy flying the Hastings. On my second dual flight I had a flight check from the CFI, and in the afternoon I was launched off on a solo flight with a slightly nervous second pilot and engineer, but all went well and I finished up by doing a GCI approach and landing. Landings were energetic but not difficult, but if one got it a bit wrong and left the hold-off too late, the Hastings would do the most prodigious bounce. But it was a sturdy aircraft and could put up with quite a lot of punishment. It certainly proved its worth during the Berlin Airlift, when Hastings flew a huge number of sorties, both day and night, to beat the Russians' attempt to isolate Berlin from the Western Powers. After three more dual conversion flights I was given my instrument rating test by Sqn Ldr Shield on 28 August and pronounced competent on type. Before leaving Thorney Island I managed to get myself a ride in the left-hand seat of Argosy XN 855, and did several approaches and landings. It was a large aircraft but so much lighter to handle than the Hastings, which lacked power-assisted controls.

On reporting to Royal Air Force Lindholme I found that as well as operating Hastings we also flew Varsity aircraft for visual bombing training. As I had already qualified on the Varsity at Farnborough I only needed a refresher check flight, which I completed with Flt Lt Perry on 14 September. Lindholme was quite a large station, whose primary task was training budding radar navigators for the 'V' Force, so a regular intake of students would arrive each month and the flying programme was fairly intense. At this time the 'Cold War' was at its height, and one of my tasks was to lecture each course and emphasize the vital importance for each one of them to face up to the possibility of finding themselves in control of a nuclear weapon, asking if they would have the moral courage to release it if ordered to do so. It was an extremely difficult dilemma with which to be faced, but as I explained, a deterrent ceased to be viable unless everyone showed a determination and willingness to use it in the last resort. This was the teaching of the country's strategy, and it was quite absurd for people like CND to protest against the very weapons that were holding at bay a possible world catastrophe.

Our Hastings were fitted with the latest H2S radar, and the navigators' training consisted of navigating by radar to find pinpoint targets previously selected at many sites throughout the British Isles. Thus each sortie was often of three or four hours' duration, and as I took my turn in flying on the training sorties I was finding my flying was taking up far more of my day than in the past. As commander of quite a large station I had wide responsibilities, and I had to engage in meticulous planning for each day of every week. Mostly my flying had to take a low place in my priorities, as my duties of running the station took up more and more time. As well as the Hastings flying, I also took my turn in flying the Varsity on visual bombing training for the navigators, which meant frequent visits to the bombing ranges at Holbeach, Wainfleet and Theddlethorpe. Each month to the end of the year I was averaging four Varsity and three Hastings sorties. I enjoyed one advantage over the other station commanders in Bomber Command in that I could fly my station's sports teams to their away fixtures in the Command competitions by making use of our Hastings fitted with passenger seats. I could also take this aircraft occasionally on overseas flights with a load of deserving airmen and airwomen as a reward for work particularly well done. These trips were usually to Cyprus or Malta, and provided valuable overseas training for my navigators.

In February 1965 the course began visual bombing at night, so I was gaining night-flying experience on the Varsity. I also did night continuation training on the Hastings from time to time. On 8 March I took the station golf team to Germany, landing at Düsseldorf and Wildenrath. In early April I was due for a Hastings type test and rating by the QFI. Lindholme was situated right alongside the old A1 main road, and when the principal runway was in use traffic lights were in operation to stop public traffic crossing the end of the runway. To separate the runway from the road there was a 'frangible' fence, as it was, as a matter of necessity, very close to the touchdown point. Having completed my QFI check satisfactorily, I brought the Hastings in over the road feeling quite pleased with myself, and seeing traffic held up by the lights on either side of the runway I thought I could do a smart smooth landing just to show them. The landing was fine, but unfortunately I collected a length of fence in the process. That taught me to show off! It was just as well that it was of 'frangible' wood and that no damage was caused to the Hastings.

A few days later we were all saddened to hear that Winston Churchill had died. I think that we surviving members of the Battle of Britain cherished a special affection for the man who had so stirringly portrayed the vital part played in the war by 'The Few'.

We were honoured and touched that some of us had been chosen to take a prominent part in his funeral procession. Twelve of us, consequently, were assembled at RAF Uxbridge for two days' drill and rehearsals, and then fitted out with ceremonial swords and belts. On the day of the funeral under the command of Air Cdre Al Deare, the distinguished New Zealand fighter pilot, we marched in solemn slow time near the head of the funeral procession through the streets of London, remembering with gratitude the great man who had done so much to bring us ultimate victory.

CHAPTER THIRTY-FOUR

Bomber Command Bombing School

1965

began April with a Hastings trip on Exercise Kinsman to Ballykelly and Cottesmore and return to Lindholme. For the rest of the month I continued with several Hastings and Varsity navigator training flights. This pleasant routine was sadly interrupted on the 12th of the month when Lindholme suffered a most tragic accident. One of our Varsitys on a routine training exercise was returning from the bombing ranges and descending through light scattered cloud when it collided with a civilian Cessna light aircraft that had recently taken off from a small airfield south of the Humber and was climbing up to its normal cross-country height. The Cessna broke up in the air and the pilot, the only occupant, plummeted to the ground. The Varsity's right wing was badly damaged and the aircraft was only kept under control with great difficulty. The captain ordered the crew to bale out and did so himself. However, the second pilot took over the controls and managed to establish a reasonable state of control and crash-landed the badly damaged aircraft in a field without serious injury to himself or to a student who had remained in the aircraft. This was a very commendable effort on his part, but he did not know until some time later that the senior instructor who was in the aircraft at the time of the collision had also baled out, but for some reason had not secured the straps of his parachute properly, and as he got out and pulled the rip-cord the chute opened but he fell through the harness and also plunged to his death.

The investigation into the accident was long and protracted, and particularly thorough as a civil aircraft was involved and a civilian was one of the casualties. Sufficient to say that the incident cast a cloud of gloom over the station and many questions were asked and had to be answered. This first tragedy at a station under my command caused me a good deal of anguish and heart searching, particularly as it involved my being interviewed by my AOC. However, normal station life had to go on, and at the end of the month I was lucky enough to get my hands on a Chipmunk again and enjoyed a glorious hour of aerobatics and low flying, a welcome change from the ponderous and clumsy Hastings. Two days later, after landing from a long Hastings training flight, I was told that one of the Varsitys was still airborne and had been diverted by Prestwick radar control from its bombing mission to search for the crew of a two-seater Lightning who had ejected somewhere off the North Yorkshire coast. It appears that the pilot of the Varsity, a Polish master pilot, had soon spotted the airmen in their dinghies and alerted the rescue services. He remained circling the crew until a rescue helicopter had sighted them. The Varsity landed back at Lindholme after eight hours in the air to a hero's welcome.

It was at this time that I had a most welcome surprise. My daughter Sue, from whom I had been separated for many years, sent me a cable from Hong Kong on her 21st birthday, just saying, 'Dad . . . isn't it time that we got together again?' It was such a generous and forgiving gesture that I felt horribly guilty that I had abandoned her, even though it had been during the chaos of the war years. We did indeed get together again when she returned from Hong Kong a few months later, and we celebrated a most loving and happy reunion when she came to stay with us at Lindholme. Happily I am still blessed with that loving relationship that was revived with so much mutual pleasure on that day of her return.

During the next three months I did regular Hastings and Varsity training flights, and also two air tests on the Hastings. The first was after a normal regular inspection, but a fairly probing air test was usually carried out to ensure that all was satisfactory. My crew and I had done all the necessary tests prior to landing except the feathering of the propellers. This was carried out in turn, but finally number four engine, having been feathered, would not unfeather, so we did a three-engine landing without trouble. Some months previously the Hastings had suffered a fatal accident when a tailplane had come adrift in the air and all Hastings were grounded for some time while all tailplanes were examined and changed if necessary. My second air test was on a Hastings that had just been fitted with a new tailplane in the Lindholme workshops. The CFI came along with me and there was obviously a little anxiety after such a major repair. However, to show our confidence, we both invited the SNCO and his riggers who had done the job to join us on the test flight. All went smoothly, and to show further confidence we did a fighter-type beat-up of the airfield, which was greeted with enthusiasm by the ground crews below as well as those aboard the Hastings.

In December Mr Ware flew in as he promised he would, and let me borrow his Cessna 310 G. ASZZ for a flight-handling trial, which I found most enjoyable. I offered Ware a Hastings, but he did not show much enthusiasm for the chance to fly it. The weather turned bad at the end of December and several training flights had to be recalled or were cancelled. In the New Year, however, the weather cleared and I was able to fulfil my promise to my station officiating chaplain to take him for a flight over his parish and take a look at his church from the right-hand seat of a Varsity at 1,000 feet. Ted was one of the nicest men that one could wish to meet, and Eve and I kept in touch with him and his charming wife over the following years.

I continued to fly Hastings and Varsity training flights during January and February and into March, when I also flew forty girls of the Girls' Venture Corps in two sorties in the Hastings to give them air experience. At the end of the month I flew the station sports team to Wyton for a Command Competition, together with the AOC, AVM Stapleton, and several senior officers. It gave me even more satisfaction to fly them all back again with our team the winners of the golf cup and runners-up of the rugby. I was able to get in a flight in a Chipmunk on the 11th, and a second-pilot flight in a Dominie XZ 128, in which I enjoyed doing several approaches and landings in command. When August came around I suddenly realized that I would be handing over command of Lindholme in a few weeks' time. I was sad that the time had passed so quickly, and I felt I had so much more to do. At the start of the month I took twenty-four of my station staff in the passenger Hastings to Luqa (Malta) and the next day to Akrotiri in Cyprus, where we stayed two nights, returning to Lyndhome via Waddington for customs on the 9th. On 16 September I took my instrument flight test so that I could walk away with my 'Master Green Card' once more, and perhaps for the last time, as I knew I did not stand a chance of another flying job for what would be my last posting.

Before my final departure from Lindholme, Eve and I were 'dined out' in regal fashion, with the AOC and several senior officers from HQ present. The evening was notable for an incident reported, surprisingly, on the front page of the *Express* and the *Mirror*, and in the *Telegraph*. 'An RAF band that had played during the evening had struck up its last number, the Post Horn Gallop, and at its conclusion Bandsman Chief Technician Titchmarsh, playing the very last note on his trumpet, hit high note "E" above Top "C", and to everyone's astonishment the opal ring worn by an officer's wife and valued at £50 just disintegrated and left only a pile of dust on the dining table.' On that note the party broke up and the outgoing group captain and his wife were escorted to the front door of the officers' mess. There, resplendent in its new paint and a floral canopy, was a bomb trolley disguised as a unique flying machine, with a luxurious double settee behind the nose and cockpit of an aircraft in which sat one of my squadron commanders, complete with flying overalls and 'bone dome', ready for take-off. As we took our place on the settee, at a given command the whole contraption set off at a brisk pace, pulled by nearly all my officers manning a pair of ropes! Thus we arrived at the door of our married quarter at the end of a most happy and memorable evening. On the 29th I handed over command of Royal Air Force Lyndholme, satisfied with the thought that during my sojourn there it had been an efficient and happy station. I could not have imagined then that it would become in a few years a far less happy place as one of Her Majesty's prisons.

CHAPTER THIRTY-FIVE

Bomber, Strike and Training Commands

November 1966 to October 1970

Anticipating that I would have to do a staff job for my next appointment, I was very pleased when I was to be posted to Headquarters Bomber Command as the Senior Personnel Staff Officer at High Wycombe. The post of SPSO was always accepted as a prestigious one, as it involved dealing with the confidential handling of all officers' postings, assessments, promotions and honours and awards, as well as disciplinary matters of all personnel in the command. It promised to be a very busy job and, as it turned out, much busier than I could have foreseen at the time. I reported for duty at High Wycombe. Eve and I were housed in a very large and grand Type One married quarter among the magnificent Bradenham Beeches, near to the officers' mess and a five-minute walk through the woods to Headquarters and my office. As well as my normal duties, I was made the secretary of the Bomber Command Association, and had to administer the association and make all the arrangements for its annual reunion. Luckily my secretary Jill was well versed in the necessary action that had to be taken for the reunion, and did all the donkey work. For my first year I wanted to do something special for the assembled members, many of whom had been flying four-engined bombers during the war and at the reunion spent a great deal of their time during their visit to High Wycombe reminiscing about those days. Before going in to their usual formal dinner after touring the operation centre, I arranged for them to assemble on the lawn outside the officers' mess, where drinks were served. An RAF band was playing in the background, and as the final notes of the Dambusters March died away a new sound arose and all heads turned to the west as the roar of four Rolls-Royce Merlins drowned all else when the Lancaster bomber flew low overhead, rocking its wings in salute before turning north into the gathering dusk. As the beat of its engines died away there was a spontaneous burst of applause from the assembled airmen, no doubt without a dry eye among them. After dinner telegrams were read out from the Queen and from 'Bomber' Harris with their good wishes.

My work was always brisk, and I very much valued my close relationship with the Commander-in-Chief, 'Digger' Kyle, who was a highly respected commander and a delightful man to work for and with. We had regular meetings to discuss confidential matters concerning officers within the command, including, to my surprise, senior officers, even up to Air rank. These confidential chats between the two of us I valued very highly, being pleased that my opinions were apparently so valued, and it was this that made the job of SPSO so interesting and special.

As often happened in the services, the exigencies were not always in favour of the individual, and our cosy and comfortable life at High Wycombe was soon to be upset. For some time there had been rumours flying around that there was to be a complete review of the Command structure of the Royal Air Force at home. It was decided that Bomber Command and Fighter Command would be amalgamated to form a new Strike Command. This had hardly been put in hand when it was decided that Coastal Command should also be included in Strike Command, so it could be seen that all the personnel matters would now be handled by one SPSO in the new Strike Command. I was the one left to take on this quite considerable task, and although my staff were increased there was still only one SPSO to control the lot, and it was some months before an air commodore was added to the Administration staff. The difficulties of taking on this extra burden were added to by another strange decision, which was to move the Administration staff from High Wycombe to the old offices of Fighter Command at Bentley Priory. For months I had to journey daily from High Wycombe to Bentley Priory, not only because we were still living at Bradenham, but also because the C-in-C remained at High Wycombe and our frequent meetings still took place there. I did not enjoy the daily drives by inept airmen drivers, and it was a relief when the AOA also did the journey and we travelled in a Bristol Sycamore helicopter – a horrid little aeroplane but so much better than those awful and ancient Ford Zephyrs and suicidal drivers.

Having survived the few months I had remaining of my tour I still hoped to get in a bit more flying, but I was far too busy in the office and only flew as a passenger on staff visits in an Anson, Pembroke or Basset, and on one occasion I grabbed a chance to fly in a Whirlwind helicopter to the radar station at Neatishead. After a staff inspection I went on to Coltishall, where I was delighted to meet Mike and Barbara again and spend a very pleasant evening with them, chatting about old times. Mike was now the officer commanding Coltishall.

During my tour at High Wycombe I remembered many happy occasions with the other group captains on the staff and their wives, several of whom I had known previously when they were commanding bomber stations and I was at Lindholme. We often visited each other's homes for drinks or a meal, but there was always a feeling of tension as during this time the 'Cold War' was causing serious concern, and nowhere more than at Bomber Command Headquarters, where, if necessary, a nuclear strike might have to be initiated. Naturally the early warning stations were on constant alert, and communications to the C-in-C Bomber Command and through him to the Cabinet Office had to be kept open, and a vigilant watch maintained, at every hour of the day and night. As part of these precautions, every twenty-four hours a general-duties group captain from the staff was on duty and had to carry the little 'white box' wherever he went. This was an important link in the 'paging' system, and if the 'box' flashed the alarm he had to take immediate action to alert the Commander-in-Chief. Although the group captains took this duty, quite rightly, with all seriousness, it was not unknown to see the 'box' being passed surreptitiously through the hedge to the neighbouring married-quarter garden, where another group captain grabbed it to take over temporarily while the first briefly took his wife shopping. Nevertheless we made sure that the guard was never broken, even for a second.

Despite the heavy work load imposed on me by the expansion of Strike Command, I left wholly satisfied with my personal achievements there. We were dined out in great style, and it was with considerable regret that we packed up our married quarter among the beeches of Bradenham woods. I was at the threshold of my last post in the service, and I made it clear to the Posters that I did not want to be put away on a dusty shelf of some backwater, but would prefer to be given some job that would still offer an interesting challenge. Group Captain Organization at Headquarters Training Command came out of the hat, a post that might be almost as busy as the SPSO job at Command and would certainly keep me fully occupied. And so it turned out, but I enjoyed the different atmosphere among the 'trainers', in contrast to the operational commands that I had served in up to that time. Eve and I had now settled in a delightful old farmhouse in Suffolk where we could enjoy a peaceful retirement in delightful countryside. We also had quite a large acreage of pasture where Emma, who had always been interested in Arab horses, could now raise them. She became very knowledgeable, edited the magazine of the Breed Association and bred several leading young Arabs, including a national champion. For a time we all became involved and excited in showing her horses at the yearly Arab shows, until later on she married and moved away from her green pastures and beautiful Arabs in Suffolk.

On arriving at HQ Training Command I was fortunate in having as my boss an exceptionally nice Air Commodore Administration and an AOC who always had time to associate with his staff officers, both on duty and socially. My satisfaction was heightened by having on my staff an old friend from Bomber Command, Jack Gilvey, who was a very smart administrative officer. I gave him the job of heading the Establishment Committee, which had the unenviable task of going round each unit in the command and cutting back its establishment of personnel wherever possible, as part of the current 'cut-back' in the services as a whole. Poor Jack was not a popular officer, particularly when he even managed to relieve the Royal Air Force College Cranwell of two of its senior staff officers.

Training Command Headquarters was at Brampton near Huntingdon, and Jack and I used to relieve the tedium of staff work with a game of golf at St Neots whenever we were off duty. Together we attended a management course at Bristol University as part of our re-settlement programme, as we were coming up to retirement in a few months' time. Regrettably we both dozed in the back row of the class during the course, agreeing that we had learned more about management in the Royal Air Force than the university could teach us. The best of our stay in Bristol were the evenings spent together down in the Harvey's cellar tasting the port and sherries.

Before I finally left the service I was determined to get into the air again, as I had not flown for many months, and I was feeling the deprivation. At the end of May 1970 I joined Flt Lt Brindle in an Andover at Oakington, and we flew down to RNAS Brawdy. While I was there I managed to fly with Sqn Ldr Stevens in a Whirlwind helicopter to do a reconnaissance of St Davids, Haverfordwest and Milford Haven. The next day Sqn Ldr Chandler and I took a Varsity to return to Oakington, when I took my turn at the controls. In June I did a dual check in a Chipmunk and had a glorious hour of aerobatics, forced-landing practice and approaches and landings in that delightful little aeroplane. In July 1970 I had my last-ever flight while still serving when I persuaded the CFI at Waddington to let me fly as second pilot in Dominie XF 739, and I had an hour handling this delightful aeroplane, finally completing three ILS/GCA approaches and landings back at Waddington. While I very much appreciated the flight, it was not what I would have chosen to mark my parting, and I yearned to have one more flight in a Meteor or Vampire to do full justice to my last sortie, with red, white and blue roundels on my wings. I was given a splendid farewell dinner in the Brampton officers' mess, and a few days later Eve and I were invited to the Mess Summer Ball, which was a grand affair, and the Commander-in-Chief kindly made a special point of saying farewell and wishing us well for the future.

So now the time had come to pack my bags and move out of Brampton and the Royal Air Force. With my blue Alfa Romeo packed to the gunwales with luggage, I drove out of Brampton's gate for the last time and turned east. I cruised slowly along as though reluctant to leave, and for a moment I felt a chill run down my spine, and I was shocked to experience a feeling of acute depression and loneliness. More than thirty years of comradeship, loyalty and a wealth of wonderful flying suddenly all gone, and no sign of what the future might hold. No wonder I felt so deeply depressed. And then I managed to pull myself together, and a warm feeling came over me with the prospect of a new and exciting challenge ahead. I slipped the Alfa into third gear and shot off like a rocket, scattering the autumn leaves and scaring a couple of cyclists as I swerved around them. I drove like the wind, not wishing to waste a moment in reaching our delightful new home deep in the Suffolk countryside, where the horses and Labradors would be waiting, and most importantly, my wife and family would be there to share what I hoped would be a new and exciting life together.

APPENDIX ONE

Aircraft Types Flown

August 1935 to September 1970

1	Gipsy Moth	1935	Aug.	Staverton	A-ABER
2	Tiger Moth		Sep.	Bristol Flying School Filton	G-ACBD
3	Hawker Hart		Nov.	No. 11 FTS Wittering	K-4951
4	Hawker Audax		Nov.	No. 11 FTS Wittering	K-4399
5	Hawker Fury	1936	Feb.	RAF Hawkinge Folkestone	K-5679
6	Hawker Fury 2		Feb.	RAF Hawkinge Folkestone	K-7280
7	Hawker Hind	1937	Aug.	RAF Hawkinge Folkestone	K-6789
8	Avro Tutor		Aug.	RAF Hawkinge Folkestone	K-3392
9	Hawker Demon		Oct.	RAF Hawkinge Folkestone	K-4540
10	Miles Magister	1938	Apr.	RAF Hawkinge Folkestone	L-5962
11	Gloster Gladiator		Jun.	RAF Hawkinge Folkestone	K-8020
12	Bristol Blenheim		Dec.	RAF Cranfield, Bomber Command	L-1125
13	Westland Lysander	1939	Mar.	RAF Hawkinge. No. 2 Sqdn	L-4699
14	Blenheim 4		Aug.	RAF Northolt	N6193
15	Beaufighter 4	1940	Sep.	Redhill	R-2079
16	Miles Master		Dec.	RAF Catterick	T-8636
17	Hawker Hurricane		July	Squires Gate	V-7751
18	Miles Mentor		July	Samlesbury	L-4406
19	Airspeed Oxford	1941	Sep.	Samlesbury	V-3249
20	Boulton & Paul Defiant			Samlesbury	T-4206
21	DH Hornet Moth		Nov.	Samlesbury	W-5744
22	Vega Gull		Nov.	Samlesbury	P-1754
23	Hudson 3			Wrexham	V-9038
24	Defiant 2	1942	Mar.	Wrexham	AA-577
25	Beaufighter 2		May	Wrexham	T-3375
26	Master 2		Aug.	RAF Wittering IR Course	DK-992
27	Beaufighter 6		Nov.	Honiley. Dihedral Tail	X-7969
28	Avro Anson	1943	Jan.	Honiley	DJ-685
29	Spitfire 5		Apr.	Northolt	AB-380

30	Mosquito 3		May Cranfield	HJ-886
31	DH Dominie		June Charter Hall	X-7392
32	Miles Martinet		July Charter Hall	HP-139
33	Bristol Beaufort		July Charter Hall	T-6531
34	Bristol Bisely		Aug. Charter Hall	BA-129
35	Vickers Wellington		Sep. Charter Hall	BJ-616
36	Mosquito 13	1944	Jan. Bradwell	HK-368
37	Spitfire 9		Feb. Bradwell	MH-819
38	Hawker Typhoon		Apr. Bradwell	R-8609
39	Auster 3		Bradwell	M-2170
40	Cygnet		May Colerne	FS-914
41	Spitfire 14		Aug. Colerne	
42	DH Mosquito XXX		Sep. Colerne	MM-811
43	Mustang 3		Oct. Odiham	FB-135
44	Typhoon 1 B	1944	Oct. Odiham	MM-979
45	Percival Proctor		Nov. Odiham	585
46	Tempest		Odiham	EJ-698
47	Mitchell B.25		Dec. Courtrai	HK-473
48	Vengeance	1945	Feb. Ibsley	HB-432
49	Wellington X		June Charter Hall	KB-6357
50	Corsair 4		Sep. Kai Tak	KD-274
51	Sentinel		Kai Tak	KJ-373
52	Barracuda		Dec. Kai Tak	MX-380
53	Dakota 4		Kiangwan	684
54	Beaufighter X	1946	Feb. Mingaladon	RD-157
55	Firefly FR.1		Mar. Kai Tak	MB-668
56	Seafire		Nov. Kai Tak	MN-996
57	Spitfire 18		May West Raynham	SM-968
58	Meteor 3		June West Raynham	EE-408 59
59	Hornet 3		West Raynham	PX-404
60	Vampire		West Raynham	VF-306
61	Brigand TF.1		West Raynham	RH-761
62	Harvard 2		July Changi (Singapore)	FS-791
63	Meteor 4		Tengah	EE-596
64	Spitfire 24		West Raynham	
65	Sea Fury	1949	Apr. West Raynham	547
66	Anson 19		June West Raynham	320
67	DH Dove		Sep. West Raynham	G-AKSV
68	Meteor 7		West Raynham	VW-570
69	Sabre F 6	1950	Mar. West Raynham	1825
70	Meteor 8		Apr. West Raynham	VZ-443
71	Spitfire 22		Sep. West Raynham	PR-575
72	DH Chipmunk	1952	July RAF Hendon	WP-803

73	Meteor 7	1953		RAF West Malling	WF-848
74	Vampire T.11		Aug.	RAF West Malling	WZ-581
75	Percival Prentice	1954	June	RAF Weston Zoyland	VR-305
76	DH Venom		Aug.	RAF West Raynham	382
77	Pembroke		Oct.	RAF Habbaniyah (Iraq)	700
78	Vickers Valetta	1955	Aug.	RAF Habbaniyah (Iraq)	490
79	DH Dove	1956	Mar.	Al Rashid (Baghdad)	267
80	Hawker Hunter 4	1957	Jan.	RAF Turnhouse	WV-323
81	DH Rapide		Aug.	RAF Turnhouse	G-AKRS
82	Gloster Javelin 5		Oct.	RAF Turnhouse	X
83	Piston Provost	1962		RAE Farnborough	685
84	F.4H Phantom		Mar.	RAE Farnborough	P-2691
85	Beagle Terrier		Aug.	Rearsby	G-ARLF
86	Jet Provost		Nov.	RAE Farnborough	HP-687
87	Airdale		Dec.	Shoreham	G-ARMP
88	Beagle 206			Shoreham	G-ARRM
89	Dragonfly Helicopter	1963	July	RAE Farnborough	595
90	Vickers Varsity	1964	June	RAE Farnborough	679
91	Hastings 1		Aug.	RAF Thorney Island	537
92	Dominie	1966	July	Stradishal	XS-128
93	Cessna 150			White Waltham	
94	Percival Proctor	1955	Sep.	Habbaniyah	291

TYPES FLOWN AS SECOND PILOT

95	Sunderland 5	1946	Jan.	Kai Tak	PP-151
96	Beverley	1960	May	Akrotiri (Cyprus)	286
97	Aztec		Apr.	Cambridge	G-RATS
98	Lightning Tr.	1964	Mar.	Warton	592
99	Viscount 800	1962		Farnborough	810
100	Britannia	1964	May	Filton	XM-491
101	F. 104		Jan.	Edwards Air Force Base (California)	C-93
102	T. 38 Talon			Edwards Air Force Base (California)	59.1596
103	Victor 2		June	Boscombe Down	XH-692
104	Vulcan 2	1965	July	Woodford	XL-384
105	Andover	1964		Woodford	G-ARRV
106	DH Trident	1962	July	Hatfield	G-ARPA
107	Piper Commanche	1965	May	Cambridge	G-ADDS
108	Argosy	1967	Aug.	Thorney Island	XN-855
109	Cessna 310	1965	Dec.	Lindholme	G-ASZZ
110	Comet 2e	1964	July	Bedford	XN-453
111	Ambassadore	1962	Apr.	Hucknall	G-373

Units and Appointments

1935	19 August	Cotswold Aero Club, Staverton Civil Flying. First Solo. Gipsy Moth.
	20 August	Bristol Flying School. Filton. Tiger Moths. Civilian.
	20 October	RAF Uxbridge. Disciplinary Course. LAC.
	7 November	No. 11 Flying Training School. Wittering, Hart, Audax, Fury. Sgt.
1936	10 May	No. 25 Fighter Squadron, Hawkinge. Fury, Fury 2. Sgt.
	27 October	No. 25 Fighter Squadron, Hawkinge. Demon.
1938	30 June	No. 25 Fighter Squadron, Hawkinge. Gladiator.
	3 October	Link Trainer Course North Weald.
	13 December	Attached to RAF Cranfield Blenheim Conversion.
1939	3 January	No. 25 Fighter Squadron, Hawkinge. Blenheim.
	24 August	No. 25 Fighter Squadron, Northolt. Blenheim.
	18 September	No. 25 Fighter Squadron, Filton. Blenheim.
	4 October	No. 25 Fighter Squadron, Northolt. Blenheim.
1940	16 January	No. 25 Fighter Squadron, North Weald. Blenheim.
	1 April	No. 600 City of London Squadron, Northolt. Blenheim. P/Off.
	2 April	No. 600 City of London Squadron, Manston. Blenheim.
	14 May	No. 600 City of London Squadron, Northolt. Blenheim.
	20 June	No. 600 City of London Squadron, Manston. Blenheim.
	24 August	No. 600 City of London Squadron, Hornchurch. Blenheim.
	9 September	No. 600 City of London Squadron, Redhill. Blenheim.
	24 October	No. 600 City of London Squadron, 'B' Flight. Drem (Scotland). Blenheim
1941	14 January	No. 68 Sqdn (Forming). Flt.Cdr. Catterick. Flt/Lt. Blenheim.
	20 April	No. 68 Sqdn. Flt.Cdr. High Ercall. Blenheim, Beaufighter.
	1 July	Headquarters No. 9 Group Staff. Sqd.Ldr.
	30 December	No. 96 Sqdn. Wrexham to Command. Defiant. Sqdn Ldr.
1943	25 March	Headquarters Fighter Command, Staff. Bentley Priory.
	12 June	No. 54 Night Operational Training Unit. Wg. Cdr. Charter Hall.
1944	1 January	No. 488 New Zealand Night-Fighter Sqdn. Bradwell, Hunsdon, Colerne Zeals.
	23 October	Headquartes No. 85 Tactical Group Brussels, Ghent.
	30 October	FRU Odiham. Test Pilot.

	29 December	No. 147 Wing. Ibsley, Ghent.
1945	1 March	No. 54 OTU. Charter Hall. Winfield. (OC)
	17 May	RAF Eshott. Spitfire O.T.U. To Command.
	5 June	No. 302 Wing. Ibsley. SOA. (For Overseas)
	5 September	RAF. Kai Tak. To Command.
	29 September	Military Governor's Staff. Hong Kong. Air Adviser.
1946	24 January	Kai Tak. Officer commanding Flying.
	20 August	No. 200 Staging Post Shanghai. Temp. Officer Commanding.
	5 September	Headquarters Far East Air Force Changi Staff (Squadron Leader).
1948	5 January	Air Fighting Development Squadron, Central Fighter Establishment RAF West Raynham.
1950	1 May	International Staff College, Andover.
1951	9 April	Air Ministry Air Staff Policy 3. Whitehall. Wing Commander.
1954	23 May	No. 209 AFS Weston Zoyland Jet refresher.
1954	July	No. 233 OCU, Pembrey Vampire Refresher.
	25 September	RAF Habbaniyah (Iraq) O.C. Flying and O.C. No. 128 Wing.
1956	19 December	RAF Turnhouse (Edinburgh) To Command. Wg.Cdr.
1959	2 June	RAF Akrotiri (Cyprus) O.C. Admin. Wing.
1962	14 December	Staff Officer Flying. Ministry of Aviation London. Gp.Capt.
1964	17 August	No. 242 OCU Hastings Conversion Course.
	12 September	RAF Lindholme Bomber Command Bombing School. To Command.
1966	4 November	Headquarters Bomber/Strike Command High Wycombe. SPSO.
1969	21 July	Headquarters Training Command. Group Captain Org. Brampton.

Index